T0322414

When Grief Equals Love

LIZZIE PICKERING

When Grief Equals Love

LONG-TERM PERSPECTIVES
ON LIVING WITH LOSS

unbound

First published in 2023

Unbound
Level 1, Devonshire House, One Mayfair Place, London W1J 8AJ
www.unbound.com

Text design by PDQ Digital Media Solutions Ltd.

A CIP record for this book is available from the British Library

ISBN 978-1-80018-227-1 (hardback)
ISBN 978-1-80018-228-8 (ebook)

Printed in Great Britain by Clays Ltd, Elcograf S.p.A.

1 3 5 7 9 8 6 4 2

MIX
Paper from
responsible sources
FSC® C018072

Special thanks to Ogilvy, a patron of this book.

Ogilvy

Bringing Lizzie to work with and support employees at Ogilvy has been a massive difference-maker as part of our offering to staff. We met in late 2019, and little did we know that our introduction would mean we would be well positioned to support staff throughout the pandemic and beyond.

From our *Ogilvy on Air* podcasts, sharing real-life and relatable stories with our employees, to one-on-one sessions with staff to help them navigate grief, I am proud of what we have achieved, and how supported our employees feel. Grief and change should not be something employees have to navigate beyond the office and virtual walls. We should all face into it together where we can and, through empathy and understanding, help people feel supported.

Gavin Sutton, Head of Learning and Development, Ogilvy UK

When I heard from my family in Australia that my younger sister had suddenly passed away, work was the last thing on my mind. Ogilvy immediately (within hours) offered an incredible amount of support, with help navigating flights in the height of the pandemic, offering extended compassionate leave and an introduction to Lizzie. I felt so looked after and comforted by knowing that Ogilvy had my emotional and mental wellbeing as a priority. Speaking to Lizzie once I was back UK-side was so helpful to navigate how I was going to learn to live alongside my grief forever.

Coby Walter, Programme Director, Ogilvy UK

Ogilvy advised me to get grief guidance after my dad's untimely death during a Covid wave. I am fortunate to have met Lizzie, as she is an exceptional guide as she comes from a place of personal experience and not just textbook knowledge.

Sessions with Lizzie were deep and full of insight into managing my grief. It was made clear to me from the start that *grief equals love*, and grief is here to stay. I could open up to her about my feelings and be authentic in the space. I am grateful to Ogilvy for their support and to have met Lizzie in the process. We will all experience losing a loved one; having support from work made it manageable for me. *Thank you.*

Gulshan Chopra, Group Governance Director, Ogilvy UK

Special thanks to Peel Hunt, a patron of this book.

PEEL
HUNT

Good mental health is key for individuals to manage the normal stresses of life, to work productively and to maintain high levels of wellbeing. This is why it is so important for us as an organisation to provide effective and ongoing support to bereaved employees that recognises individual circumstances and provides utmost compassion and support in the workplace during such a difficult time.

Fatima Badini, HR Director, Peel Hunt

*My grateful thanks to the following people for their
generous support of this book:*

Jez Stone
Francie Clarkson
David Lightfoot
Mark Watkin Jones

For Hugo, Harry, Cam and Emilie

This book is for those going through grief.
And for anyone who might need to support
someone in grief; I hope it will encourage you to
hold your loved ones tighter and be more courageous
about being alongside those who need you.

CONTENTS

Introduction: On Sorrow and Joy

When we talk about grief it is natural to think about grief for someone who has died. But as the world is finding out now, grief is experienced in so many situations: death, divorce, diagnosis, workplace change. The ripple effects of Covid-19 on individuals, on society and our shared loss of freedom. The refugee crisis with loss of home and community. Racial grief and ancestral grief. Loss of the past, present and future. Anticipatory grief through a terminal diagnosis. And the big one – cumulative grief, when many of these come one after the other and life experiences pile up and become too much to bear.

Over the last twenty-two years, through working for twelve years in the children's hospice world, and more recently helping companies deal with change, I have listened to many people describing both the mental and physical effects of grief and, most importantly, what has helped them survive their grief; in many cases finding a healthy relationship with it from which to grow and even thrive. Each and every one of them has required a different toolkit to survive, experiencing different effects and responses depending on their situation, DNA, neurodiversity, metabolism, diet, family and their individuality. Each of these responses has created potential difficulties for those around the grieving to cope, to walk beside them and to empathise. I have seen people turn away from the grief of their friends and I have personally witnessed friends walk away from me and turn the other cheek when they couldn't cope with my grief. I have also felt the bonds of the friends who could withstand the effects of my loss, and the strength of the community around me. I have listened to my 'grief tribe', those of us living in a parallel world to those who don't understand, tell their stories of survival and I have marvelled at the depths of sorrow and the heights of joy we humans can endure.

I have also witnessed and experienced survivor's strength; the joy of breathing again, the joy of living and thriving when it was never deemed possible. How I personally went from the moments just after my eldest son Harry took his last breath, when part of me died, through the panic attacks and physical symptoms, not being able to drink, eat or function, and slowly, over many years, not only learning to breathe properly again, but feeling so lucky to be alive.

I found a new energy which I channelled into family, my surviving children, and into work connected to my son. And eventually into other projects and people, all connected to this grief experience and the great desire to use it to help others.

When Grief Equals Love is the result of my investigation, telling the story of how I learned to live alongside loss, navigating a new landscape and accommodating grief into my life, both personally and professionally. I start with an account of Harry's life, followed by entries from the diary I started just before his death in November 2000. Leading on from those, I look at the myth of closure, survivor's energy and cumulative grief. I interview some of my friends and family about their unique experiences of grief, before discussing my current work, with advice on supporting others and a range of resources to enable the further exploration of grief.

It took a long time and much investigation into how to survive my own grief, and that is a work in progress, but I hope that some of what I have learned so far might resonate.

Part 1

Harry

Diagnosis

Harry was born in July 1994, resulting in medical records which read 'A vigorous, responsive infant'. My husband Hugo and I had a pretty idyllic life at the time – we were surrounded by close family and an incredible circle of friends. We had set up our own video production company in London but a year before Harry's birth had moved out to the Cotswolds, renting a gatehouse to a deer park, while we discovered whether our business could function away from the edit suites and recording studios of London. To boost our income while we established ourselves in the country, I was working on the first year of *The Big Breakfast* for Channel 4, which I absolutely loved – an exciting time for us all round.

I left Channel 4 a few weeks before Harry was born, feeling absolutely ready to settle down to our new life as a family, with our own production business and plenty of time together in breathtakingly beautiful surroundings.

When Harry was born, he didn't seem to have any problems; he was a slightly skinny but very energetic boy who just loved life right from the start – he smiled constantly. Looking back, his only problem was that, as I was a new mother, I would never put him down – I was far too scared! That first year, Hugo worked from home and I would help out when Harry had a nap; we had endless time together and friends and family visited regularly – everything in our lives was good.

Seventeen months after Harry's birth our second son Cameron entered the world and right from the start Harry and Cam became a team – there was never a hint of jealousy. I look back on that time now and just feel grateful we had it – it enabled us to resent what was to come less, and it gave us a solid foundation from which to deal with the blow when it hit.

Six weeks after Cam's birth, our health visitor came to carry out a routine check-up. While checking Cam, she watched

Harry crawling around and noticed that he could only pull himself up onto his knees, not his feet. I was completely relaxed about this since I didn't walk until I was two years old. The health visitor suggested we should make an appointment at the John Radcliffe Hospital in Oxford as, 'Harry might just need some physio to get him going.'

A week later we spent a day at the hospital while Harry had various tests. By the end of that day we were instructed to go to the Radcliffe Infirmary in the centre of Oxford for an EMG test (electromyography) to see whether Harry's problem was due to a flaw in either his muscles or his nerves. We still thought at this stage that we were simply ruling things out and I felt quite confident that there wasn't much wrong. The first test was fine – a muscle test involving a series of external electrodes placed on the skin and muscle reaction read via a monitor. This all seemed fine.

The second test – with little warning – was absolutely horrendous. Poor Hugo had to hold Harry on his lap, while the consultant inserted electrode needles directly into Harry's calf muscles. Harry screamed and screamed in absolute agony; I will never forget the horrified look on his face. This was nothing like the vaccination jabs children tolerate – this was intolerable for all of us.

Devastatingly, the consultant thought a mistake had been made and that the machine wasn't working as there was no signal whatsoever, even though Harry was in such pain. We both realised the machine was working and at that moment we looked at each other with the dawning realisation that there was something seriously wrong with Harry's nervous response. The consultant, of course, was not allowed to communicate with us until all the test results had been collated and analysed. We left the infirmary pushing Harry in a buggy, walking round the frozen fountain in the front courtyard of the hospital, both of us inconsolable – at this stage I think with a dread and fear of the unknown.

I don't know how we survived the following weekend. Dr Pike, the consultant paediatric neurologist at the Radcliffe, phoned us on the Friday, asking us to see him on the children's ward, without Harry, on the following Monday at the unusual time of 9 p.m. By this time, through our own research, we knew at best Harry may have a form of spina bifida; another option was a tumour on the spine and the worst option was muscular dystrophy. At that point I thought there was one type of MD, but was soon to learn there are many, many different forms with different outcomes.

On 4th February 1996, in Dr Pike's office, accompanied by Jane Stein, whose badge read 'Muscular Dystrophy Care Officer', we were told that Harry had (and I wrote the words down on a sheet of paper) an 'incurable, untreatable, terminal' condition called spinal muscular atrophy (SMA Type II). A severe form of muscular dystrophy, worse than our darkest fear, because (alongside our GP, it turned out), we didn't even know this condition existed. In addition to this was a fact we could barely absorb – all our children, male or female – had a one-in-four chance of having SMA. Harry would probably never walk, would need a powered wheelchair and may live into adulthood ('adulthood' being sixteen in the medical world), but that would depend on the condition of his lungs and curvature of his spine. However, surveys had shown that many children with SMA were particularly bright and used their minds to a greater extent than their peers due to the weakening of their bodies.

Aftermath

I remember our return home that night – the devastation, the traumatic shock of the diagnosis and the realisation that everything in our lives had changed. That was the moment our grief started; we were experiencing anticipatory grief.

In those days, the prognosis for SMA children was bleak. Thankfully it can be different now; thanks to medical advances and drug trials, there is more hope, but at the time it was still the leading genetic cause of infantile death. I tried to feed seven-week-old Cam, only to discover that my milk had dried up due to the trauma (it disappeared instantly and never came back). The great irony was that I had been advised to always keep a tin of formula milk in the house even though I was breast-feeding and the tin I had was the brand SMA.

Neither of us could go and look at Harry that night. He was fast asleep and was of course oblivious that our lives – especially his – had been shattered in one evening. We gradually phoned friends and family to let them know our awful news.

Again the next morning, when we heard Harry waking up, neither of us could bring ourselves to go to him; we let him play in his cot for a while. We simply couldn't face him, now that we knew the difficulties he had ahead and that his life was to be short. Everything had changed.

My parents were devastated. I am an only child – the offspring of parents who suffered fourteen years of multiple miscarriages and two stillbirths in order to have me. I was born into grief and through that into an appreciation of what matters in life. We have always been inseparably close, and they gave me the most blissful childhood with unconditional love.

Thank heaven they were also paranoid about spoiling only children – if anything, they went the other way with discipline, second-hand toys and a strong work ethic instilled at an early age. They were incredibly sociable and our house was always full of people – often my own friends visiting them whether I was there or not – just wanting to chat to my mum. I discovered the meaning of 'chosen family' at an early age. Later, Hugo became like a son to Mum and Dad, and when their grandchildren were born, their earlier struggles to have a larger family seemed to fade. Our news was a terrible blow, but we knew they would support us through thick and thin.

In fact, soon after Harry's diagnosis they moved from Kent, their home of twenty-five years, to a village in the Cotswolds just ten minutes away to be able to give practical help and their time. The ultimate gift.

Two weeks after Harry's diagnosis we decided to have Cam tested. We had been on an emotional rollercoaster, at first trying to get our heads around Harry's life expectancy and condition and not actually being able to face more potentially devastating news. Cam was still only nine weeks old, and so much had happened to us during that time. But after two weeks we felt we couldn't go on without knowing the full story: whether both our sons had the same barbaric condition.

I took Cam to the Radcliffe for a simple blood test – that tube of blood holding the key to his future and life expectancy. We would have to wait a few hellish days – possibly up to two weeks since the blood had to be sent to Cambridge. We existed through that time, waiting to find out whether our two children were going to die, not 'just' the one.

At this time I did experience suicidal thoughts. I would lie awake at night trying to work out how I could end all three of our lives at the same time; if both my children were going to die, then I wanted to die too – but in those dark hours, I could never quite work out how to do it.

On a Monday morning, a week after the test, Dr Pike telephoned. Hugo was just going out of the door to a meeting and my parents were out walking with Cam and

Harry in a double buggy. Cam was fine; he didn't have SMA. Hugo and I were overjoyed, yet it was mixed with guilt and horror – how could we celebrate the health of one child when Harry was still going to die? Only three weeks on from Harry's diagnosis this was all too much to take on board. I don't think either of us had even been able to contemplate life without either child – we needed Cam to help us through what Harry was to face and give us a reason for carrying on. I don't know how we would have coped if the results had been different, although now, I know other families who have experienced the deaths of two and even three children through genetic conditions. I have been to their funerals – the family's pain was unimaginable and to this day they are never far from my mind. Now at least Cam had a future – but one without his brother.

Living Grief

Although the shock of Harry's life expectancy was hanging over us, there were many smaller hurdles of grief which hit us gradually. I had been waiting for Harry to learn to walk before buying his first boots – these were essential for life in the countryside. I now realised he would have no use for them and this really hurt. I tried to rationalise Harry's death versus wellington boots but couldn't – it was still painful! So we bought wellies anyway and I cried in the shop as I paid for them.

The first time Hugo took Harry to buy shoes, the shop assistant asked Harry to stand up. He was sitting in a normal children's buggy so she didn't see a problem. Hugo was barely able to explain and nearly had to leave the shop as another wave of grief hit him. The sales assistant ended up in tears too. We began to realise that this had no end, that grief wasn't going to be only after Harry died; we had a living grief, which I sometimes felt was almost more painful. Being with Harry with the knowledge that his life was to be cut short was too unimaginable to comprehend, but we had to try and learn to cope with the waves when they hit us and to sometimes be able to shelve them until later. We also had to deal with other people and constant explanations – sometimes in front of Harry, which became increasingly difficult.

During the following year we met with Jane, the Muscular Dystrophy Care Officer, who in turn was able to put us in touch with other people we would need to know. Our lives became a round of appointments – consultants, physiotherapists, orthotists (for standing frames and callipers), wheelchair assessors, dieticians, educational psychologists, social workers, occupational therapists and many, many more. Sometimes the meetings would be with one of these people, often a group together – all of them discussing our child. Not only were we coming to terms with the life-shortening aspect of Harry's condition but we also had to take on board our lack of privacy and how we no longer seemed to have much control over any aspect of our lives.

As we tried to move forward through our sadness and grief, it became obvious that we must make the most of every second with Harry, for all our sakes. Harry was here now and this time should not be wasted – to quote Sister Frances, founder of the children's hospice movement in this country and worldwide, *it was not the length of his life which was important – but the depth*. The impossible aspect of living with a terminally ill child is that you always have their death on your mind. From the moment Harry was diagnosed, his funeral was never far from my thoughts, particularly on the way to our many hospital appointments – I would constantly wonder how the end would come: would we be at home or in hospital? Would he be in pain? Would we be able to speak to him? How much longer did we have together? Would Cam be old enough to remember Harry or, even worse, would it happen in teenagehood and prove even more devastating for Cam?

I worried for Cam more than any of us. Would we as a family ever recover? Of course, none of these questions could be answered; we just had to live with them whirring round and round in our minds while trying to make the most of enjoying our beautiful children. Ironically Harry always looked very well – even during hospital visits or soon after life-threatening chest infections he would look bright-eyed and a picture of health. He was a 'cup half full' child and always thought of other people – he just had a naturally sunny disposition, which stood him, and us, in good stead.

With two small children who knew nothing of their future it was vital that we carry on and the more energy we put into them, the easier it became. But sometimes grief would hit me when I least expected it – usually during a truly happy time; seeing Harry enjoying himself with his friends, laughing ecstatically at another appallingly bad joke, could force me to leave the room, engulfed with sadness, hurt to the core that this life had to end. I became adept at quite literally swallowing my pain, letting the grief subside, taking deep breaths and 'putting it away' till later. It wouldn't be until I put the children to bed after a happy day that I would allow the grief out again; I knew it had to surface and then I would give way to my pain. I would cry in private until there were no more tears, I was constantly drained physically and emotionally, yet by day I could carry on and enjoy every minute with my young children.

Life Lessons

In some ways I was aware that our appreciation of life had been changed and was even enhanced by what was happening to us. Our world had caved in and yet our grief-stricken state allowed us to appreciate the smallest things, the truest friends and the unconditional love of our family.

Some friendships didn't stay the distance and others proved to be strong. Throughout my grief I was aware of the privilege I felt in looking after Harry and I realised how much we were all learning from him. I have always had a huge awareness of the fragility of life – maybe due to my miscarried and stillborn siblings. As a teenager I read war poetry and prose avidly, *Testament of Youth* and Primo Levi from cover to cover, and had a fascination with illness and death rather than a fear of it.

I remember when I was fourteen, one of my parents' closest friends, Lionel, suffered a slow and early death in his fifties from Alzheimer's. On the day of his funeral, I asked his widow Gwen if I could stay with her that night. I realised that she was going to be alone and desperately wanted to be with her. Thank heaven my parents allowed me, and that evening we sat up, the pair of us crying, laughing and talking about life, death, the universe, the bigger picture, and also about Gwen's son who had died years before. How she would never recover from her son's death and how even her husband's death could not hurt her in the same way although they had been happily married for years.

I suppose that was my first hint of the pain of the death of a child, straight from the mother's mouth, yet here she was now, on her husband's funeral day, allowing me, a fourteen-year-old, to be alongside her and share it with her. It was a night I would never forget.

I have also always believed that nature will continue to outwit us and this was never more evident than with the advent of Covid-19. We live in a society where so many people are driven by money and status, people don't have time for death any more; it is seen as failure, rather than part of life. The unthinkable.

Cures for disease are quite rightly being sought, but there is scant care for those who are long-term, terminally ill; those who can't be cured. That is left to the many families like us to administer behind closed doors; at least that is how it can seem when you are in that position. People are frightened of this horror among them, especially when it is a child who is facing their mortality. Death is hidden now in the UK (with the exception of the Irish wake). Even pre-Covid, bodies were hurriedly taken away by undertakers, nobody given time to say goodbye, to linger over and accept the benefits of mourning. We fight illness until the final moments, a denial of what is inevitable, rather than celebrating the life that has been lived.

So in facing Harry's death, once we were able to think coherently we wanted to make the most of every second, to love him and relish our time with him, however painful that was going to be, and also to give him as normal a life as possible, to appreciate friends and family and have fun.

We were inundated with letters from friends during the early weeks of Harry's diagnosis and they truly lifted us. They were proof that there were people who were prepared to join us on this terrifying journey into the unknown.

Sharing the Load

Within days of Harry's diagnosis, two of our closest friends, Ben Hall and Polly Steele, made a suggestion which was to influence Harry's life and all our lives in the most wonderful way. Ben and I grew up together (we're still trying to grow up!) and have remained life-long friends and when he met Polly at university she became like a sister to me. Ben phoned to suggest that if we would agree to it, he and Polly would like to set up and run the 'Harry Fund'. Ben wanted access to our (pre-digital) address book and the phone numbers of our friends and family. We agreed to this and within a couple of weeks of Harry's diagnosis he and Polly had sent out a letter giving news of Harry's condition and prognosis and giving people the chance to be involved and help – firstly to buy the £10,000 powered wheelchair that Harry was going to need. Harry was not yet two and at that time the government would not fund powered chairs for such young children.

The Harry Fund helped us on so many levels. It allowed friends and family to feel they were addressing Harry's problems with us and that they could make a real difference to his life. The fund also enabled us to give out information about Harry's condition so that most people we came into contact with had quite good knowledge of what we were facing as a family and could discuss it with us without us constantly having to start from scratch; they felt involved and informed – and that helped us to feel less alone.

It was good for our local community too. Many people we didn't even know contributed to the fund and local children became more aware of how lucky they were to have good health, and not to be afraid of disability. Harry was recognised everywhere he went and no one felt embarrassed about approaching us for a chat.

We also had fun with many of the events – sometimes we didn't feel up to attending them, and everyone seemed to accept that, but when we did feel able, we could join in the sponsored walks, barbecues, fetes, etc. The Harry Fund was so successful with its initial fundraising that we were able to give money away towards other children's wheelchairs, equipment and research into SMA. The fund organisers also agreed that we should have a holiday while we were able to travel with Harry – this was wonderful advice because only a couple of years later this was impossible due to his deteriorating health and the sheer amount of equipment needed for each day.

On Harry's second birthday in July 1996, just five months on from his diagnosis, he greeted all his friends, whizzing around in his powered chair to see them as they arrived – he beamed and radiated freedom. No one would ever have imagined he had a care in the world. We were as ever struggling – in fact, at that party with twenty of Harry's friends and their parents, I had to leave the room in tears as they sang 'Happy Birthday'. Harry was about to blow out his candles when I handed the cake to my friend Cath and ran out. Luckily most people and certainly the children didn't notice. Everything seemed double-edged – buoyed up by the love and encouragement of so many, and aided with equipment bought by the Harry Fund, we could carry on as normal a life as possible, but still our living grief knew no bounds. It is also hard to see your child in a wheelchair for the first time.

Our GP had told us about Helen House Children's Hospice which was situated just twenty miles away from us in Oxford.

Helen House was the first children's hospice in the world. Founded in 1982 by Sister Frances Dominica, a member of the Anglican Society of All Saints Sisters of the Poor, it is open to people of all faiths or none. Helen House offers respite care for families of children with life-limiting illness. Many families use Helen House for short stays over a period of several years and on average are offered an allocation of respite care per year which can be taken over weekends and as longer breaks of up to a week. Alongside these planned visits, emergency care is offered – amazingly, any time of the day or night, 365 days a year, and for as long as it's needed. This was a lifeline for us and to this day I don't know how we would have coped if we had not been introduced to the work of Helen House.

My first meeting at Helen House was incredibly hard and Carol Hughes, our respite carer and dear friend, came with me, thank heaven. Walking through those doors for the first time, knowing we desperately needed their help, but that this was a *hospice* for our eldest child, was horrendous. We were shown into a room at the front of the building where we were able to talk before we looked round. I explained our situation to the staff and soon felt at ease with them. I had a dawning realisation that these people had experience over many years of dealing with children like Harry; they probably had more care expertise than any doctor we had met to date and were deeply perceptive, intuitive, highly intelligent and FUN!

The staff explained what they could offer and I couldn't believe that this independently run charity could give us so much compared to Social Services, who at the time gave us help (from Carol) for one and a half hours, twice a week. It seemed too good to be true, but over the next four years the staff were as good as their word and Helen House really did become our second home.

We discovered during our first few visits it was up to us to use Helen House exactly as we wished – we could lead the way. Some families prefer to leave their child with the staff while they go away, or stay at home to get on with things they cannot normally do. We loved staying at Helen House all together and each of us enjoyed our time there. In fact, if we didn't visit for a few weeks, both Harry and Cam would ask when we were next going. They thought of it as a wonderful hotel totally geared to children and with every toy imaginable on offer. It was heaven for them, especially since they didn't have the extra knowledge of what it represented; they could just enjoy their holidays there without an adult's emotional baggage associated with the word 'hospice'.

We would hand over Harry's care entirely so that we could enjoy time with our son without worrying about medicine, enemas or physio – that was not our responsibility here. Even on emergency visits usually due to chest infections, I felt comparatively relaxed. At home we were dealing with collapsed lungs and often near-death situations on our own but at Helen House we could benefit from experience and medical knowledge second to none. We felt safe and always knew that whatever the outcome of any visit, we would have the best care available and be consulted on everything. We could always be there as a family too, whereas on previous hospital visits, pre-Helen House, we would have to leave Cam with friends, often in the middle of the night, while we rushed Harry into hospital. It was such a relief to be able to be at Helen House together. I felt as though we handed SMA over to the staff and enjoyed Harry as our son.

Facing Reality

Over the years that we used Helen House I realised how very cleverly it had been planned. The building is mainly single storey; it feels like a giant eight-bedroom bungalow with light airy rooms and vibrant colours everywhere, and it is set in beautiful gardens. Off a long, wide corridor are six bedrooms usually available for planned respite care and an additional two which are kept for emergencies. Parents and siblings stay in one of the four flats. These are the only rooms to be found upstairs – this is to encourage families to spend a little time (even if only at night) as they will be in the future. Siblings who sometimes have to take second place due to their brother or sister's needs can have time with their parents.

At the end of the eight bedrooms, facing us all on our visits to Helen House, was the Little Room.

Based on the idea of an Irish wake, it is a vital part of the building design that this room is placed near the bedrooms. On first visiting Helen House this seemed hard, even cruel, but over years of visiting, it became strangely comforting. The Little Room is a chilled bedroom where a child's body is laid once they have died. The family are given total control over when the body is moved to the Little Room from the bedroom in which they have died, or sometimes children have died at home or in hospital and are subsequently brought in. Nobody will enter the Little Room without the parents' permission and the child will most often just be laid out on the bed there, a candle burning on the table next to them and with things they loved around them. They will not normally be put in a coffin until the day of the funeral. This gives family and friends time to be with them, to say goodbye and to grieve by their side; nobody is rushed and the body is not taken away from the family by undertakers, a thought which to this day fills me with horror.

Although during early visits to Helen House I tried to think of it as a child-friendly hotel, the inevitability of

Harry's death was of course always on our minds. It was important for us that the Little Room was there; it offered the comforting knowledge that I could now picture where Harry would be. Prior to Helen House I used to constantly wonder where Harry would die. I would picture him in a morgue at the Radcliffe, us having to drive away without him, but this was now so very different, and somehow easier to bear. We would all be in familiar surroundings, and even if Harry died at home, we knew we would bring him straight there. I always hoped he would die at Helen House, though, with us, his family and the staff he eventually knew and trusted so well by his side.

For some of the children or young adults who knew that their families would use the Little Room one day, I think on the whole that realisation worked for them too. I heard of a teenager who was staying at Helen House without his parents, when a child died there during his weekend visit. The staff gave him the chance to go home if he wished, as it may have been too hard for him to witness this so closely, but he chose to stay. During the weekend he observed the child's family entering the Little Room whenever they felt the need and he saw that through their tears they could still breathe and even smile; they were still a family, although a very different one. He had a meal with them in the main kitchen and chatted to them. The teenager found comfort in this and told the staff. Since diagnosis of his condition he admitted that he had mainly worried about how his family would cope after his death; he simply couldn't imagine how they would carry on, and now he knew that they would survive – he had witnessed it.

Emergency visits didn't always have to be an emergency for the sick child; they could also be due to another member of the family not being able to cope.

We always loved our ten-day summer holiday there too; we looked forward to it as much as, if not more than, other families going to exotic places. It was a complete rest for us from everything – especially in some ways from the outside world where we felt the odd ones out. This was our 'normal' and we were protected, with the addition of expert medical care.

In November 1998, after much soul-searching and genetic counselling, I was lucky enough to give birth to our beautiful daughter, Emilie. She too of course had a one-in-four chance of having SMA but thankfully we were able to have her tested in vitro and we were told she was clear. We were so thankful that Cam would have a sibling left when Harry died, that Emilie would have the privilege of knowing Harry and being part of our bigger family. We knew it would be hard bringing a baby into the world where already our time had huge constraints caused by SMA, but whatever happened, we knew we were doing the right thing for us all.

Part 2

Grief Diaries

I have included these diary entries because they illustrate what we went through twenty-two years ago, and because they also tell our story, which mirrors that of many other bereaved people whose grief starts on diagnosis, and carries on beyond the death of their loved one. At the time I felt the need to write and remember, partly for my own peace of mind and partly for Cam and Emilie should they wish to know what they had lived through when, due to their young ages (nearly five and two, respectively), they might not remember it all. I wanted them to know that they really grieved and honoured their love for Harry. Writing, with no pressure or timescale, and only when I felt like it, was cathartic. In some way it helped me to make sense of what was happening to us, when at times it felt like an extremely bad dream.

5th October 2000

Harry's lung collapsed this morning. It has been a long day. We decided under guidance from the staff at Helen House to put Harry on IV as soon as possible. Yet again we have come straight here rather than consulting our GP or the hospital. We are now at a stage where there is no point in going anywhere other than Helen House – we do not want Harry resuscitated or put on life support. An impossibly hard decision to make, but one we both feel strongly about. Harry has been depressed this summer about not being able to join in everything with his friends and some of his friends are not around as much as they were; they are fit and active – this is so hard for him. This situation can only get worse and worse and the thought of him deteriorating with a bright mind but failing body is horrendous.

Every part of me screams 'Let's do everything we can to keep him here forever!' With some medical advances, this would be possible, but I don't feel this is right for us. We would be keeping Harry alive for ourselves as parents, not for his quality of life, which to Hugo and me is the most important thing.

I have a constant sick feeling in the pit of my stomach, a nagging reminder of what we are facing; a reality check. It's the pathetic knowledge that we have no hope. As a parent I would do anything to protect my child – to make him better, but I can't. I suppose that is the main thing that parents at Helen House have in common: we cover a whole host of different illnesses, but in order to walk through the doors of Helen House, your child has to have no hope of a cure. We have had all hope taken away; they are incurable, untreatable and terminal. We are stripped of our maternal or paternal rights to protect our children.

Harry is breathing quite well and is in a deep sleep, I feel relieved and know he is in the best possible place. We seem to be entering a new phase with Harry as his lungs collapse more frequently and with less notice.

21st October

I haven't had the energy to write since our stay at Helen House. We came home last weekend, on the 14th, but since then have been inundated with phone calls, visits, good wishes, support and appointments. All much needed and appreciated, but completely draining. This week was the first anniversary of my mother's death. I couldn't visit her grave because I felt we came very close to burying Harry next to her this week and I couldn't contemplate going there. As an only child, I was inseparable from my mother – we were incredibly close in every way, and now I can't face visiting her grave. She is in my thoughts all the time, she had a huge influence on every aspect of my life and I miss her desperately, but with what I am dealing with now, I can't even grieve for her properly. It is just too much.

Note: Having selflessly moved from Kent to the Cotswolds to be near us to help when Harry was diagnosed, in another really cruel blow, Mum soon found she had terminal cancer and was given a year to live. On the same weekend I found out that our unborn baby Emilie was clear of SMA, Mum had started symptoms which led to her own diagnosis. It felt as though I was being told 'You can keep your daughter, but you have to sacrifice your mother.'

(Undated)

Harry nearly died again last week. He didn't respond to the IV for five days and seemed to be withdrawing from everything.

We were all so low last week, we barred all visitors and phone calls.

Thank heaven we are home now and let off the hook this time.

13th November

Harry is at home with another severe chest infection since the last bad spell.

I shopped in Witney today, while Carol stayed with Harry and Emilie. As I purchased Christmas presents I wondered if Harry will be here to receive them. How much pain can we endure?

At the Helen House Remembrance Service yesterday, Revd. Mike Williams mentioned men at war seeing things 'no man should ever have to witness'. I feel I am seeing things now that no parent should ever have to witness.

Pain all the time; tearing, wrenching pain. At its worst when I dry Harry's hair before bed, or kiss him goodnight and absorb his smell – that overpowering maternal instinct linked with scent which I know one day soon, I will never experience again.

14th November

My birthday.

Following a bad day yesterday Harry woke this morning desperate to go to school. 'I want to see my friends,' he said. We had already dressed him in his body brace and jeans ready for another day at home, but duly changed him into school uniform. He was determined. I felt a deep dread in the pit of my stomach but didn't know why.

I took Harry to school and then had a lovely sunny walk with my friend Cath, the dogs and Emilie in her yellow Tweenies boots. I still felt sick. I kept my mobile on throughout the walk, having guaranteed to the school that I would be nearby to pick him up quickly if necessary. This is hard for them too, frightening for us all, not knowing what is going to happen next – or in fact whether this will go on and on. No one knows and there is no one we can turn to for an answer. We just have to carry on.

We received a phone call from Rosemary Klee, Harry's dedicated school helper who has also become our friend. She has tried to persuade him to come home most of the morning because of his persistent cough and shortness of breath but he didn't want to until now.

I pick Harry up from school. It is lunchtime play and he whizzes up to various friends to say goodbye. His beloved Claudia (Cath's daughter and also my goddaughter) is playing with another friend and when he calls goodbye, she doesn't hear him. He looks upset, but carries on to the van. Claudia then sees Harry leaving and runs up to him, calling goodbye; this time Harry doesn't hear and Claudia looks devastated. The bell rings and Claudia rushes off. I have a fleeting thought: *I hope they see each other again to put this right.*

Initially at home, Harry doesn't seem too bad but his shallow, dry coughs get worse. Lying on the sofa with his head on my lap, his pulse races and he passes out.

I ring Helen House and two of the staff are sent out from Oxford to escort me there. Harry won't be able to sit in his chair, so Alison from Helen House sits with him lying against her in the back of the van, while I drive. Harry has said he will only go to Helen House this time if we promise no needles. No intravenous antibiotics. With a heavy heart I agree.

Harry has become really depressed about the increasing chest infections and use of IV lines. He has suffered with chest infections from the age of two, sometimes turning quickly to pneumonia and often lasting for weeks on end. Children with SMA (like many other conditions at Helen House) often find it difficult to cough. Harry has not been able to cough properly for the last few years, due to muscle weakness and scoliosis. His spine pushes on his lungs and we have to assist his coughing with physio in order for him to clear his airways for a short time. In the last couple of years we have often had to turn to IV when oral antibiotics have failed. For Harry being on IV means his arm is in a protective splint covered in bandages to protect the cannula. This means he cannot move or use that arm at all and sometimes hasn't been able to drive his powered chair. For someone who has very little use of his arms anyway (he has to ask us to lift his hand to his face to scratch his cheek for instance, or take a pen lid off a pen) this is devastating. The process of finding a vein in his puffy hands is agony too. He has had enough of this, and is generally exhausted and low from this constant treatment which has a short-lived effect.

A few weeks ago I had a very difficult but necessary meeting with Dr Justin Amery, old friend and Medical Director at Helen House. Justin sat me down one day and said we needed to look properly at Harry's chest symptoms and the way we were treating them. Together in Justin's notebook, we went through them one by one as I answered his questions.

He wrote:

Dry, weak, breathy cough
Lung collapse
Choking

For which we were using:

Drinks
Antibiotics
Physio
Nebulising with saline solution

Justin pointed out that most of the time these days, Harry is not really having chest infections; it seems that his lungs are collapsing each time when they get stuck with congestion and deflate. Through physio sometimes we can shift the blockage and his lung will re-inflate (we often manage this at home), but when we can't shift it then an infection can start. But really the infection is not the primary factor. Therefore antibiotics, although acting as an aid against infection, are not really the answer. Actually THERE IS NO ANSWER. This is of course what we have known all along, but by having this very difficult conversation in this room right now Justin is hinting to us that we might be facing things sooner rather than later. My gut feeling is that Harry may not see the end of this winter.

This conversation is followed up at the Radcliffe with our consultant Dr Pike, at our six-monthly check-up, and as usual a handful of other people were there too (a registrar, Harry's orthotist, muscular dystrophy care officer and his physiotherapist). Luckily we were the last people on the appointment list that day, as we broached the subject of future treatment. Dr Pike gave us all the time we needed and our appointment ended up being close to two hours long. Jane Stein from the MD group took the three children out while we covered all issues, all options and touched on the possibilities of artificial ventilation; the fact that we could, if we wanted, probably keep Harry going by hook or by crook, but possibly with little quality of life and much intervention.

We reach Helen House and Harry manages to drive in using his powered chair. I find myself apologising for coming in; it briefly seems unnecessary. Harry whizzes around and asks if he can use the computers while he is there. Bizarrely, it now seems, I speak to Harry and point out that we are here because he is ill, not to play! As I type this up now from my handwritten notes, I would give anything for him to play on those computers. Within half an hour of this initial energy surge, Harry becomes exhausted and we lift him onto the bed [not knowing then that this was to be the last time].

Blyth, the doctor on duty, arrives and confirms what we suspected: that there is very little air in one of Harry's lungs. Over the years it has always been the same lung that has collapsed; one has always been fine.

We find some privacy with Blyth in another room, away from Harry, and in a surreal way discuss our wishes at this stage. I can't believe we have come to this conversation. Since Harry's diagnosis at seventeen months to this day my life has felt like an out-of-body experience. Suddenly our lives took an irreversible turn, we lost control over many aspects of our lives from that point, and now here we are reaching the end of this part of the horrific journey. I am dying with Harry, my heart is bleeding and I feel my head exploding.

I feel sick, I have no air in my lungs and I keep forgetting to breathe. [As I copy these notes I forget to breathe now; I'm so easily back to square one; I have tears streaming down my cheeks.] We don't know what this is, but I have an awful sense of foreboding that simply won't leave me.

Harry, having been assured that he will not have to have IV again – 'Please, no needles, Mummy' – lies calmly asleep.

15th November

Hugo slept in with Harry last night; both had some sleep and they seem in good spirits this morning.

The good spirits don't last. Harry sleeps fitfully for only minutes at a time. When awake he coughs incessantly – breathy, airless, congested coughs which he is powerless to prevent and which don't shift anything. It is as though he is being strangled.

As the day goes on, I feel Harry withdraw completely. Hugo and I alternate sitting on his bed acting as his armchair; he leans on my chest [just the thought of that possibility now makes me cry again]. Harry only wants to watch television, no talk. Endless insubstantial coughs. An 'I don't want to know' and 'This isn't happening to me' attitude from Harry. No connection with us except for our assisting his breathing with physio.

At one point I tried to leave the bed to eat in a chair next to him but Harry wouldn't let me. He suddenly seemed to switch on again – 'Don't move because I love you,' he said.

Hugo's sister Louise arrives and is very upset. I take her upstairs and explain the situation. She was coming to see us at home originally today; this is a big change of plan. Louise has told Harry about a Pikachu toy that his cousin Olivia has. She goes into Oxford to try and get one for Harry – a mission.

My father and Kate Day (a close friend) arrive with birthday presents for me and flowers.

Suddenly Harry has the most horrendous choking fit and almost stops breathing. As it happens (it seems to last forever), he can't speak or breathe and his huge pleading eyes look deep into mine. A single tear runs down his cheek. I will never forget that look. He pleaded with those eyes: 'Do something, Mummy.' I was helpless, as I have been helpless for five years to do anything to save our boy. That is the worst feeling in the world. My heart practically stops. Eventually we clear the blockage and Justin is called. Harry sleeps, worn out.

The only thing that will stop that choking from happening again soon is morphine and a sedative to relax the muscles. I feel at once numb and hysterical inside. I want to die with Harry. Nothing can hurt this much. A morphine drip must signify the end.

Harry wakes as the syringe for the morphine driver is inserted into his tummy. He cries and begs us to take it out, pleading with scared eyes and voice, 'But you promised no needles.' I want to die even more. Not only am I helpless, but I have gone against my word.

Justin gets us all through this. He takes his watch off and gives it to Harry to hold. He promises Harry that if the syringe hasn't stopped hurting his tummy in fifteen seconds, he will take it out. Harry holds it and counts the seconds. He dozes off but thank heaven when he wakes he says excitedly, 'Mummy, this is working!'

We hold him, a parent on each side, and tell him all his Christmas presents. Harry's face lights up as it would on Christmas Day. I tell him about the Junior Monopoly for his computer – with animated fairground rides (he loves Monopoly but finds it hard moving the pieces on a board), about the Pokémon Fact File with 150 stickers. I almost feel I have given these things to him as he wide-eyed asks exactly what they are like and grins.

My head feels as though it's about to explode.

Harry asks for Cam and Claudia to be brought in tomorrow morning (they are together with Emilie at the Stebbings' house). He feels two-year-old Emilie shouldn't come because she might pull the syringe driver out – he laughs fondly as he says this. He adores his sister; they are very alike in character and he always puts her first.

15th November

I ring Cath (the first person I've spoken to since the morphine was attached) and can't speak. Silence. 'Is that you, Lizzie?' I hear. I just can't make my voice work. Eventually we make arrangements – thank heaven Cath and Libby, another good friend, have given us all this time by having the children.

Harry is refusing all food and other medicines today – we explain that he must try and drink, but he just doesn't want to. Fair enough; I certainly can't eat or even manage a drink of water.

I'm so grateful that having disconnected from us all day yesterday, with the fitting of the morphine he genuinely feels relieved – we have him back for a short while.

Harry is such a huge force in our lives; I don't know how we will cope without him. I'm desperate for Cam; they are inseparable. He loves Emilie so much and she will never have the chance to experience this properly.

The constant chatter in our house – I so often want the children to be less noisy as the levels rise through the day. How I long for that noise now. Harry's chair swinging backwards and forwards, nearly knee-capping us in the process.

Cam and Harry are always hilariously witty together – a comedy act. Will Cam and Emilie ever replicate that? How will we ever manage for Emilie to know Harry? Will we ever be able to speak without tears? I hurt all over, ache,

ache, ache. These thoughts are unbearable; I just want to switch my identity and feelings off.

We were meant to be a family of five – we felt complete. Now there will be a void, irreplaceable, irreparable.

Is it survivable?

11 p.m.

We have three beds in a row in Harry's room.

Everything is bright and warm. The staff at Helen House have always insisted that nothing appears clinical – this is so important for children who are used to spending time in hospital. This really does feel like home.

I talk to Harry. 'Do you know how lucky you are to have a brother and sister and parents who love you so much? We are so proud of you for doing brilliantly at school and being so clever. I love you, Harry.' He grins.

In the months after Harry's death I'm so glad I wrote this diary. At times I would become desperate, needing to remember this whole sequence of events and needing to know that Harry had been OK through all this, not scared. It really helped me look back and know that we had talked to him throughout. We also asked for our camera to be brought in and took a few photos of us on either side of our now unconscious Harry; these have given me strength and the knowledge that he was peaceful.

3 a.m.

Harry has an energy surge and is able to chat briefly but lucidly. He's excited about Cam, Claudia and Grandpa coming in tomorrow. He would love Emilie to come too, but is still worried about the morphine driver in his tummy. He talks so lovingly about Cam and Emilie. Harry asks to see the driver or 'butterfly'. We sit him up to look and he says, 'Cam wouldn't like it, it's not symmetrical.' He tells Welly (one of the care team) that Cam makes fantastic Lego models. This is to be his last conversation with us. It sums up how he and Cam fit together as a team, like twins. With only seventeen months between them they have always been inseparable. Harry creative, fluid and free-spirited; even with all his problems he was born with an enormous capacity to enjoy life. Cam has from birth been more careful and considered with everything, a meticulous eye for detail and unable to rush anything until it is carefully completed – and usually with perfect symmetry!

The gurgles in Harry's chest have moved across to the other lung now – the first time in all these years. He is really struggling with his breathing, but still manages to kiss us. We laugh with him – his eyes sparkle. He puts both hands up as much as he can and gently waves them as he always has done to ask for a hug. Me first, then Hugo. Sleep.

Hugo and I ask for privacy and stay alone in bed with Harry between us. We talk about how much it's going to hurt doing all the things we will now be free to do, but couldn't do with Harry. What a price to pay.

But we must do things for Cam and Emilie. Theatre trips, cinema, museums, long country walks and ongoing fun. We owe it to them, but right now I cannot imagine even breathing again without Harry in the world.

What must this be like for parents with one ill child and no other children? We are unbelievably lucky having Cam and Emilie; they will be our reason for carrying on. Our way forward. They will lead us now.

Harry looks so peaceful. I'm lying beside him but I cannot shut my eyes. He's cuddling the Pikachu toy while propped up on cushions, still in his school uniform which he simply wouldn't change for pyjamas. A beautiful patchwork quilt covers him.

My head aches, my eyes sting and I still can't take proper breaths. My teeth are permanently clenched and my jaw aches.

The staff move us into two huge bedrooms with wide dividing doors that can be closed, or left open for the whole layout to be used. I know that these are often the rooms used for families when their child is very sick. Their design means that we can have our three beds together and on the other side of the room is another single bed for Cam with a large sofa right next to it. This way we can be with Harry through the night with Cam right there in view, but slightly removed in case the going gets tough. Dad and Carol can have the sofa and be near us all but particularly with Cam. Dad must really be suffering watching us in this state, having so recently nursed my mum through cancer and watched her die; he now has to suffer this on his own. Carol has also been through so much with us – she has been with us unconditionally; part of our family.

During the evening Harry's godfather Jon and his partner Dale arrive – we sit on chairs around Harry's bed, listening to his laboured but peaceful breathing. Tears all round. Jon's brother Siggy died when Jon was eight. He has been through this with his own family and I know will be a tower of strength for us all. Sister Frances arrives and sits with us for a while; her presence is peaceful and calming. Later, our friends Brian and Ann arrive. I'm so pleased to see them and appreciate how very hard this must be for them because their own son Tim died from leukaemia at the age of eleven. I also know they want to be with us and say their own goodbyes. They are such extraordinary people that maybe they took some comfort from seeing the peace that Helen House is offering us, so different from their own experience with Tim in a large hospital. I wish they could have had the same care we are having.

Friday 17th November

During the night, the calm goes for a few hours and we all lose control for a while. My worst fears are confirmed as Harry's lungs fill completely with fluid and it starts pumping out of his nose with every single rasping breath. We increase doses of morphine. Harry's heart is strong, only his lungs are weak; his pulse rate is hardly changing even though he is drowning. This is HELL. I lie with Cam for a while (he's in a deep sleep) and can only get back to Harry when things calm down. My father bravely stands with Harry while I lose the plot, and wipes every breathful away; he too is doing his bit for Harry at the end. Staff give Harry an injection to dry the secretions – and finally things calm.

9.50 a.m.

After thirty-six hours on the morphine driver, Harry stops breathing. During the last hours Hugo and I hold him and keep telling him, 'It's all right, Harry, you can let go now.' We so wanted this to stop; there was no way back. All the way through this I could understand the links people make with birth and death. During labour that intense pain and fear of the unknown, the longing for it to stop and the complete lack of control over any part of it, just a waiting game. We waited and waited and even though the intervals between each breath became longer and each breath weaker, they still didn't stop. I couldn't hold Harry by this time. I lay next to him, but he was so full of morphine that when I put my face close to his, he didn't smell like my child.

A base, territorial feeling took over; his scent had gone and had been replaced by chemicals. I couldn't get any trace of my child's smell. I have always been very maternally aware of my children's scent; each one is different from birth. When they were babies, if someone else held one of my children, I could always smell the 'impostor' scent on my baby. As they grew older, and I knew Harry was going to die, I would lie with him at night, breathing in the smell of his hair and back of his neck, knowing it might be for the last time. Now I was there and my fundamental sense as a territorial and protective mother had gone.

Almost when we were least expecting it and beginning to think it would never happen, Harry took one last breath, a big pause and then the death rattle, the big sigh as the last air left his lungs FOREVER. At that moment part of us died too. I cried out but couldn't release any more tears just then; I was painfully dry-eyed, having cried so much for days.

What to do now? He's gone. We are hysterical inside, our grief indescribably painful. We have to tell Cam. Since he arrived at Helen House yesterday morning, he has spent his time with us on Harry's bed or playing with Carol or Helen House staff elsewhere in the house. He happened to be out of the room when Harry died. He looks sad and bewildered when I tell him and his first response is, 'Harry will be dreaming of marrying Claudia.' My grief is hard-hitting now, I can't function at all; it's like an out-of-body experience. I want to die too.

Cam comes into the bedroom to see Harry. He moves straight over to him and puts the Pikachu soft toy back into Harry's bed with him, nestling it under Harry's arm. This toy seems to have been symbolic of the boys' relationship over the last forty-eight hours. Harry loved it in the short time he had it and wanted to cuddle it in any lucid moments before he died. Cam eventually took it from the bedroom once Harry was permanently unconscious and constantly had it with him as Harry was dying. By that stage we all felt Harry was gone, just a fragile body barely functioning. Cam occasionally looked worried and guilty about taking Pikachu away but we were able to say, 'It's yours now,

Cam, Harry would want you to have it' – giving him and ourselves a hint of what was to come. Transition.

I manage my first meal in days – I haven't even been able to drink water, so feel dehydrated too. I was living Harry's death as if it were my own. My lips are dry and cracked like Harry's. We swabbed his lips all the way through. All those hours of listening to his body filling with fluid. His lungs were so weak and his body immobile but his heart so strong.

In the end those breaths were only every few seconds, but huge and gurgling, each one. Harry wouldn't let go until it was his time. No more enemas, Harry, no more hoisting, physio, endless hospital visits, no more waiting for other people, no more red-tape-bound professionals.

For us no more infectious laughter, no more weak-bodied hugs drawn from the depths of that strongest of hearts. No more crazy banter with your little brother. Those imaginary games you played with Cam, the two of you either using the wheelchair as part of play, or just forgetting it was even there. You loved each other so very much. I hope Cam and Emilie will find love like that for each other. You loved us all. Your adoration for your tiny sister, the way she would climb onto your lap (she knew at one and a half that she had to do that gently) and sit there as you drove around the kitchen – a look of ecstasy on both your faces.

But you are giving Cam and Emilie a different childhood now. We will have more time for them – particularly at bedtime when it used to take so long to carry out physio, enemas, etc. I found bedtime hard, as though we were taking away your freedom. During the day you had a lot more freedom, but nothing like that of your friends or siblings. From the minute your exhausted body was put on your bed you were then in our hands, totally dependent on us even to turn you over or change position. You had little choice in all this – even those horrendous enemas. I hated having to do that to my own child every night for years. You were so accepting, only occasionally questioning these things, but seemingly realising that we, like you, had no choice. It even hurt you when we lifted you; the pain showed in your face but you always tried to make us feel better about it. You spent your life reassuring others about your own condition. You were selfless.

18th November

Last night the Helen House staff were wonderful. They have watched families go through this process for twenty years, so they almost know what we need more than we do. We had to have our first meal without Harry. We chose to stay up in the flat with Cam and Emilie; we couldn't face joining other people downstairs. A trolley was delivered laden with delicious things and we laid the table upstairs. I lasted about ten minutes sitting there with the wrong number of places laid and the wrong number of us sitting there and couldn't do it any more. I left the table and found myself wandering around the flat in a daze. Miraculously the staff arrived back in the flat, knowing exactly what would be happening, and took over with the children – finishing the meal with them, bathing them and getting them completely ready for bed. By the time they were ready for bed, we were instructed to go and kiss them goodnight; they then gave us a glass of brandy each (Jacqui literally had to feed it to me like a toddler), and then we were tucked up and the lights put out. I really did feel like a child.

I worry about my father – a widower of only one year, and with no other children but me. He lives next door to us and I know he will have driven home to his dark house (there is no street lighting in our hamlet) and will face the evening alone. There is, for once, nothing I can do; for myself, Hugo, Dad or for anyone else. We are all unreachable. I do, however, feel I want our support group of Dad and our closest friends to be together, so I ring Cath Stebbings and ask her if she would invite them all over for supper. She obviously doesn't feel up to it after what has happened, but won't say 'no' to her bereaved friend! I hear later that they have had a good evening, laughing and crying together. I know that will have been good for Dad and hopefully for all of them to share this.

Staff and pupils at Harry's school have created a memory tree. On hearing of Harry's death, they stopped all lessons for the day and the head teacher visited every class talking to them and answering all their questions. Each child in the school cut out a paper leaf and wrote a message for Harry on it. At a special assembly later in the day the children placed their leaves on a memory tree in the school hall. We hope to have it in place for Harry's funeral. We owe much of Harry's happiness in the last two and a half years to Kingham Primary School and particularly to his one-to-one helper, Rosemary Klee. They made it so easy for Harry there, enabling him to participate in just about everything, including school plays and sports day. The children particularly used to think about how Harry would do things and join in and would always be concerned if they thought he may not be able to. Rosemary was so sensitive to Harry's every need and ours. We couldn't have wished for anyone more perfect to be with Harry; they shared the same sense of humour and Harry could confide in Rosemary. Like our respite carer Carol Hughes, she really understood what our life was like behind the scenes and is now part of our extended family.

Cam has made a junk crocodile out of milk cartons and has placed it on Harry's bed in the Little Room. He would have loved it. Emilie has painted a bee, now hanging on the wall next to Harry. A candle flickers gently on a small table. The Helen House staff are so considerate, constantly giving us back some choice over what happens with Harry now. This is so important when we have had all choice over our child taken away in the last few days and even years. As parents it seems our right to make decisions regarding our small children, yet when your child is terminally ill, from diagnosis onwards you lose much of that choice, as they do too. Always other people making decisions for you, hospital visits, constant intrusion at home and at school. Now, with Harry's body alongside us, just for a few days, we can all take stock at Helen House.

When Harry was moved from the bedroom in which he died, we asked the staff to use the room again; we didn't want to be taking up precious bedroom space with our things once Harry had been moved. However, the staff, after nearly twenty years of observing bereaved families like ours, knew differently. The next day, I was really suffering badly and felt a really strong urge to go back to the room in which Harry had died. I knocked on the door and walked in and everything had been left just as it was. All Harry's things were still in place, the same quilt on the bed – nothing at all had been disturbed. I spent quite some time there, going over the last few days; the state of the room helped jog my memory as to the order of things. I needed to do this and thank heaven Helen House gave me time.

The Little Room is very cold (for good reason, of course) and gives everyone a shocking 'chill' on entering. The sound of the refrigeration system sends shivers down my spine too. I find I need to see Harry, but it is also so very hard to enter that room and all it represents. This is the start of us facing our pain threshold and trying to battle through it without running away. I don't at any time feel I want to take any medication to numb these feelings – I want to feel this pain, every bit of it.

Hugo's family arrives together as requested. They wanted to come separately, but we are not up to many visits. We can barely speak or function on any level; grief drowns out all ability to give out to other people. Cam is thrilled to see his cousin Olivia and they play beautifully with Emilie. I take comfort from this; it provides a tiny glimpse of a way forward – through the children.

I take Hugo's mother Rosemary to see Harry and we stay a while – we also revisit the room where he died. We all talk upstairs, but they want to know too much about arrangements and we can't cope – we become exhausted again. They understand and leave. It has been a good visit; I'm glad they all came. I feel sad for Hugo's brother Aidan, who came immediately from LA, but not in time to see Harry. He is staying very close by in a hotel on his own, but we are not up to seeing him, or anyone. We appreciate him just being there and Hugo asks him to go with him to register Harry's death.

The staff are visibly stricken too. Nobody expected Harry to die yet; he always looked so well. They are also in shock and I love the fact that we can witness this. I would hate to see that hidden. They remain professional but show us their feelings too. Maggie the cook brings trays of food up to the flat – constantly trying to tempt us!

Hugo takes strength from spending time in the Little Room with Harry, but increasingly I find myself getting so mentally and physically distraught when I am there that I almost can't recover. How are we ever going to survive the funeral on Friday?

The Harry Fund founders, our beloved friends Ben and Polly, arrive with their children – we spend a little time with them and all visit Harry's body. Cam is keen to take Josie and Toby in – it helps him to share this with his friends as it helps us too. Carol and Roly are here too and although I am surrounded by people, I feel isolated and removed from my own body, yet at the same time comforted by this shared pain, seeing friends together – representing our life outside.

Since Harry's diagnosis, I have been an avid reader of the doctor and psychiatrist Elisabeth Kübler-Ross. Through more than forty years of working with terminally ill adults and particularly children, she has helped the hospice movement in America to evolve and has influenced the way death is dealt with in hospitals and the wider community. She is published in many languages and has transformed the way her readers think about death and dying. Throughout her writing the thing that comes across most clearly is the regret people feel (doctors and families alike) when they realise retrospectively that they didn't LISTEN to what the patient wanted until it was too late.

In so many of her case studies, the patient seems to know when death is near and has a need to put affairs (emotional and practical) in order. Kübler-Ross also insists that the greatest need for a dying adult or child is LOVE and good unconditional care, not, as she has witnessed so often, the avoidance of a difficult subject. I was certainly helped by my knowledge of her writing and, as with the staff at Helen House, we were able to benefit from years of experience of people who have worked alongside the dying.

Kübler-Ross had a great influence over the way I tried to listen to Harry, and still does to this day as I try to answer Cam and Emilie's questions with honesty, remembering that children go through the same stages of loss as adults. If not assisted, they get stuck and develop severe problems, which could be prevented. I can relate this to Harry and his gradual grief over loss of strength, his struggle to keep going, and Cam and Emilie with their profound and incurable grief over their brother.

I will always live with the knowledge that possibly, if we had given him more IV antibiotics – like last time and the time before, and the time before that – he might have gone on longer. If we had used external breathing devices he may have lasted even longer, but with discomfort, invasive procedures and poor quality of life. We knew that Harry didn't have the strength to fight again and that is what he was saying to us. We were all able to LISTEN. With Helen House alongside us, we could carry out his last wishes.

However hard, what a privilege it was to be able to do that, to have some element of choice.

While Johnnie and Cath Stebbings are writing the address for Harry's funeral, their daughter Claudia, Harry's soulmate, has had her not-quite-ready wobbly tooth pulled early. A brave act, but one she felt she had to experience. Claudia wants the Tooth Fairy to visit Harry and feels this will make it happen. She has made a tiny yellow bag in which to place it, and has written a letter.

23rd November

It is the day before the funeral and time to leave Helen House for the last time. Although we will be leaving Harry here and the next time we see him will be at the church, I feel ready to go home now. Another clever and subtle piece of reasoning by Helen House has taken place – as usual without us realising. During the first two or three days after Harry died, I felt hysterical every time I entered the Little Room and saw Harry's body, looking so 'normal' and peaceful – as if he could just sit up at any moment. I couldn't accept on any level that he was really dead. But as the days have progressed during this strange week, Harry's body has deteriorated – I realise now that he doesn't look the same; there are just subtle changes which mean he is not Harry any more and I will be able to leave. His eyes have sunk into the sockets and his fingernails are slightly changing colour – darkening. That's all, but it is enough to enable our departure.

The staff ask if we would like to place Harry in his coffin ourselves, but neither of us can face it. So they lift him in and we enter the room for the last time once this has taken place. Marie, one of our greatest friends at Helen House, stayed up late last night stitching simple white cotton into the coffin. The lining sent by the undertakers had a glossy synthetic sheen, which was not what we had asked for. We insisted it was fine and didn't matter, but Marie knew this would be our last sight of our child and that it should be just what we had asked for. The consideration of our every wish is quite incredible here. Nothing has happened all week without our consent. The coffin contains Harry's favourite soft kangaroo, Claudia's tooth and letter, Cam's enormous junk crocodile, Emilie's painting and our eldest child in school uniform – beautifully laundered by the staff. This is an image no parent should ever see and I can't look for long. I can't really take it in.

The day we have dreaded is here, as we leave Harry in the knowledge we will never ever see him again. Our pain is simply indescribable and I feel as though I exist on another plane – none of this can be happening. The staff wave us off and no aspect of my life seems familiar. We are in Hugo's tiny car – the four of us, not five. The big VW Caravelle van with its side lift has already been driven home by Carol and Roly – I couldn't have faced leaving Helen House today in that, without Harry, without a wheelchair.

The next few days are a blur, and my first handwritten diary entry leaps from 23 November 2000 to 13 December 2000. However, parts of the funeral on 24 November are still clear in my mind.

I remember leaving Cam and Emilie at home with our friend Jo Astor; we had asked her to stay with them since Cam was adamant that he didn't want to go to the church service or see the coffin. We respected this wish since both Cam and Harry had been quite traumatised by my mother's funeral the year before. Cam had strong memories of this and I felt we should listen to him. Jo would bring them along to the village hall in time to meet us straight from the service. Our friends Jayne and Martin stood helplessly in our driveway, waving us off as we left in a black limo. 'See you there,' we called, as if we were going to a party.

We chose, as Dad had at my mother's funeral, to greet everyone as they arrived at the church. This meant we would actually see everyone who entered the church and speak to them. We both took great strength from this and it kept us busy, welcoming everyone as they filed through. We were then on the outside with all our friends and family inside as the hearse arrived with Harry's coffin. We walked over and looked at the flowers – just one bunch of simple sunflowers on top and family flowers to be placed on the grave. I remember Hugo's brother Aidan's handwritten message – 'Harry, my hero'.

We entered the church walking behind the coffin. We managed to sing, I don't know how, and strangely I didn't cry then. I took a lead from our elderly friend Mamie Magnusson whose son Siggy had died and who had travelled all the way from Glasgow with her family to be with us. She sang heartily just behind me, one of the few, as most people were too choked, and we joined her. I was aware all the way through that in such a huge congregation, and many of them with strong musical talent, the sound didn't represent the numbers. I looked around occasionally, lifted by the sight of our grieving friends, knowing our pain was shared. For most of them the reality only hit on entering that church and seeing the coffin.

At the vicar's suggestion the congregation were encouraged to write a message for Harry on a yellow star. These would be collected and put in his grave. There were many children among us who needed help through the service; Harry's school had closed early so that those families who wished to attend could be there. The stars gave the children a focus. Ben, my kindred spirit since childhood, appeared in front of me, tears streaming down his face but giving me an ironic smile; he had been asked to collect the stars in a basket. On the day Harry died, Ben had been in an important investment meeting for his TV company. He took the call, explained what had happened and asked for a ten-minute break. He left the building and sat on a pavement in the heart of Soho sobbing. He then collected himself and managed to return.

Harry's head teacher gave a beautiful address and Johnnie's eulogy enabled laughter and tears. As we left the church behind the coffin, Ceredwin, the music therapist from Helen House, sang. We walked out into a grey November drizzle. Freezing cold and soaking wet, it somehow seemed fitting. The churchyard was packed with people standing among the graves as we said our final goodbye.

I found myself among a sea of faces at the village hall. I stood in one place and didn't move for the whole time we were there. Libby and Cath had organised the whole thing. Parents and staff from Kingham Primary School had made cakes and many of them served tea and cleared up the hall. Around twenty friends joined us that evening for a spur-of-the-moment wake, including Aidan before his return to America and our Scottish friends before their journey home. We went to bed exhausted and drained – thankful for the end of that day and naively unaware that our worst grief was to hit in the coming months and years. Thank heaven I didn't know then that the death of a child gets worse, not easier, as time goes on from when you last saw them. You just get better at dealing with it.

The weeks following Harry's funeral are a blur on the whole, but interspersed with memories of Cam and Emilie's grief. Every day for a few weeks Emilie (aged two) would wake and stand in her cot in the morning saying 'Where Harry?', or 'Harry not here.' Cam would run in and explain to her patiently again, 'No, Emilie, Harry's dead, he is never coming back.' It was agony.

Cam was terrified of being alone; he couldn't go upstairs on his own even in daylight; we constantly had to be with him wherever he went. He didn't want to accept invitations from friends to play and even when we were all invited to lunch with our friends the Ways, whom Cam had known all his life, he fell apart. On that particular day Hugo and I were feeling quite positive and looking forward to venturing out again, especially with such close friends. Poor Cam, however, couldn't deal with this at all; it was one of his first outings without Harry. Normally Harry would have whizzed in first to greet everyone with Cam riding on the back of his wheelchair, happy to have the social shield of his big confident brother. Now without Harry, Cam suddenly found himself having to play the role of big brother and we soon realised that we would have to take things very slowly. The Ways' three children tried every possible method of tempting Cam to play, but he couldn't speak the whole time we were there and spent much of the time under the table; he just sat, staring into space. I look back now with horror as I remember telling Cam off for this behaviour on the way home in the car – I just wanted something to be normal in our lives and nothing seemed to be. Three years later I witnessed Cam just beginning to emerge from his shock and grief, which is completely understandable. I don't think at that time I had any ability to rationalise any more – we could all cope with different things and all be hit by our grief at different times; this made family life very difficult.

On another occasion I went to visit friends and their four sons in Wales, with Cath and her three daughters. Cam had really looked forward to this visit, but again when we arrived, he couldn't speak to the other children and was miserable all day; he just couldn't join in, although everyone tried to tempt and persuade him. I cried all the way home and vowed to stop accepting these invitations – they were miserable for us all and isolating, but especially impossible for Cam. We hunkered down at this stage and tried to see people at home, rather than at their houses – this was better for us all. We had all lost confidence and it would take a long time to return. I felt very alone.

13th December

Cam at bedtime: 'I hate being on my own without Harry, without anyone.'

Me: 'But you still have Emilie?'

Cam: '...and you, Daddy, Grandpa, Pingu and Nibble [our dog and Cam's rabbit]. I can't remember what Grandma looked like though.' We go downstairs and look through photo albums, sitting by the Christmas tree broken-hearted, the pair of us. Cam decides to go up to bed after all and is peaceful.

3rd January 2001

Walking along after our first Christmas without Harry (last Christmas was my first without my mother, this, my first without my son), Cam is on a spending spree with Christmas money. Suddenly he says, 'I wish I could show Harry my Christmas presents.' I don't know what possesses me – just a desire to make Cam feel better, perhaps; to protect this small child from the horror he has already witnessed and give him hope – but I answer, 'Maybe Harry can see them somehow.' Cam looks quite horrified and slightly scared – he doesn't actually like the idea of Harry being anywhere other than with us. 'Mummy, maybe I will have to be very good if Harry is watching me all the time.' I don't really know what I believe, but I do know that some of the things other people say in order to placate me, and to protect themselves from my pain, are quite hurtful. They mean to be comforting as I do now, but actually I hate the thought of Harry being anywhere other than in our hearts and memories if he can't be with us. The idea of him being 'happy in Heaven', as some have suggested, is too distant for me and maybe for Cam too.

I discuss this with Marie, our friend and bereavement support at Helen House. She, as always, gives me advice on dealing with Cam's grief based on many years of observing families like us.

Marie's advice is to always tell the truth and try not to protect Cam from his own grief. I could have turned to him and said, 'Yes, Cam, I wish you could too.' That was all that was needed and that way I would have shown understanding of his pain, without trying to take it away. Marie asks me if anything anyone else ever says to me comforts me, and I answer no. This is the same for a child: we can't make it better for Cam and have to accept that. He needs to live through his pain alongside us and get through his own pain barriers with our support, not hindrance.

4th January

On entering our bedroom, Cam's very first thought of the day is, 'What do you do on a dead person's birthday?'

Me: 'You can do whatever you feel like doing. I don't really know; what would you like to do?'

Cam decides he would like to do something with the Prices and the Stebbings and others who loved Harry – a picnic maybe.

5th January

Emilie wakes and calls for Hugo who has already left for work. She phones him on a toy phone and babbles away. Minutes later she calls for Harry. 'Where's Harry? Dead,' she keeps saying, then picks up the phone and tries to call him. 'Harry, Harry, Harry.'

6th January

Cam: 'Harry and I were twins, weren't we?'

14th January

To Helen House for our first visit since Harry died. Supper there with Cam and Emilie and some of our favourite staff. It is lovely to see them as we sit once more at that kitchen table. Lots of crying and talking. Cam is so happy to be back and is fine. Emilie walks along the corridor to the children's bedrooms, opening doors and calling for Harry. More tears from me.

I ask advice and tell them how confused I feel about how to deal with Cam, constantly wanting to protect him and make him feel better. The staff reiterate that we must just let him grieve and be there for him, never protect him or placate him. Only tell the truth.

15th January

I read the second part of *The Death of a Child* to Cam this evening. I wanted to give him other people's words, not just our perspective all the time, yet so many of the children's books on death that I have seen are patronising. He listens intently to every word in this one. When the mother in the book says that the brother will die soon and the child asks, 'What will happen?' Cam, aged six, says, 'His heart will stop beating and he will go cold.'

As we walk out of the room having read the book, Cam says, 'I've got tears all down my cheeks,' but he hasn't – he is crying inside.

16th January

I see the bigger picture more easily: we can try with all our might to create the perfect race through genetic science, high-tech medical research, etc., but nature will always outwit us. It is part of natural selection, culling; and whichever illnesses or conditions are cured there will always be new strains around the corner.

The perfect race would be unbearable anyway, a horrendously selfish society, even more so than now. I look at the community in which we live. Harry's death has made our friends cherish their own children even more and question their own mortality. Some have even re-evaluated things in their lives through Harry. There are those who are untouched by it; they have been scared and have denied themselves those feelings. They have no understanding and are, I feel, poorer for it. These people don't deal with life and death or imperfection, they are often in denial till either they die or something happens to them to change the course of their lives.

Late February

Harry's godfather Jon, along with his sister Margaret and the rest of the Magnusson family, have paid for us to have a holiday in Sanibel, Florida, an island off the west coast. Their generosity is selfless; they understand. It will give us a chance to be together, this changed family, away from everything at home. They have suffered this same pain themselves for their brother Siggy.

It feels strange going away anywhere. I feel as though we are leaving a child behind while the rest of us go on holiday. I have to take a framed photo of all three children with me on the plane.

Emilie constantly phones our friend Nancy from imaginary phones and ends each 'call' with, 'Back home now.' How two-year-olds love routine – she is totally confused by all this, but then her life to date has been pretty confusing, and so has mine!

We swim in the sea right in front of the apartment and sit on the beach as the sun sets and the children play. I pick up perfect shells and cry silent, invisible tears: Harry loved shells. I will take some home for his grave if I don't die with the pain I feel at this moment. My pain always seems to be worse when we are having a wonderful time. I hate the fact that we are able to be here without Harry, somewhere completely inaccessible to him in his lifetime. We are here with two of our three children and it hits us all hard. I feel incomplete and can't believe that we have to live with this pain for the rest of our lives; it seems impossible right now.

An elderly American lady wanders over to talk to me on the beach – she chats about children and families and I long to tell her that this is not how we are, there is one missing, but I can't. I would burst with uncontrollable grief if I even mentioned Harry.

During the night I lie awake thinking about home, and our life at the moment. We are lucky to have such loving friends and family and so much support but I can feel isolated much of the time through my profound loss, especially in a crowd. Cam has been angry with Emilie since Harry's death and I understand this. She is so young and a girl; Cam probably compares her to Harry – an older boy, a natural leader – and it's hard. This holiday might help them be together with sea and sand and minus outside influences. Cam said last night, 'I'm not going to pick on Emilie any more' – I think he is beginning to realise. When we return to England we must continue to have quiet times just as a family and not accept every invitation under the sun; we need to give the children time together to get used to being just two.

26th February

Cam is annoyed that Emilie is copying him. Hugo explains that when you are two or three years old it is good to have someone to look up to and admire. Cam replies, 'Well, what I really wanted was a big brother – like Harry.' We all did; Emilie did too.

Emilie still wants to go home!

Lunch at Fernandos, a beautiful restaurant with a deck overlooking the sea. This whole scenario seems so perfect, yet so alien. I think the pain of Harry, the fact that our eldest child has died, is just as strange and surreal to me as it would be for any of our friends if they try and imagine never seeing one of their children ever again. It is unimaginable torture, like living your worst nightmare for ever more. There is no way out, no escape for any of us.

Will we ever enjoy experiences like this again, without this chronic, all-consuming pain?

28th February

A much better day; we explore the Everglades by airboat – alligators everywhere, blue cranes and wild boars (luckily not the human kind!). At bedtime Cam cries, 'I feel sad about Harry. I'll never forget him; he was my best friend.' We must not placate, only empathise. I suggest that we take shells back for Harry's grave and Cam's face lights up. A long and loaded hug follows.

26th March

Hugo's goddaughter Maria comes for tea. She asks if she can play on the My Little Pony CD on the computer. It hasn't been used since Harry died. We switch it on and the last date Harry used it appears on the screen – June 2000. All the names of the ponies are there – Claudia, Wind-whistler, Sweety-pie! The music makes Cam and I feel very sad, and we have a big talk when Maria leaves. Cam says it was like having Harry here again.

16th June

Three months ago I read Cam a book I wasn't sure about called *Water Bugs and Dragonflies*. I found all the heavenly references of leaving people behind for another life hard, but thought Cam should have all the options in order to form his own opinion. When I read it to Cam he seemed distracted and I didn't think he had really been listening.

Just a week ago at Cam's second Helen House Club meeting (for bereaved siblings), this same book was read to the children. In a group discussion afterwards, apparently Cam didn't say much about the book; he was more interested in talking about the sand sculpture that he had made that day.

Today I was sitting at the kitchen table with Cam, when he looked across at our tadpoles in their tank (about to lose their tails and turn into frogs). He related their change to the dragonfly book and repeated the whole story to me; how the water bugs become dragonflies and are free to fly, but can't get back to the bugs remaining below to tell them what it is like up there. He had clearly understood and taken in the whole story, but had stored it away until now.

We spend the morning at the Cotswold Farm Park, our

first visit without Harry. As we step out of the car, Cam sees a big puddle and says, 'If Harry was alive he could whizz me through that.' So many things remind him of Harry; it is wonderful that he can remember all these things even though it is seven months since he last saw him. It's such a relief: Harry lives on in Cam's memory as well as ours.

27th June

At breakfast Emilie suddenly says, 'Mummy, Harry not better yet,' shaking her head very sadly. I feel gutted for her that she thinks Harry might still come back after all this time, with a heart-wrenching lack of comprehension due to her young age.

5th July

Harry's seventh birthday

We have a surreal but beautiful day. Last year a big party with Mark Andrews, the children's favourite entertainer. This year Harry's gravestone is put in place.

Many friends call by with flowers and good wishes. I appreciate their courage in facing us today.

9th July

Cam wakes up and says, 'Daddy – when Harry died, you bought me a Push Pop.' (A lolly.)

Emilie wakes up again with, 'Harry not feeling better, Harry dead, we not going to see Harry any more.'

And so it goes on.

August

Over the summer dear, brave friends ask us to go away with them – we are spoilt by all and appreciate them asking us when we are not in a very sociable state. We could ruin their holidays and probably will! We are also very aware that we must attempt to holiday on our own too – just to try being together with our different dynamic. I look forward to the holiday on our own in a friend's house in Scotland, but when the time comes, we rush back from that holiday days early – we are not ready to be on our own yet, as the four of us; we are better with other people, if they can cope with us! We have a fabulous holiday in Menorca with friends Jeremy and Francie Clarkson, whose three children are the same age as our three. Cam and Emilie play happily all day long with Em, Finlo and Katya and I find this incredibly comforting. There are plenty of tears from us, but we are helped by being part of their larger family. We also have the most wonderful week with Ben and Polly and their children Josie and Toby in France – I feel I can let go of yet more tears with them; we all spend as much of the holiday crying together as we do laughing. Josie, who is just younger than Harry, is a real strength to me. Just what was needed.

7th October

Emilie asks for the millionth time, 'Is Harry coming back, Mummy?' 'No, darling, Harry's dead, he can't come back.' More tears till I run dry.

Cam wakes up crying during the night, devastated, having dreamt that Harry was alive and they were playing together. He cries and cries. I haven't had any realistic dreams like that and I almost envy him.

24th March 2002

I attend the first of eight sessions of a bereavement course for parents held at Helen House. It has been painstakingly organised by Marie, Jan and Erika. Fifteen of us went in feeling fine and all came out complete wrecks. On leaving later in the day, I wonder if I may have done the wrong thing by going. I am back to the state I was in the week Harry died. Shock, trauma and gut-wrenching grief. Although I have a good cry every week it isn't that sort of cry. This is really letting the plug out and it takes me a few days to come out of it.

The course opens with us all showing the person next to us a photo of our child and talking about our own story for five minutes (timed). They reciprocate.

We discuss as a group how that felt. Here, I feel that I've been honest whereas normally in discussing Harry with a stranger I would skim over emotional detail and instantly try to make them feel better about the situation, quickly moving on to something else. Everyone admits that they spend their lives protecting other people from the truth, from the real state of their minds. This happens every day.

We are a mixture of parents. Some women on their own, one man on his own and a few couples. One whose child died nine years ago, another just last year and another couple whose two children died and there was no test to enable further 'safe' pregnancies. Our guilt in protecting people tends to creep in where they are concerned – I feel I shouldn't be complaining about anything when I have two healthy fantastic children. I simply don't know how they get out of bed each day, which is probably how people with healthy children feel about us.

During part of the day we carry out a simple but powerful exercise which sends us all into the depths of despair. A picture of a tree is placed on an easel. We can see its roots below a line of grass, a heavy, thick trunk and substantial lower branches reaching out to tiny twigs up to the sky. We are asked to dig deep and think about how we really feel at this moment in our lives. If we want to, we can take stickers from a table in the middle of the room and write our thoughts down and stick them on the tree in a place appropriate to how we feel. We all sit in silence and withdraw inside – we take it seriously. The grief in the room is tangible – indescribable and not only surrounding us all but within us all. I have tears instantly pouring down my face and have to leave the room to gather myself together when I think honestly about how I really feel. Some are very quiet, eyes closed, pain etched all over their faces. My head is banging and three or four of us take stickers and place them on the tree; others just sit in contemplative silence. I write 'pain', 'sickening grief', 'tears', and put them on the outer branches of the tree, where they are in my mind: close to the surface, never far away but always covered from view. I write 'happy memories' and place it not near the roots but close to the main body of the tree; not buried, but fairly deep, sometimes hard to reach through the constant pain and bad memories of Harry's death.

We all break down after this exercise and the rest of the afternoon is spent in discussion. Many cry openly as they speak – the main theme being the constant and forever missing of our children; the fact that this will never change; how after nine years one couple feel worse now than ever before; how the man whose only daughter has died does not know how to cope at work: he has lost all meaning to his life now. How we would all give anything just to hold our children again.

I come home and cry and cry once the children are in bed. I can't stop. I often do that in the middle of the night, always on my own, but not like this. This is raw again and I wonder if it is the right thing to have done. Three days later, though, I feel a real sense of being able to cope again and a sense of relief. Maybe it was good to let go and have the luxury of being honest in a safe and understanding environment.

After lunch the staff show us 'comfort' boxes they have prepared for us in the hope that we will make our own for next time. Again this is very moving and also helpful. People have placed anything from chocolate to music, candles to photographs – or very special items related to the person they love.

15th April 2002, 2 a.m.

Douglas House turf-cutting ceremony

Note: Helen House was eventually renamed 'Helen & Douglas House, Hospice Care for Children and Young Adults'. Douglas House became the first dedicated hospice in the UK (rather than a wing or floor of an existing children's hospice) for young adults from sixteen to thirty-five.

I've been awake so much tonight – on a complete emotional high all day, but now coming back to reality, some good, some bad. I feel strange about it – I was there in a dual role and it felt a bit odd. I was mainly looking after Graham

Norton, who was there to cut the first turf. He is such a star; the energy he gives out at something like that is phenomenal – people grabbing him constantly for the next autograph, press going on and on at him – even at something like that asking too many questions. He was so giving and polite and I loved him for it yet again. Jon (Harry's godfather, who works closely with Graham) and Hugo were finding it all very hard, I think. Hugo for obvious reasons and Jon – his first visit to Helen House since the night before Harry died. And then all our Helen House teenagers – having a great time as usual, but for them this is such a loaded day. Hugo summed it up last night when he talked of Helen & Douglas House reaching people on so many levels. When I took Jeremy Clarkson and Graham around the house yesterday, I felt they really understood the place better. Jeremy was visibly touched when we reached the room where Harry had been laid out and looked at the Book of Remembrance. For people like Jeremy and Graham, Helen House perhaps gives them a way of making sense of their strange position in life – fame, wealth, etc.

Care team member Erika spoke of the emotional impact of today for the staff. The fact that she would never again (once it's finished) have to turn away children because they haven't died yet. 'Sorry, you've reached sixteen and you shouldn't have – you can't come to Helen House any more, you're too old – oh and by the way, no one can provide anything else.' For us as bereaved parents – our children will never use Douglas House and sadly we will never stay there, but we understand the need for such a place. I used to lie awake at night wondering how we were going to cope as Harry grew towards adulthood (sixteen in medical terms). But now our teenage friends will have that provision.

As Sister Frances said yesterday, some of them want a soundproofed music room so no one will ever complain about the noise, the biggest and best Jacuzzi because it's so annoying at Helen House when you have to wait your turn, huge bedrooms so they can all get together for chats late at night, and a bar – with FREE drinks. She has made all this possible. Please let our friend Nick Wallis be there to see it and use it. Although even if he doesn't get there he'll have had so much fun and enjoyment anticipating Douglas House. And Jeremy and Graham were there because of Harry and yet again that made me very proud: the ripple effect of all those children who stay at Helen House is so powerful given their often-short lives.

It's 5 a.m. now and I haven't slept much at all; I feel elated and devastated all at the same time. Such mixed emotions. I miss Harry as usual, so much; I miss his conversation. I'm reminded of our last summer in Kielder Water. Sitting at the kitchen table with Harry, the others were all out and we just sat opposite each other chatting about this and that. He was so animated about all sorts of things, and we laughed constantly. Suddenly a wave of grief hit me as we chatted and I had to make an excuse about going to the loo, where I went and had a quick and silent but massive cry from the pit of my stomach, then I went back and we carried on. In those moments I was acutely aware of how little time his lungs were going to give us (just from their general state) and how I was going to miss out on those chats – each time thoughts like that hit me I wanted to die. That is the only way I can describe the pain I feel now and felt then. But today I saw my other beloved teenagers and we must fight for them. Harry can't be here but they are and we must carry on in their names.

[Devastatingly, Douglas House closed in June 2018 due to struggling finances and staffing issues. They had severed ties with Sister Frances in 2015. There is now little or no respite provision for the young adults and their families who benefited from it, and Douglas House staff lost their jobs. Helen House remains open and much needed.]

We parents of terminally ill children did not have the luxury of just enjoying our children in a pain-free way.

Every time we did something happy it was also acutely sad – that living grief for what we were about to lose – almost the most painful feeling I have ever had.

Last week we were driving along in the car and Cam told me that he keeps remembering the week Harry died and how he kept going into the Little Room to look at Harry. He described it perfectly even though he hasn't been into the room since Harry died. He was nearly five at the time and six and a half now.

Flashes of memory seem to come from either Cam or Emilie most weeks. Emilie asked me if Harry was run over last week. I had been teaching them about the road outside school and telling them yet again about Jon's brother Siggy being run over. This has stayed with Emilie. She's constantly muddled about Harry and trying to make sense of it in her three-year-old mind. It will probably hit her harder and harder the older she gets as she does make sense of the great void in all our lives.

28th April

One and a half years on, we have our first really OK day as a family since Harry died. The sort of day most people take for granted but that we have never been able to. We get up late, reading in bed while the children play. Breakfast reading the papers while Cam paints. Then out with the children's bikes where Cam overcomes another huge hurdle and learns to ride his bike with Hugo's help. Cam is ecstatic – absolutely euphoric – and we all laugh, cheering and clapping in the sun – Emilie is pleased for Cam and Cam is proud of himself. This is so good for his battered confidence.

Back home for lunch with Dad – a lovely family lunch, but as always missing Mum desperately. It is still so strange to sit at a lunch table with no Mum and no Harry, it doesn't bear thinking about, and yet we are all strangely happy today. How can we be so happy sometimes through a simple day like this and yet we are at the very same time devastated, forever? The depth of our sorrow is the height of our joy. We appreciate the small things.

Maybe because we were lucky enough to have the unconditional love of them both and that will stay with us always, enabling us to live day to day even though our hearts are broken. We are lucky enough to feel that we did all we could for them. I had the most wonderful relationship with Mum all my life till the day she died. She taught me to live for each day, each minute, each hour. We weren't perfect and we would argue, but it never lasted beyond that day; we always made up by bedtime and started afresh, each day a new day. We taught that to Harry too: if we'd had a bad day with doctors or brace fittings or lung collapses, etc. we would always try and just put it behind all of us and start the next day anew, constantly trying to rise beyond our heartbreak and make the best of what we had together. How lucky we have all been to share those relationships at all, but how heartbreaking it is to have lost them now.

26th May

Second Helen House Bereavement Course day

We start saying how we felt after the last day we spent together. Most people felt awful for the next few days and then much better for a while. One father talked of the relief but then went downhill again a couple of weeks later, finding it hard to talk to people at work, finding no common ground at all with his colleagues. He talked to friends, but became too honest – having felt relieved at letting his feelings be known with us, in a safe group, he tried the same with friends and soon realised it couldn't be applied there; they couldn't cope.

One mother feels she's calmer having come through the slightly mad euphoric stage that we went through just after Harry died, the adrenalin kick. Erika writes down key words and sentences that come up – a common thread. We all feel a huge bond with each other, having been together before. We open our comfort boxes, which are interesting and moving. One mother has her son's diary from when he was ten – full of words and pictures. His teddy, then classical music, bubble bath, etc. A father has chewing gum which he always hated people chewing, but now finds to be relaxing for his tightly stressed jaw – he still hates to see other people doing it! A can of beer, a key ring with a Ferrari – he loved driving his blind daughter around.

I share mine. The pillow Claudia made me last Christmas to represent sleep. An empty box (Harry's pencil box) to represent the part of me that can never be fixed. *A Grief Observed* by C. S. Lewis. A photo of Cam and Emilie and Hugo (I say I feel strange about that one, knowing there are people in the room whose only children or two children have died). A knife and fork to represent getting round a table with good friends. Mum's favourite serenity prayer, which I find I can't read out as I'd planned as I'm crying too much, but it represents Mum's strength and wisdom and all that Mum and Dad gave me in security and family. How much I miss her now, but how that prayer (I've put the word 'God' in brackets and explain my agnosticism to the room) will give me an answer for any situation as it did for her.

Grant me the serenity
To accept the things I cannot change
Courage to change the things I can
And wisdom to know the difference.

I'm crying a lot by the end of this, but we all cry on and off all day.

We break for lunch, which becomes completely hysterical as Marie and Erika start telling stories (to lighten the load). One father and I are crying with laughter – a fine line of release. We all go mad with laughter and for a while can't get back to serious stuff when we go upstairs. We place tissue-paper blossom on the tree drawing for the good things in our lives. Not everyone can put any on but two of us place a piece on for liberty and freedom to do things we couldn't do before, simple things like sleep and reading and endless other things that were curtailed for many years. A double-edged freedom we all agree.

13th June

Breakfast: Emilie: 'When is Harry going to come alive again? I wish he would come alive again.'

Note: In 2002 I knew financially I had to go back to work but didn't feel I could go back to my old TV and corporate film work now I was in a state of deep grief. I also had two young children and lived in the countryside, which wasn't practical. Since Harry died, I had co-organised various fundraising events for Helen House as a voluntary way of thanking them for their incredible care for us all. Together with the Clarksons and their friend Lucinda McFarlane, we produced a power-boat race at Cowes with companies paying for their management and clients to take part with celebrity team captains. Dinner and an auction would follow in the evening, with Jeremy as an utterly brilliant, comedic and ruthless (where raising money was concerned) auctioneer and Francie, Lucinda and I attacking the detail of production. I was asked by Sister Frances to do some consultancy for Helen House to look at marketing, fundraising and communications and eventually this led to me helping Tom Hill, the newly appointed CEO, to set up the fundraising team. We found our first six members of the team and at that point Tom and our newly appointed Head of Fundraising, David Pastor, asked if I would like to stay on and produce events, a paid role. I knew I couldn't quite work full time so suggested I introduce casting director and old school friend Kate Day into the mix. I knew she loved Helen House and wanted something to do in addition to her casting. We came up with a plan where I could take the holidays off with the children (all our events were in term time) and I could cover Kate when she was casting. It worked brilliantly and we were there for twelve years, working together as a very happy team.

One of the highlights of our year was *Childish Things*, a comedy and music event that was originally the brainchild of actor Tom Hollander, whose niece Immie was a Helen House guest. Tom founded the concept at the Oxford Playhouse with his well-known actor friends (the first line-up included Steve Coogan, Mel and Sue, Jude Law, Hugh Laurie, Griff Rhys-Jones and we even presented Bill Nighy singing 'Love is All Around' backed by members of Radiohead!) We took it forward with Tom's blessing and help, and produced the show for ten years, giving audiences Rowan Atkinson, Rob Brydon and Ruth Jones, Michael McIntyre, Jimmy Carr, Stephen Fry and the cast of *QI*, Miranda Hart, KT Tunstall, Jamie Cullum, James Corden, Jo Brand and many, many more. Each year we would have ten or more acts per night and one year we managed three nights with a varying cast. It took months to organise with just the two of us until the night of each show. From year 2, we moved the show to the 1,800-seat New Theatre in Oxford who took it to their heart, donating the space and many staff volunteering their time if they were able. Over the years we raised huge amounts of money, not only from the show but many other events throughout the year. Celebrity karting, power-boating, Jeremy Clarkson's Taxi Treasure Hunt, the Big Top Ball (we put up a massive Big Top for 700 guests, opposite Temple Island, Henley) and art shows with professional artists from all over the UK, hosted by then BBC arts editor and good friend Will Gompertz.

Two decades on, through working and walking alongside so many bereaved families, I realise that I was naturally, without knowing at the time, creating my continuing bond with Harry. There was no closure; I simply don't believe in it where grief is concerned, especially grief for a child. But there were certainly new beginnings. A way of living my life deeply connected to Harry through my work at Helen & Douglas House, and particularly volunteering with the bereavement team, helping to develop peer-to-peer support for bereaved parents. I always felt in those years I had two thirds of my maternal energy for Cam and Emilie and my other third was for Harry; no longer with us physically, but still so much a part of our lives.

23rd June

Helen House Remembrance Service

Hugo (understandably) doesn't feel up to coming; he took a long time to get over the last one. Rosemary Klee offers to come with me. We meet there and as always are welcomed with open arms. I start to cry as soon as we walk into the garden and barely stop the entire three hours we are there. Now I work at Helen House, when I'm there for fundraising meetings or for a function, I can put on a metaphorical mask and get through it all on a professional footing – for the children and young adults who need it now. But when I return on any personal level, I'm instantly back to week one of Harry's death. I feel ripped open again but always pleased to be there at the same time. It is lovely having Rosemary there with me, and after the service we sit in a swing chair with a glass of wine and lunch. We talk, uninterrupted for once. It does us both good and it's just the right place to do it. I know she has her own grief for Harry, through her very special relationship with him, but sometimes she tries to put herself in my position and wonders if it was her adult children, Paul or Laura, what would it be like? I cry again and say she must never try and 'go there'; I don't want any of our friends to even try and imagine it because it's too bad a place to be. I have to live with my grief every minute of every day; it never goes away. Sometimes I can feel genuinely happy (even though it is always there) and other times it eats away at me during the day, right at the surface of everything I do. I feel I could run from a room in a panic attack at any given moment, but I try to take a deep breath and stay put, facing whatever it is.

I get huge strength from being productive for Helen House – it brings all aspects of my life together, my work as a producer, and Harry. I feel I have to carry on with my life and find a way of moving forward. I remember Ruth Picardie, who wrote about her terminal cancer diagnosis in newspaper articles and eventually a book, *Before I Say Goodbye,* calling it the 'spikey minefield of grief'. That resonates now.

Monday 1st July

As Harry's eighth birthday approaches on Friday, I feel the now familiar veiled and surreal feeling coming over me, whenever there is any anniversary or Harry-related hurdle ahead. Sitting at my computer this morning I realised that it is two years since Harry's last living birthday and ONE AND A HALF years since he died. It is so gut-wrenchingly strange to say that I haven't seen my child for a year and a half. My child who still lives completely in my mind and my heart and sometimes in the sick feeling of grief that I get in my stomach. We spent this weekend with old family friends, the Longfields. They used to scoop me up as an only child and take me on their large family holidays or outings to be part of a family of four wonderful children. It was strange to stay with them this weekend and for us all to have our own children there. It made me realise once more how much my mother has missed out on her grandchildren and her chance to have a bigger family. It was very emotional being with friends with whom I share such a history but who didn't get to know Harry very well. It was incredibly comforting, though, to know that they are still there for me after all this time.

5th July

Harry's birthday. Flowers arrive during the day from our inner sanctum of friends – and some from people I hardly know, parents at the school who still remember his birthday even though their own children weren't in his class. It is quite overwhelming. The open wound in my heart is raw again and I just can't stop crying from morning to night. Hugo and I go to the grave while Cam is at school and Emilie with a friend. How is it that I spend my child's birthday visiting his grave and my friends get to make cakes and wrap presents for theirs? I could die with this gnawing pain. As the day progresses, I feel supported by friends' phone calls but also feel very alone with my memories and pain. When I feel like this nothing can make me better, but equally when I feel fine and happy memories surface, I can't imagine feeling this bad. I have learned to just enjoy the times I feel fine and merely exist through the other times, knowing they will pass eventually, until the next. On picking Cam up from school, we go to Libby's house – others join us: Carol, Rosemary Klee and various friends of Harry's. We chat, cry and watch Wimbledon while the children play; it is very restorative. Hugo's sister Louise arrives later that evening with her husband Matt and children Olivia and Allegra and I feel quite sociable again by then. Harry's cousin Olivia was born twelve hours before Harry, so we celebrate her birthday and also his best friend, my goddaughter Claudia's birthday too. All born within hours of each other.

6th July

We co-host a party for around 150 friends at Merriscourt, a local art gallery. We drink, chat and dance till the early hours and I wonder how I could possibly have felt so weighed down with grief yesterday and be ecstatically happy and full of energy to dance all night now. Thank heaven it works like that, though. Joy and sorrow, the depths and the highs. The confusing messiness of grief.

Note: 17th November 2020 (twenty years exactly from the day Harry died and during England's second Covid lockdown, where once more freedom has been curtailed).

Looking back at that last entry, I would say twenty years on that feeling has not changed. I still feel the same – I live a happy, fulfilled life in so many ways. I love my family, my friends, my home and feel so lucky – but alongside those happy feelings exists grief. Grief for Harry, now for both my parents (Dad died thirteen years after Mum) and for my marriage, which very sadly ended with separation sixteen years after Harry died, through us grieving very differently and growing apart. Also grief for the many children I have come to love at Helen House, their families and the grief we share. Yet take me to Glastonbury, Wilderness or any other music festival, gatherings with good friends small or large, and the joy I feel in community balances the darkness. So much has happened, so much sadness and so much joy, and somewhere there is peace in-between.

27th July

Emilie as usual walked into our room this morning and climbed tousled into bed, burrowing down under the duvet still half asleep. I found myself appreciating her ability to do this; the fact that she had a one-in-four chance of having SMA but was clear. Harry's morning started without being able to get out of bed. He would call for us, stiff and uncomfortable, at around 6 a.m. I would then get him dressed immediately because he had to sit straight in his chair and brace; he couldn't support himself on our bed even with cushions. Harry's own bed was an electric hospital bed. He would use a wee bottle, we would dress him – in clothes and a body brace – and then lift him into his chair. Then he would come into our room but couldn't play with much from his chair, so we would all end up going downstairs early so that he could access special tables and things to enable play. What he would have given to do something as simple as climb into our bed on a Saturday morning.

28th July

I am reminded of Harry on the last day of one summer holiday. All his friends were going swimming and he desperately wanted to go too. Not possible though! We were off to the Nuffield, Churchill and Radcliffe Hospitals for three separate appointments in different locations spread throughout the day, so lots of waiting around. Having had tubes inserted in his throat to test his swallow function, he then spent the afternoon on a rack having a plaster cast of his torso made for a new body brace. It was a very hot day and we had to lift him in and out of his chair all day, messing him around. The consultant turned to him and said, 'So, Harry, how are you enjoying the summer holidays?' Harry replied, 'It's bloody bugger shit!' He'd never said anything like that in his life and I told him off massively in front of the consultant, but as soon as we got in the car I told him that he must never say those words again but I completely agreed with him – we laughed and laughed! I used to feel so often that it was only our world that had stopped turning and everyone else was at full speed.

3rd–10th August

Summer holidays, near Tavistock, Devon

We've rented a holiday cottage in an area we know quite well through staying there when the boys were very small and Harry was newly diagnosed. We retrace our steps through places last visited with Harry and Cam in backpacks – pre-wheelchairs. It feels strange to come back after all this time, but lovely to describe previous visits to Cam.

I still feel terrible going on holiday without Harry and going to a cottage that would have been completely impossible for him. Most things we do now would have been impossible in Harry's lifetime, and while I feel grateful for Cam and Emilie that we don't have to think like that any more and they can enjoy things freely – long walks by the River Tamar, pub lunches in pubs with steep steps, boat trips, days on the beach, etc. – I still feel strange. I also miss Harry desperately for the part he played in our family which just isn't there any more: his interaction with us all, his conversations with me.

I read Philip Pullman's *Northern Lights* at long last. I love it and it captures so much of my own awareness of the 'bigger picture'; how small we are and how little we really know.

Driving home in the car from Devon I feel suddenly flat, and desperate to get home. The children are also keen to return home and even though we've had a great holiday, they both state that they much prefer being 'home'. I think it's a huge security blanket for us all still – I feel the same if I'm honest and although part of it is living in such an extraordinarily beautiful part of the country surrounded by good friends and being part of a strong community, it is also to do with Harry – we are still just beginning to venture out and every part of this journey hurts.

In the car I experience that sudden sweeping, all-engulfing grief again, which I can now 'do' silently, but it is just as strong as always. No one sees, but it's there again. I haven't had it that badly all week, but it suddenly hits me again. It's as though my heart bleeds, having been stemmed for a while, that lurching sick feeling as grief, hurt, pain envelop me once more. That feeling of panic that I know I can try and ward off with superficially positive thoughts or maybe I shall just cry openly and not ever stop. I have to take the obvious route; I'm in the car with the children and Hugo, so Choice No. 2 isn't really an option.

1st September

Twelfth wedding anniversary

I've loved this summer – I feel we've progressed. We haven't run away like we did last year and have had five weeks at home. The children have become much closer, played well together and we've all relaxed. Although Hugo is at last frantically busy with work, he's happy and on a high because it's all interesting work that he's enjoying and best of all he's doing most of it from home. During the past few summers we have dealt with a new baby, my mother dying and Harry getting worse with no hope and finally the worst summer of all last year, our first without him. Given all of that, this one, remarkably, has been good.

4th September

A setback day, broken hearts all round. I don't know what to do or how to help Cam; maybe I just can't help him through this one. Cam's term started today – nerve-wracking for him and for his peers. But the others were just facing a new form teacher, while Cam, aged six, nearly seven, had to face his brother's last classroom, his brother's last teacher and every playtime in the big playground, where he last played with Harry and where a tree is planted with a beautiful plaque which reads: 'Harry Pickering, much loved pupil'. Last night Cam was upset in bed; 'I just want to be with Harry,' he kept saying over and over, 'I feel sad inside.' What can I say? I don't try to placate him; I hate it when people try and make sense of it to me. I know it hurts, it hurts all of us, but there is nothing we can do. We just have to try and carry on. I say, 'I love you so much and so did Harry – he would want you to have the best time possible. I'm sure after a while you'll feel that it is your own classroom, not just Harry's – your friends will be there with you.' Heartfelt, desperate but hollow words. We try and think of all the good things we can but he looks small and lost in his top bunk, alone in the room they shared, and I feel helpless. I was unable to make Harry better, and now I am powerless to help Cam.

This morning Cam was up at six thirty. He dressed himself and appeared by my bedside in his school uniform – still looking lost, but with a determined expression. We arrived at the classroom and the first thing we saw was Harry's tree, laden with bright yellow crab apples. A sharp intake of breath. In the cloakroom I automatically went to Harry's peg. No – wrong – bad move. We find Cam's peg and then go and see his form teacher – she asks if I'm OK, I falter and ask her the same, her eyes well up like mine. Cam seems happy to see all his friends and I leave feeling confident again.

The positive attitude has changed dramatically by the end of the day and Cam comes out of school looking forlorn. I ask him how the day went and the first thing he tells me is that he didn't want to join in any of the games his friends were playing at lunchtime, so instead he sat on his own looking at Harry's tree – my heart lurches and I feel sick at this image. He tells me that as you get older all you want is peace and quiet! So unlike him – he's always joined in all the games in the playground and never minded how rough they were. All summer we have been more free – Cam lost all cares, looked so well and strong and HAPPY. We all progressed and came out of it feeling as though we were moving forward, but it's only surface healing and the wound always opens again. I feel as though the progression we've made over the summer has gone in one day – for Cam and for me. I feel sick with grief for the whole situation, but most of all for Cam and his beloved brother who were never meant to be apart, never separated; as Cam has voiced before, 'almost like twins'.

Cam is now five months older than Harry was when he died – a strange thought. He is bleeding inside and I just don't know what to do.

27th September

I managed to live to the age of thirty-four without knowing the painful depths of grief – first I faced it through the death of my mother and then Harry just a year after that. My life will never be the same again. Cam managed to live to the age of only four and now has to live with his grief for the rest of his life. Sometimes I look at him and wonder quite how he is going to get through this; I can see him riddled with pain sometimes, just as I am, but he is too young for this. But then I see the other side – his appreciation of the smallest things at such a young age, his strength in knowing what he does or doesn't want to do with his life already. He told me today when he decided to give up karate after only two weeks that he felt he was doing enough already – he said he loved tennis, didn't want to do football, rugby, karate or anything else like that, and he was happy going to places with us, seeing friends, visiting people and going for tea after school. That was all he wanted to do. Fair enough! I think after all he's been through in his short life so far, he can at least have some choice over that. Tonight we snuggled down on the sofa, Cam, Emilie and me, and watched a wonderful film: *My Dog Skip*. Cam and I both cried at all the happy and sad bits and loved every minute. He has an appreciation of life that I discovered through Harry in my thirties; he has it already. I hope he uses it well – he is so far, and that gives me strength and hope.

29th September

Helen House Bereaved Siblings Club visit to Blenheim Palace for a picnic and then to Kidlington Airfield for flights in small planes! I drop Cam off with the others at the entrance to Blenheim – one of the boys greets us with, 'Maybe I'll be able to see my dead brother up in the clouds in Heaven.' Cam joins in, 'Yes, maybe I'll see Harry – oh no, I won't, he's in a coffin down on the ground!' Jocelyn takes them off for their chats, picnic and to get lost in the maze. These bizarre, black-humoured chats are only possible for them in the safety and understanding of other siblings.

We join them later for the plane rides – I'm terrified but by the time we get there Cam has already been up once and is preparing for another trip. He refused to go with a member of staff from Helen House – he wanted to go up with just the pilot! His confidence is boosted by being with his fellow Helen House siblings. Hugo, Emilie and I venture up in a 1960s Russian plane. As we soar I lurch from pure pleasure to a sudden wave of grief. Harry would have loved every element of this day and SHOULD be here. I have tears in my eyes as we fly over the spires of Oxford.

26th October

We have a wonderful holiday in Devon on the Flete Estate estuary with friends the Prices and the Duffs. There are ten children there with us – Cam's confidence grows as they experience a real *Swallows and Amazons* holiday, wonderful to see. As it grows and he becomes free and happy, I witness his added grief too – just like mine. In safe surroundings, blissfully happy, he can let it out more – at some stage in every day of the holiday I find him for a few minutes each day, on his own, away from the pack of children, tears in his eyes thinking of Harry. One day I find him on a window sill, behind a curtain, gazing out at the beautiful view – bereft and missing his brother.

Back home and in the Co-op today, I bump into a friend with many problems – she talks on and on and on about her family and their various challenges. My head spins and at the very end she says, 'So how are you?' I feel like saying, 'How do you think? Harry's dead!' but answer only, 'We're fine, thank you.' I wouldn't know where to begin!

30th October

I know that it is when I am at my happiest now, safe and secure, that Harry's death often hits me hardest. I wonder how I would have been without the guidance of Helen House. My anger, grief, frustration and hurt has never been buried, but neither have I had to burden friends, family or even Hugo too much with it. They probably think I have, when I share snippets, but the full force of it, the truth of how I really feel, is reserved for Marie. That is because I have known for the last two years that every so often I would have a bereavement visit where I could store up worries and voice them all in that session. Marie is thankfully there for that purpose and it has taken me a while not to feel guilty for dumping on her! Importantly it's not therapy of any sort, it really is just conversation, but with gentle grief guidance and knowledge. That support started from the moment we set foot in Helen House for respite care – that was the point I was beginning to flounder, from sleep deprivation and the exhaustion of living grief. At nearly every visit we had at Helen House, I would arrive, go through Harry's medical notes, hand over, see Cam and Emilie happily playing and know for the first time since the last visit that I could collapse – and I did, every time. I would undoubtedly either break down at some stage with one of the staff or just use the space in the flat to go and have a good cry on my own. This would come out during the weekend and eventually, armed with help, support, love and advice from the staff, I would set foot into the outside world again. That is how it is now and I feel so lucky and appreciative of this safety net.

14th November

My birthday. The anniversary of our last journey to Helen House the week that Harry died two years ago. Today I helped at Kingham Primary School and experienced the morning from his perspective – it was agonising and distressing to the core, but also comforting. Cam's class even wrote about the coronation – the last piece of work Harry produced on this same day, before saying goodbye to his friends and coming home. At times this morning I thought I was going to have to leave the classroom and indeed the school, but I stuck it out through a wall of silent tears, a fug of grief, and got through it for Cam. Cam knew it was the last piece of work Harry wrote and I needed to be there with him.

Outside, in the school grounds, Harry's tree was still laden with yellow crab apples, appropriately in their last stage now, about to fall and degenerate – but amazingly they have been on the tree since the first day of term, nearly two and a half months; clinging onto life, just like Harry.

17th November

We spent this anniversary weekend away – with friends and all without our children. I didn't want to burden Cam; in future years he will probably realise the date, but this year he is sad enough without having this to add to his grief. I cried so much on my birthday that by the time today arrived I was all cried out, not a tear left to shed. Friends have been more tearful than me over this – I think because for them it focuses their minds on Harry's death for a time, while for us it is every day; we are never free of this pain.

20th November

Cam is desperately sad at the moment and has been for weeks. Most evenings after school we end up talking about it – thank heaven he feels he can. The trouble is that he is six, nearly seven. I feel although he voices such strong feelings and identifies with them, I don't know how such an old head on young shoulders can cope with this. I suppose all we can do is keep him talking and deal with each thing as it arises. Most of it is pure devastation that Harry isn't here. How can other adults or other six-year-olds relate to his feelings? Most adults have not been to the depths of despair and life experience that Cam has – how do we deal with this? All I can say is that I agree with him – in the car on the way home I say, 'But, Cam, you love life, don't you? The main thing is that we all have each other and we are healthy and happy.' He replies, 'But we don't have each other, Mummy; Harry is never coming back.' That is the bottom line for him and affects everything he does at the moment. I just have to hope that at some stage he will get through the pain in some way.

Cam's school photo arrived back today and it is the saddest photo I've ever seen. So different to the last one taken with Harry as a duo. Or even last year's when I think the finality of death had not landed in quite the same way. I hope that by next year, when he is out of Harry's old classroom and Emilie has started school with him, that we will see a happier, more free face. He has the weight of the world on his shoulders at the moment and is haunted. How can he cope with so much? I feel powerless.

22nd November

A very good session with Marie at home. I cry constantly and tell her all my worries about Cam. I can really trust Marie's judgement because as a founder member of staff at Helen House, she has twenty years of experience, observing families like us and the effect on siblings, parents, grandparents, the whole family. Marie feels sure Cam will come out of this OK and that, although painful to watch, it must be seen as a positive thing the way he is able to talk easily about his grief, his extraordinary depth of emotion for a six-year-old. He was probably in shock for a good year and it is only now in this second year that reality is hitting hard and that in becoming more mature he is able to address the whole situation. Marie has seen children close right down emotionally, parents who feel all the way through the illness that the other siblings' time 'will come', but of course when the sick child dies, the siblings have no relationship to build on with the parents; they have often been ignored, and it is too late by that time.

Also, those parents are often so taken up with their own grief they cannot channel energy into the remaining children and it all begins to go wrong from there. I feel so grateful for her sharing this with me, her wealth of understanding and experience. I feel better than I have done in the last two weeks, just through this session with Marie. In some ways I need these visits more now than I did at the beginning; it's strange and so lucky that we are still able to have them. Marie also feels it will be important for Cam later on to know how he grieved aged six. Later he may have feelings of guilt that he is enjoying his life and has good health (hopefully) when he had a one-in-four chance of having SMA too – he will only need to read this to know that he suffered as a child and can go ahead with his life liberated, having been the best brother in the world, and having suffered so much grief now. I hope Cam and Emilie will feel lucky eventually that they had such a great relationship with Harry but that they now have each other. I know the pain will never really subside for any of us, but just hope we can deal with it and live with it.

23rd November

Dinner with friends who have invited people we have known a little over the last eight years, and whose son is a friend of Cam's at school. We get on brilliantly and have a great evening with lots of silliness and laughter. Later on in the evening, though, we turn to more serious subjects and they eventually ask how Cam is doing (in relation to Harry). Normally unless people are my 'inner sanctum' handful of friends I would just say, 'Fine, thank you, he's coping really well.' But somehow because I like them so much, I go in quite deep and probably talk in too much detail. I worry the next day that I said too much. I never know whether people can cope with the whole child-death thing and all that it entails, but they were so supportive that I felt safe going there. It's a difficult subject, because in some ways by saying 'he's fine' I would be fobbing them off and not telling the truth, but in others to go into too much depth is just wrong for certain people.

It's like the great conversation stopper, 'How many children do you have?' 'We did have three but our six-year-old died; we now have two.' People simply don't know how to react, but I can't say we have two and bypass Harry completely, eradicating his life! I'm tired of constantly protecting other people.

25th November

I have a long phone call with Pete Griffith, whose daughter Misha gave me strength after Harry died. He and his wife Rach [two of the interviewees in this book] have become good friends. He rings to tell us that Misha is now on morphine, due to a terrible chest infection which is moving in the same way as Harry's. They are devastated and we talk for ages, Pete asking about Harry's last week, and we also talk of happier times. I feel deeply, deeply touched that he should phone at this time. Pete says we can go in and see Misha if we feel up to it. I think long and hard but know that I can't face it. I long to go and see Misha for one last time, but I just can't face seeing her in the same state as Harry and probably in the same room. I feel cowardly because I would give anything to be with them, but I also feel in my heart of hearts that they should have space to be on their own at this time. It means so much to us that they phoned and offered this.

28th November

We left the house at 7.30 this morning to join a coach party from Helen House for their Christmas outing. I haven't been on the coach long before I have to ask about Misha – a member of staff tells me she died yesterday afternoon. I feel devastated for Pete and Rach and their remaining children – Natalie (who also has Batten disease), Zak and Sophie – and in awe that they have two children with the same condition. Words fail me then and now. I hope that in time we will see more of them; I like and admire them so much.

A wonderful but emotional rollercoaster of a day follows. A tour of Hamleys is the first stop. Cam and Emilie's faces are an absolute picture of ecstasy! We then go via Trafalgar Square to the Houses of Parliament where in the Great Hall, Father Christmas makes an appearance, with named presents for each Helen House child or sibling. Cam and Emilie both get things they have wanted for ages and can't believe their luck. I chat to a wonderful lady who is there with two of her gorgeous children. As we talk, she tells me that her eldest son had an accident when he was young, hence using Helen House, and then her husband died last year, suddenly and completely out of the blue – a brain haemorrhage. I'm lost for words again. Why does so much happen to some people? She has an infectious laugh and sparkling eyes, a visibly strong character.

I also chat to another lady; her son Harry died only nine weeks ago and her two children have just joined the Helen House Club with Cam. In talking to her I realise she is completely raw, facing the first Christmas and trying to keep going for her other children's sake. It makes me realise that I am stronger than I was two years ago when it first happened to us. But looking at Sam I remember it so clearly, that early grief; the shock, trauma and agony. I still have the same depth and level of pain, but in between it hitting me, I feel OK.

We go to the London Eye at dusk and see the lights over London. Then back via Regent Street and Oxford Street to see the Christmas lights. Cam has tears in his eyes as we listen to music in the coach, and says he misses Harry. 'Mummy, I always feel sad for Harry when we are with Helen House. I have the best times with Helen House but miss him, and this music and Christmas make me feel sad, but happy too.' I know exactly what he means and agree with him. He often mirrors my own feelings, without me saying anything.

It is so important for us all to be invited back to Helen House in this way. To catch up with other families, to still feel included and to have these treats in a safe environment, where we can laugh, cry but know that we are with completely kindred spirits who understand. We all talk openly because we know we are part of the same 'club'. One you would never wish to join, yet if you have to, you couldn't be with better people.

29th November

Letter to Pete and Rach

Dear Pete and Rach

We are so truly sorry to hear your news; thank you for letting us know. Thank you too for taking the time to talk the other night; it meant so much to us both. I now know how our friends probably felt when Harry died; completely at a loss for words, and helpless in reaching you in your horrendous pain. All I can say is make the most of everything Helen House can offer you in giving you time with Misha. I absolutely cherish the time we had there with Harry after his death, and the time Cam and Emilie spent with him too. While nothing can take away the pain, it really helped allay their fear of death and that has lasted through to the present day. I know too that at the beginning of the week after he died, I became almost hysterical when I thought of the funeral and all it represented, and leaving Helen House for the last time. However, by the time I had spent all those days with Harry there, I was prepared for the funeral, and ready to go home. I'm so glad we had that period; it turned around the panic of leaving. I don't know whether that makes sense, but it was so important and is still a period that I relive regularly. You are rarely out of our thoughts at the moment – if only that could help. With our love to you all and see you on Friday.

Lizzie, Hugo, Cam and Emilie

22nd December

Cam's seventh birthday. He's had a nightmare for some weeks about his birthday, saying how it was going to be the saddest day because we'd never had a seven-year-old before. I've tried every which way to convince him that I'm so lucky to have a seven-year-old NOW, but he won't believe a word of it. He's mentioned it at school and at the Helen House Club.

We spend the day in London with Hugo's family – Cam has a Harry Potter cake, great presents and a lovely day spent playing with his cousins. But when it comes to blowing out the candles, everyone tells him to make a wish and he just looks at me with huge sad eyes and mouths silently H A R R Y, spelling out his name. I say out loud, 'Cam, wish for something that's possible,' and he takes an age with everyone waiting to try and find something to wish for. I don't know what he did wish for, but he found something eventually.

He then played happily again, a game of hide and seek all around the house, but later as I pack up our things to leave, he comes to find me upstairs, sits on my lap and cries and cries, enormous tears, saying he looked at the Christmas tree downstairs and it made him feel sad. He doesn't feel he fits in the family any more without Harry and he feels 'stupid'. I try and console him and say that we all miss Harry and it's even worse at this time of year when we are supposed to be happy, but we have to try and find good things to focus on. He seems a little better having released some emotion and returns downstairs.

23rd December

A good day. Cam and Emilie play all morning, completely happy, uninterrupted here at home. Late morning we set off to take Cam to the pantomime in Oxford with the Helen House Club. He loves it and comes home happy. We watch the film *Monsters, Inc.*, all sitting together cuddled up on the sofa, and later put the children to bed in the same room in Cam's bunk beds. Emilie falls asleep immediately but an hour later Cam is still awake and when we go upstairs to see what's wrong he becomes completely hysterical like I have never seen him before. He says he is selfish, stupid, he hates his personality and he wishes he could kill himself. He is absolutely inconsolable and for an hour Hugo and I take it in turns trying to talk to him, lying on his top bunk with him.

In the end we get him to go to sleep. I feel devastated and for the first time genuinely frightened about whether he or we can deal with this level of grief and emotion in a seven-year-old. Hugo wonders if he needs some further help with counselling. During this outpouring from Cam I ask him if he would like to speak to Jocelyn from Helen House if I ask her to come over tomorrow, or Mrs Klee (Harry's helper at school who is a close friend) or to Jon Magnusson, Harry's godfather, whose own brother died at a similar time in his life. He says he would like to talk to Jon.

I call Jon at around midnight and he offers to come over to see us. We sit in the kitchen discussing Cam.

Jon says he is so impressed with the way we, as a family, under the guidance of Helen House, have managed to be open about our grief and have encouraged our friends to be with us through all this. He feels Cam will be all right and that it is wonderful that he can talk to us in this way, even though some of it is so impossible to listen to. We have encouraged him to be open and he is doing exactly that. He says, 'Lizzie, you seem to have forgotten that is what you do!' I laugh and he's absolutely right – he reminds me that one minute we seem able to party and have fun, and the next I'm in floods of tears over Harry – we get it all out in the open and then carry on till the next wave of grief hits us. He says that's just how Harry coped and it's how Cam is coping too. I feel safer, though it still worries me that he talks about wanting to die. I must speak to Helen House about that tomorrow.

I hope Cam will wake in the morning and feel he has let go of some of that grief. We must stay very close to him in the next few days and do everything together.

5th January 2003

What a lot has happened since that night. Cam woke the next morning quiet and subdued but OK. He said he was feeling a bit better and I assured him it was good to let these things out sometimes. The next night, Christmas Eve, he was extraordinary. We went to our neighbour's house for supper; there were about eighteen of us in all, including Harry's godfather Jon, and everyone there he knew well, so he felt safe and able to be happy. Cam spent the evening attached to Jon, but joined in everything. Games, singing, even offering to do something he'd never done before: he sang his Nativity song on his own in front of everyone. I couldn't believe the difference twenty-four hours had made, but also the shedding of weeks of build-up to that.

Christmas and New Year carried on in the same vein – free and happy with no more major mention of his trauma, only the normal missing Harry, but in a different way, as though a gear had shifted. Over New Year we rented a big camper van and drove up to Scotland with my dad and aunt to stay with Jon's family, his parents and sisters.

Amazingly Cam was confident with a large crowd of children he didn't know well (all Jon's nieces and nephews); he joined in music and games, and was absolutely fine. He was with us, loved the mobile home, but was also helped I think by being with people who understood our situation – the Magnussons having been through the death of their son and brother Siggy.

February 2003

We hold the final bereavement group at Helen House. I feel sad to leave the group, but ready to stop now; we have covered so much. We look back at our past sessions; we know there are no answers to our grief, no changes in our feelings and ultimately we realise that this pain is for life, that few friends in the 'outside world' will ever truly understand that. In this group we have shared our deepest thoughts and experiences and it has helped. If anything I find memories of Harry, photos, etc. more painful than a year ago; a year ago I would allow myself to wallow in them and even get strength from them but now they are almost too painful.

We all agree that we live with reminders of our dead children around us, but can't look too closely without that searing pain returning. In fact, as we speak of this we all break down again. There is no upbeat ending to this last session, but that is to be expected. We have to deal with our private pain and cannot expect others to understand. Most people want you to be better and expect it especially after time has passed, but we all know from others who are much further on (my friend Ann after fifteen years) that this never changes. We must just protect other people from it but it helps to share with those that know. This is why we all need Helen House.

20th March

The war against Iraq started last night. Knowing it was imminent I spoke to the children about it yesterday, not wanting them to get scared by TV or other children's comments. Cam looked terrified to start with but then asked some pertinent questions about Saddam Hussein. Later in the evening he said, 'Mummy, do you think his weapons will reach heaven and hurt Harry?' He was saying it quite tongue-in-cheek, testing but also feeling vulnerable I think.

2003: three years on – thoughts on grief

This has been an extraordinary journey. No doubt it will continue to be, since it has no end. The only end for my grief is the day I die, but then grief for Harry will still continue in his brother and sister, I hope in a diluted form as the years go by.

I remember many years ago, way before we had children, a friend's baby died through a tragic freak accident. A year on from the accident my friend's mother said to me when I asked her how they were, 'Oh not so good – I really think they should be able to move on with their lives now, especially since they have another child.' Even then, with no personal experience, I was shocked to the core at these words – amazed that anyone could think for a second that time would make any difference with the death of a child. I felt quite chilled by those words and instantly wanted to ask her whether that would be the case for her if one of her children died. I didn't, of course. But now, years on, having suffered the death of my own child, I know that I was right. Time does not make any difference at all, in fact if anything it gets worse. I could just about cope with saying that our eldest son died six weeks ago, or even a year ago – it sounded close enough – but try saying, 'I haven't seen my eldest child for three years.' I still find that impossible to compute. Yes, maybe I've become better equipped in coping and living alongside my grief, but that grief has not lessened; it gets deeper if anything. I just have better methods of dealing with it – I've become practised with some of them in order to face certain situations. I surf the pain, face it full-on and feel the relief when I've managed to master it without cracking up completely. It is a constant state which takes a downturn when I stand looking too long and too deeply into Harry's eyes in a photo – I have to try and skim certain issues, certain things in order to keep going, until I find myself staring for too long and that's it, the pain surge hits me again as if my heart might break. Grief is not able to be fixed, I have to face that.

March 2004

I often lie in bed going over everything, the whys, how-on-earths?, etc. Through our journey with Harry we have gained so much – and discovered the strength of our true friends and family – and the weakness of others! But the greatest gift, I've realised, is acceptance. I can't criticise those who were not able to be with us on that journey; it pushed us all to our limits of endurance and some stayed alongside. But those who didn't quite make it with us had their own reasons which I completely accept and I try not to feel bitter. Harry enriched our lives beyond measure and taught us many valuable life lessons. We are so lucky with the life we lead and the time we have as a family.

I filled in a bereavement sheet for Helen House recently and interestingly, but not surprisingly, three quarters of the symptoms apply to Cam. The ones I tick are: sadness, inability to sleep, nightmares and fear of sleep, fear of being alone, inability to concentrate or focus, drop in school performance, asking repeated questions about death and repeatedly speaking of joining the deceased.

In some ways in filling this in for Helen House, I feel comforted to know that this is all quite normal in Cam's situation. This seems obvious when you think of the trauma he has suffered at a young age, yet school seem to think he should have 'moved on' by now.

24th March

Listening to Eva Cassidy's *Songbird* album while doing the VAT returns for our business, I'm constantly reminded of all the extraordinary children and young adults I have met in the last few years through Harry and the way they have influenced all the adults and other children around them.

Cam for the way he was the perfect brother for Harry; his soulmate, his playmate; for the fun they had together and the way he and Emilie have coped with their profound ongoing grief – I am so proud of them both. Nick Wallis, one of the most courageous, heroic and witty people who has influenced my life more than he will ever realise. Rob Heywood, determined to live the most normal of lives as a student and artist. Ally Craig for his musical talent and wit and his wonderful family. Marni and Evie Smyth, so similar to Harry and Cam in their unconditional relationship – Marni, uncannily like Harry, his female twin; clever, artistic and honest about her feelings whether having fun or feeling fed up with her condition.

Eva Cassidy brings me closest to Misha and Natalie Griffith, the two sisters who died within a year of each other, both close to Christmas and whose funerals were unbelievably beautiful, yet devastatingly sad. We were shown video footage of the girls through all stages of their Batten disease – they ran on the beach as normal healthy children in some of the images and then were rendered speechless, powerless and disabled by a barbaric condition, while still exuding their radiance and smiles. All this to a background of Eva Cassidy's 'Fields of Gold' and Roberta Flack's 'The First Time Ever I Saw Your Face'. In many ways while I would give anything for Harry to be here now with us and for him never to have suffered the indignity he had to go through, I would not like to go back to being the person I was before all this. I feel we have the privilege of living our lives alongside those who can teach us – constantly reminded at every get-together how lucky we are to move our hands, to breathe without pain, to walk and to talk. It makes it very difficult to enter the able-bodied parallel world each time and I would love to pass on this knowledge, this privilege to others around me, but some are untouchable. I live alongside and suffer with these children; this is their profound gift to me, the constant reminder which in turn helps me to enjoy the life I have – but they are always with me, and always will be.

In writing about life with Harry, and our bereaved lives, it is easy to make things sound so hard – life at that time *was* hard – but the truth is it was the greatest joy for all of us to live with Harry – none of the procedures, the appointments and the equipment could really ever take away from that. We did everything we possibly could as a family to make life good for Harry and for us all; four years on, our house is only just verging on having the atmosphere it had when Harry was alive when it was filled with laughter. He instilled in us all a love of life and for that I will always be grateful. I think we are beginning to get some semblance of it back.

27th June

Emilie, aged five, has for weeks been deeply upset about Harry; she is being hit by waves of grief for the brother she remembers through photographs. Today she and I attended the annual Remembrance Day service at Helen House and she blossomed before my very eyes – this was, as I suspected, just what she needed to help her through this period.

I was able to show Emilie the toy cupboard where she played as a toddler, the bedrooms, the Little Room where his body stayed for a week after he died, the flat we inhabited on many visits and even the cot where she slept. We entered the convent chapel and cried our way through the service alongside many other similarly suffering families; here she understood that we were not alone. Emilie went up to the altar and sombrely lit a candle for Harry, solemnly but happily feeling she could offer him something, some part of her heart.

We shared lunch at Helen House and wandered through

the grounds chatting to staff. Emilie sat in the craft room painting a t-shirt; Cam and Harry carried out the same activity in the same place only four years ago and Emilie has seen this many times on video. Now she knows she has joined in too. Helen House is a real memory for her now and she seems more relaxed since going there. In recent weeks she has asked questions like, 'Why is no one at school upset about Harry? Why does no one in this family cry about Harry? Why does no one at school notice Harry's tree?', etc. So much time (three and a half years) has lapsed since the funeral and our constant massive state of grief that Emilie was too young to remember our tears. Now they tend to be in private and at strange, unexpected times, rather than being constant. The service gave Emilie a chance to grieve quite publicly, which she needed.

Helen House staff have invited Emilie to attend the latest siblings club in the New Year which I feel sure she will benefit from and we will read some of the books we read to Cam three years ago with Emilie now. We are all at different stages of grief, but Emilie's is strong and tangible, so we must respond.

2nd July

Show and Tell for Emilie at school – again she takes in a framed photo of Harry. It will be his tenth birthday on Monday and Emilie wants to take a card to his grave.

6th October

During the journey to school this morning through heavy showers and bright autumn sun we raced towards a huge rainbow arching perfectly with us in the centre. The children were amazed and wondered if Harry was sitting on top of it, or playing up there. They laughed excitedly and chatted happily. As it eventually disappeared from view, Cam said, 'Bye, Harry!' in a totally happy, normal voice. Maybe four years on I can cope with this sort of image; maybe the reality of death is fading and I can be led by the children's imaginations. It engulfed and cheered me all at the same time, but I felt better for them voicing it. Long may they continue to do so.

6th March 2005

Cam (now nine), while practising his spellings, suddenly burst into tears and came and sat on my lap. He sobbed about Harry and how hard it is without his brother around – he couldn't stop. Tears are often close to the surface for Cam – not in a babyish way over silly things, but in the deepest way possible over serious hurt. This never ends and probably will never end for any of us; it is just a deep-seated pain that we live with every day which surfaces sometimes uncontrollably. Sleep always helps us to deal with this, and Cam, after a really good sleep, was much better this morning.

4th January 2006

Five years on from Harry's death

Emilie lays the table for supper while I am cooking. When I turn around she has organised five place settings – this one is for Harry, she says. Cam walks in and together they decide to make place setting cards, including one for Harry. I go along with it – finding it comforting for us all to see the right number of places at the table and not wanting to spoil it for them. I put my foot down at serving Harry food, but through my absolute sadness, I love the fact that he really is with us all still; I don't think a day goes by when either Cam or Emilie doesn't mention Harry.

Finding Neverland, film

In the film, J. M. Barrie describes to the young Peter Llewelyn Davies, following the death of his mother Sylvia, the way she will always be there in his imagination.

His words reduced me to uncontrollable tears, resonating with everything I feel about my mother's death; she is with me all the time and I 'visit' her each day, although it hurts. However, where the death of a child is concerned, I do feel it is possibly different. When Harry died, all the images in my head were of him when he was ill until gradually those faded to reveal the real Harry, full of life, fun and wit – sometimes I can almost smell his scent once more. But the truth is I can't always visit him fully, not each day, because each visit is devastating, it hurts too much; just one look too long at a photo, or one thought too many can reduce me to the gibbering wreck I was on the day of his diagnosis when my hope for Harry died and when that part of me died. I will never heal, and as a mum, why would I want to?

'Closure' is a challenging idea when someone you really love, deep in your core, has died. But if I think about the pain representing my love for Harry, alongside my equally unconditional love for Cam and Emilie, then I can live well with it. They are all here. The pain equals love.

And that was my last diary entry.

Part 3

The Myth of Closure: Time Doesn't Heal

Twenty years on, what has changed? I look back and I feel that my own personal grief moved in phases rather like changing gears. The first three years were unbelievably hard; I was constantly putting all my energy into surviving the pain – primarily for my remaining children Cam and Emilie, for Hugo, for my widowed father and for our friends. And that was exhausting!

I feel the 'early' stage for me was the first two to three years, the deep traumatic feeling of shock, and then a gradual emerging into a new way of being over the following years until I felt I had accommodated the knowledge that I wouldn't see Harry again. But having said that, if I think too hard now, I can feel the depth of that sorrow and it can become unbearable again. It is a constant work in progress managing my grief alongside my joy and absolute appreciation of life, as it is now.

From 2002 I also channelled energy into Helen House as my work built there. I realise now that I was very naturally finding strength in 'continuing bonds' – the idea of bringing the memory of your loved one through into your new life without them, accommodating their legacy into every day. I felt connected to Harry in that way; the part of me which would have been active being his mother could then help other people going through the same challenges.

Eight years on my friend Polly Steele insisted that I go away with her – I don't think at that point I had left the children and she could see it would be healthy to have a weekend away. I never minded the children going for sleepovers or being out with friends, it's just I felt I couldn't 'abandon' them. Polly wouldn't take no for an answer and she and I had a long weekend in Tarifa, Spain, staying with friends of hers, Paul and Mei Ling, in their beautiful annexe, usually rented out to honeymooners! I know that this was the first time, eight years after Harry's death, that I allowed myself headspace to really switch off from family, work, everything, and allow Harry back in fully. I was too scared to do this before: I didn't want time to think; I wanted to fill every waking hour. Being busy was what helped me survive.

In Tarifa I had my first dream about Harry since he died. I half woke the next morning with a soaking-wet pillow and tears streaming down my face. The dream was so real I felt he was with me, and woke to the truth. But somehow I could cope; it was as though eight years on I could find the strength to live with the pain, with the knowledge – just about.

I worked at Helen & Douglas House for twelve years, from 2002 to 2014. I loved the fact my job mixed fundraising and production (large-scale events) with being alongside other bereaved parents, their families, siblings and the care team staff I knew so well from our time as beneficiaries. It also connected me with my old work in TV and the corporate world since our fundraising was across Corporate, Major Donor, Community, Events and Activities. I worked closely with the bereavement team, connecting donors with the stories of the bereaved, and volunteered, helping to run peer-to-peer support, weekend workshops and get-togethers for families. Many of the children, young adults and their families also attended our events.

The greatest full-circle feeling came in 2007 when I oversaw a BBC documentary, *The Children of Helen House* – an eight-part series for BBC2. We spent a year negotiating the contracts (to ensure protection of our families), a year filming (the team staying in Oxford for that time) and three months of the BBC team editing over 400 hours of footage in three edit suites! It was well received and, alongside having made some life-long friendships with the team, I had a feeling of life making sense – the bond with Harry, with my old work for Channel 4, my production knowledge and love for my grief community of parents, children and carers. It was definitely a time of full awareness and gratitude for that.

After twelve years at Helen House, and by which time as a team of twenty-four professional fundraisers (supported by many volunteers) we had to raise nearly £5 million a year, I felt exhausted and jaded and knew that period had probably come to an end. Sister Frances, our dear friend and inspiration as founder of the worldwide children's hospice movement, was going through challenging times and didn't have the support of the trustees and new CEO. That meant my heart wasn't in it any more. And combined with my dad dying and our lives changing, this led to me handing in my notice in 2014.

Survivor's energy and renewal

From 2015 I had the chance to work with film director and friend Polly Steele. We spent a few months workshopping different projects she had in the pipeline and working out which would be a good fit for us, which one could work. It's no surprise that the one we both felt most strongly about was a memoir called *Let Me Go* about generational trauma. Polly had optioned it and written the screenplay six years before. It is about the life of Helga Schneider, whose mother had abandoned her during the Second World War, leaving her (with no explanation) with her younger brother Peter. A story of hidden family secrets, the psychological effects of war and the legacy of that trauma on future generations many years on. Set in the year 2000, Helga has discovered the truth, that her mother was a Nazi war criminal, and the film takes place when Helga meets her mother Traudi.

To cut a long story short, Polly and I set out to raise the money (£1 million in the end) to produce the film and spent the next three years working on it. I was interested to see if I could raise money for something that I had a less obvious connection to; an arts project rather than a children's hospice. To do that I had to find the right roots and belief and for a while it didn't feel obvious. I don't believe you can raise money for anything unless you truly believe in it. Polly took me to stay with Helga Schneider in Bologna, Italy, where she now lives, and at the end of that week, we knew we had to share her story with the world; whatever it took we would make it.

In Helga I witnessed survivor's energy and in her case creativity – her flat was full of her own paintings, photography and books. She had used her storytelling capability to work through her grief. Here was a true connection with a grief survivor. At the time I don't think I realised the synergy and why I felt so strongly about it, but I can see it now.

Cumulative grief

Eighteen years after Harry died, Hugo and I went through divorce. We were married for twenty-six years, but Harry's devastating diagnosis came just five years into our marriage. We came through those years together, but grief took its toll. We are wired very differently and as we processed our grief separately over many years, we grew apart. Initially, from September 2016 we lived side by side, taking Gwyneth Paltrow and Chris Martin's idea of 'consciously uncoupling', Hugo moving into my late father's cottage next door. We eased into separation while still sharing our office, eating together with Emilie (Cam was living independently by then) in the evenings and even happily giving each other lifts if we were going to the same events! But it was difficult to maintain this once Hugo met his partner Martha and they wanted to live together. After a lot of heartache, huge hurdles and the many challenges of readjustment, we now get on fine, have coffee together occasionally and swap news. We will always be family.

For me, divorce, although a mutual decision, was the

tipping point of my grief. In those years leading to 2016, as an only child from a very small family, I had experienced the deaths of my son, my beloved parents and now the break-up of our marriage, for which we both took responsibility. At a time when I thought I had a robust grief toolkit, I had the shock of cumulative grief and the realisation that I had reached a new low where I couldn't cope. I found for a while I couldn't practise what I preached. Post-separation and leading to divorce, Hugo and I argued badly, which was unusual for us. I didn't reach out to friends; I put up a wall. I felt full of shame for not succeeding in facing our issues. When Harry died I truly felt we had done everything in our power to give him the happiest life; with divorce it felt that there was no resolution – I couldn't reach Hugo emotionally and he couldn't reach me. He has, since our divorce, been diagnosed as having Asperger's, which explains so much. If only we had known, it would have helped us both to understand why we couldn't grieve together; we experienced Harry's death differently, even more than most. I am more emotionally and empathetically wired and Hugo sees things literally. But the diagnosis, while it has helped all of us, including Hugo, to understand why our emotional dialogue was so different, came too late. These days we find it easier to communicate, now that we have this knowledge and I have to remember (when I can) to leave emotion behind. We were just speaking a different language.

Note: Hugo suggested I include his diagnosis in this part of the book.

Part 4

Community

Over the last twenty-two years, partly through my work in the children's hospice world and partly through having open conversations about grief, I have made many friends who have experienced great loss in different ways. Perhaps we were naturally drawn towards each other because of that. I feel I have a tribe of people around me I can talk to on a deeper level because we have shared some of the same feelings around our unique situations. I wanted to include some of their stories too, their insights and knowledge gained from investigating their own grief. They are people who have helped me to navigate my own path, but also to understand my clients' situations better. We all learn constantly from each other. There are others I could add, but I have tried to choose people who represent different aspects of grief. I hope these insights with their varied time perspectives will give you hope, especially if you, or someone you are supporting, is in the early throes of grief.

The following interviews were audio-recorded during various stages of the Covid-19 pandemic. I have edited the interviews with the blessing of each interviewee, largely taking out my voice, to present the real gems of our conversations.

Cam Pickering

Music producer, pronouns they/them

Cam, who, along with their sister Emilie, is mentioned so much in the memoir part of this book. Cam (twenty-five at the time of interview) is seventeen months younger than Harry and was nearly five when Harry died. We talked about what Cam remembers from that period, and the amount of disability equipment we had in the house – the hospital bed in their shared bedroom, special seating, standing frames, two wheelchairs, the through-floor lift, the bath hoist. It was our 'normal' at the time and the children's friends loved playing with it all, especially when it came to the lift and riding on the back of Harry's powered chair.

ॐ

I remember there being a big bed in our room, not necessarily a 'hospital' bed, and then it not being there. I remember riding around on the back of Harry's powered chair, loads of us being crammed in the lift.

At Helen House the week Harry died I remember being in the craft room and not being sure if I was actually on my own, but I feel like I went into the Little Room to see Harry on my own when everyone was eating. It's a strong memory – there was probably someone with me, but I felt like I was alone with him.

I know the staff wanted all of us to be able to access Harry whenever we wanted to after he died in the week leading up to the funeral, so the fact Cam remembers being there alone is just right: a member of staff would have been nearby watching over them, but letting Cam have precious time with Harry.

I remember going places, on outings with the Helen House Club and being called 'Camera' by the children there, basically fun memories of being with people.

I asked Cam how Harry's life and death affects life now.

In everything really; it's immeasurable. It affects the way I think, everything I do, how I've developed as a person. Early life is your personality. I was reading an interview with Sophie [the experimental music producer and musician who died a few days before our chat and who had influenced Cam massively]; it was about transhumanism. She said, 'Your body isn't a story that's finished at birth.' So the idea of nature or nurture is bullshit because your decisions are a part of your nature. Nature is before birth and early life, but so is nurture. They are both the same thing, just different sides of it; it's what you can control that defines you.

You make decisions based on experience. I think some of my friendships and relationships are less deep as a result of what I've experienced because I tend to deal with stuff myself. It's easier to get on with life in that way. It's a good and bad thing.

In the film *Jodorowsky's Dune*, Jodorowsky says, 'Thing come, you say yes. Thing go away, you say yes.' It's forward momentum.

We talked about when Harry died, how I had felt immediately afterwards a heightened awareness of my every breath counting, so while the worst thing I had ever experienced was happening, I was also aware of life being amplified in some bizarre way.

As Cam and I were talking (on Zoom because of lockdown), we both ended up laughing and crying, totally illustrating 'the depths of sorrow and the heights of joy'. I shared with Cam that now that more than twenty years have passed, I tend to visualise this phrase these days as not a low point and a high point vertically, but two dots on the circumference of a circle, matching each other, side by side, horizontally. How the tears and pain can be there again instantly (as they were during our conversation) but how we always end up laughing and can be completely happy at the same time. They have shifted from high and low to being hand in hand.

I also wore black as a teenager for about five years! The aggression in the music I listened to, punk and metal, I always needed a bit more of that. I was definitely angry for a few years.

I was able to talk to Hebe [see the interview with Hebe Campbell] because I relentlessly asked her questions about her sister dying; it was just normal to be able to do that. Harry's life and death were just something we talked about throughout my childhood and it wasn't ever something we covered up.

Visually for me, grief is like sound waves. Each time something happens, death, divorce, each difficult event, the cumulative grief maybe sends the sound waves higher and lower, so if they get too high and low you can really lose it. So I'm trying to get better at stretching and breathing with exercises to counteract the build-up. Dealing with stuff in my head isn't always great; I've had a couple of times when I've really lost it and broken down, especially during the divorce. I remember Dad was talking to me and I just shut down and couldn't hear anything, I couldn't move. A flatline; I just froze and couldn't feel. Post-teenage hormones, that's a rare time I really remember that happening, so that's the accumulation of everything, not just one thing.

We discussed and agreed that however far the sound waves fluctuate, because we've demonstrated that we can survive Harry's death, and that we had and still have a happy family life, then hopefully we can get through it all. We get better at dealing with the lows and highs.

www.ineedsound.co

Emilie Pickering

Actor, set assistant on films

Emilie (twenty-two at the time of interview) is three years younger than Cam, and she was two years old when Harry died.

❧

I don't really have many early memories, just specific memories of events and moments, but I can't really place when they were.

I found it hard growing up that Cam had memories of Harry and I didn't at all. I liked having photos of us together everywhere, but they also made me sad because I didn't have any memories of having a relationship with Harry. There's a video of me putting my finger in Harry's mouth, him laughing and making a popping noise, and me laughing; that was always one of my favourite things to watch and I used to think I could remember it but I don't think I could really as I was under two.

Thinking of Harry doesn't really distress me so much now – obviously it does that he's not here, but I don't really think of him and feel upset or sad. It used to, but not any more.

Emilie felt really strange saying that last paragraph, but I pointed out to her that it's helpful for people to know that. I speak to so many parents who are worrying about their two- and three-year-olds and how their lives will be following a major loss and it might help them to know that at twenty-two Emilie can think of Harry in a positive way. We worried so much at the time. Especially when, through the diaries earlier on in this book, we witnessed how she missed him, but not in her real memory. I think that might be helpful to people.

I remember being upset at primary school when a girl picked the last daffodil by Harry's memorial tree. I remember being around the tree and also looking at photos of Harry with one of the teachers, Mrs Randay – and sitting alone on the buddy bench often. But looking back I don't remember how it really felt.

I think I'm very realistic about life and death as a result of Harry. Most people don't know what to do when they are around bereaved people, or people going through something major. I would never say 'I'm sorry' to anyone because I don't really get that. I don't like the wording; I would rather say 'That's really shit!' and talk to them about it. I'm not awkward about asking questions, but I also understand if they don't want to talk about it. I'll try and help them through it in a practical way – I'll make them food or cake!

We discussed animals: Emilie's cat Pinkle who died two years ago, along with our old dog Daisy, each producing a tsunami of grief for Emilie who bravely held both of them as they took their last breath. Through the last few years Pinkle was Emilie's rock; through a break-up and our divorce, she was the one constant at a time of traumatic change.

After Pinkle died I felt weirdly detached because I was still grieving for Daisy and still dealing with my break-up, so it made me feel worse because I couldn't grieve properly for her. Now we have our new kitten Roo, I feel awful because she's making me forget Pinkle more. I don't think grief gets easier, it's just up and down. In a few months I might feel differently, but then I'll probably feel upset about something else, or it can be triggered.

I have mainly happy childhood memories. But what takes over is Cam being so angry for so long. I don't know whether that's the same for other people with siblings, but it felt more severe, that he was traumatised and angry. Anything I would do that might be even slightly irritating, he would react. I know I was very lucky compared to many people, in terms of having an amazing home and a stable upbringing, with good friends and relationships, but it was hard. I can see why he was like that; Cam had it worse than me in many ways growing up, because of his memories of Harry. I'm not as traumatised by Cam attacking me as he is probably by what happened to him through being older. We both suffered the effects of trauma. Everyone has someone they take it out on and for Cam it was me; for me, it's you and myself.

You have to be honest with children and not sugar-coat anything. It will make them grow up faster if you tell them the honest truth about the world and I think that's a good thing. There are some people who are mollycoddled their entire life and not told the truth, not exposed to enough and have not experienced grief yet. I definitely find it harder to be around those people because it's more difficult to relate to them and I often feel I have to filter some of the things I say. I understand why they are the way they are. When I'm around people who have experienced loss, it's a lot easier and you can be totally honest, and they can too. I know that can also make people awkward. I know I can be quite pessimistic and blunt sometimes, but that's how I am! I would rather not look forward too much and then be happily surprised.

There are people I have been close to in the past, as a teenager, who didn't understand what I had gone through so they would say things that upset me, but they probably wouldn't realise how much that affected me. Now that we are all older, they wouldn't say those things and everyone has experienced life a bit more, so they are more sensitive.

Claudia Stebbings

Occupational therapist

Harry and Claudia were born just six hours apart and I met Claudia hours after her birth, with her mother Cath, in the Maternity Unit at Chipping Norton Hospital. As they grew up together, Claudia and Harry were best friends, inseparable, and our families are forever linked as chosen family. Claudia is my goddaughter.

❧

My job is to help people who are in hospital get back to doing the things that are most important to them following physical or mental illness, head injuries or post-surgery. I also work in palliative care where my role is to help people choose their preferred place of death and then problem solving to try and make that happen. Recently that has included oncology with the backlog of complications due to Covid, so more people are choosing to die at home because their relatives can't be with them in hospital or hospices. It's been very hard with Covid patients not necessarily having that choice, and very hard for their families not being able to be with them.

I was on the Covid wards for eight months, with patients who had been in ICU and needed rehab to get back on their feet, or patients who weren't appropriate to be escalated to ICU, either because they were not for resuscitation, or they were elderly and the risks and complications outweighed the benefits.

During the pandemic it has been particularly hard because we haven't had our usual resources of family, friends, social life, the gym – all the things that help after a stressful shift. Then everything on the news has been about healthcare so getting headspace has been very difficult. There is definitely more support needed.

One of my colleagues has worked as an OT in New Zealand, and out there, every member of her team has six weekly 1:1 sessions with a psychologist. They can talk about anything in those sessions, personal or work-related, anything big or small, and she said it was so helpful in preventing people being off work; fewer sick days. It's crazy that not all companies do it!

Claudia shared some of her memories from growing up with Harry.

We had a lot of fun: going to school together; the Cotswold Wildlife Park; the silly things we shared, like playing with Harry's invisible chickens. I felt we were always playing outside; I remember you drawing a hopscotch for us and I wondered how Harry was going to do it but he just whizzed through on his powered chair – he loved it! So I always remember thinking about how Harry would do things, how he could be included.

I reminded Claudia how she and Harry would be colouring together, and while Harry was dextrous, he didn't have the strength to take the lid off a pen, but without stopping chatting, he would just hand it to Claudia, she would do it for him and they would continue seamlessly. Disability didn't get in the way of their fun. Equally, if Harry became unbalanced and his head fell forward onto the table, Claudia would just push it back up without either of them even drawing breath!

I wondered how aware Claudia was of Harry's illness and life expectancy.

I remember Harry getting his body brace and that was the first time I remember thinking, *This is different, perhaps this isn't a good sign.* Mum and Dad were very matter-of-fact and open. They told me that Harry might die much younger than other people, that over time parts of his body would stop working, so I did clearly know that Harry was going to die. It was quite harsh really, but it was just presented as a fact.

I also remember going to Helen House, and being quite overwhelmed by the amount there was to do there; the toys and the sensory room. I loved the garden as there was so much to absorb inside.

I remember when Harry was dying, someone took me aside with Cam and said Harry was going to become an angel and go to a different place. He didn't use the word 'die' or any words I knew, so I was very confused! He was obviously speaking to a six-year-old and a nearly five-year-old, but I had been told that you die, your body rots in the ground and your soul might go somewhere else, but different people have different beliefs. So the talk of angels was confusing to me.

When Harry died, I remember having my tooth pulled before it was quite ready, because I wanted it to go in his coffin! I loved making the pouch and putting it all together, writing the note.

After he died, I used to think Harry could hear my thoughts and I found that comforting, so I used to just chat to him. There was a school nurse who had also worked at Helen House and she made a memory box with me and I could talk to her about Harry. It was helpful that she wasn't family.

At some stage, she suggested I write a letter to Harry and that was when it clicked with me that he couldn't see it and I wasn't going to see him again, so it finally registered that he had really gone.

When you're a kid you don't have control over your routine, but I knew I could talk about Harry whenever I wanted with Mum, Dad and my sisters Imogen and Polly. It didn't need to be scheduled, it was just part of life, and they were grieving over him too. If I was upset I didn't ever have to hide it. It's very different if it's your sibling and your parents are also going through grief. Talking really helped.

It was hard moving to a new school where nobody knew Harry and I had to explain who he was. I had never been with people that didn't know Harry because we had always come as a pair for the whole of my life.

On cumulative grief:

I feel like I have a certain resilience, but with everything that happens it slowly gets chipped away. Especially during Covid. I was talking with a colleague who has been on intensive care wards during this period and we were saying that when you first graduate, you can cope better with the bad things that happen, you are more able to switch off and compartmentalise, being more self-protective. But in just five years we find it so much harder.

I think there are pros and cons to having that early experience of loss. You are very aware that life isn't forever from a young age and that is a good thing, but also daunting. At primary-school age, I accepted death as a normal part of life, and I was not scared of dying myself. It makes things more matter-of-fact. You know that the worst thing can happen to you, but you will be OK eventually. So when people around you are going through grief, you know that things can be OK in time.

It definitely made me reluctant to have one best friend. So I've always had a big friendship group since Harry died. When my boyfriend Rufus and I got together, that brought up lots of stuff about Harry, and I would never have expected that. It felt like I was investing in one person again and you always think they are going to die.

People tend to think that older people don't have the same mental health problems, but of course they do. Particularly if they lose their spouse or life partner in their eighties or nineties – they go through huge grief – but people brush it away and they don't get the right support so loneliness sets in. I see that a lot in my work.

Claudia's toolkit:

The memory box was probably the most helpful tool because I could visit it and focus my sadness while looking at nice things to remind me of Harry.

Marie Murray

Bereavement support

Marie, now retired, worked on both the care and bereavement teams at Helen & Douglas House. She is co-founder of Dads.care, which provides support for bereaved fathers.

Marie is mentioned throughout my diary entries so will be a familiar name if you have read that part of this book already. She often looked after Harry on the care team at Helen House and afterwards she looked after all of us as our main bereavement contact, visiting regularly for nearly two years after Harry died, guiding me with conversation and knowledge (rather than counselling or therapy), delivering the courses in which I participated and developing the work of The Elephant Club for bereaved siblings which helped Cam. We then collaborated closely for the twelve years I worked at Helen House. We are now 'just good friends' although we both volunteer for The Good Grief Project. I don't think I would be doing the work I do today if I had not had the quiet, expert but informal help, support and advice (when I asked for it) that Marie gave me.

≈≈

I started as a carer at Helen House, the world's first children's hospice, in 1982 from day one when the doors first opened. At the time I thought my role would be looking after the children, but of course the parents were equally looked after. I was there for thirty-three years up to my retirement. It completely changed and enriched my life. I feel very privileged to have been part of the development of the work.

In those days it was Helen House (Douglas House was opened in 2004). The priority was always the children: your aim each day was to make that day a good day if you could.

Making things as easy and comfortable as possible and to distract them from all that was going on at that time. But with the parents, you're alongside their worries and fears and in the early days I used to think, *I don't know how to support them. I can play board games with their children, but how can I support* them? I felt inadequate. In time I got better at hearing their concerns; not just the illness but the many issues around having a very sick child. At the start I was fearful of saying the wrong thing and making things worse for them. There was no blueprint at the time for the work we were carrying out; we grew it organically and we learned what was needed directly from the families.

I was surprised in the early days of Helen House how much access parents had to their child once they had died. They could visit the body in the chilled Little Room whenever they wanted to in the week up to the funeral (like an Irish wake). But I soon realised how important it was. We had one dad who wanted to lie by his child's coffin overnight. But what we learned early on was that we weren't going to say no to things; we would explore them together and see what felt right. For that dad who repeated that for seven nights, it's a huge comfort to him now that he was able to do that for his child. We were able to facilitate it and we learned from him what a difference that made to his ongoing grief.

Many people have wondered over the years whether this aspect of our work was necessary. With thirty years of witnessing the effects of that time, I can honestly say it was absolutely beneficial. Seeing those natural changes in the body helps parents to find some acceptance in the physicality of death. It is about having the privilege of choice, to make those decisions when every other choice for your child has been taken away. Occasionally someone might not have wanted to visit their child in the Little Room and we would never push that even if we felt it would help. We had to be led by them; being told what they should do is never helpful, without exception.

I learn so much from you parents, it is an absolute privilege. When I visited you at home twenty years ago, I would never have thought you could be doing what you are doing now. I have seen you come through your journey, not fixed, but reintegrated into your life as it is now and bringing up your two children to be balanced young people, who have been through a very, very sad household as all bereaved children do. As good as you are on your good or bad days, you are still not the Lizzie you were before Harry died. They have lived with that difference. You don't know how they know it but they do and they go home to a grieving household. It's not all bad; it can be beautiful in the way it can unite families, but no one should have to go through that. Seeing all of you parents get life back alongside (not replacing) your grief is a real privilege and is what has helped me to continue in the work for so long.

On grief:

There's no rhythm to grief; it's not predictable. It's like a tide; it ebbs and flows and is often chaotic.

We learned the art of conversation-based bereavement support from Sister Frances; she used to say, 'Don't be worried about what you are saying – there aren't any magic words; you can't make them better. Just be alongside the parents; be natural and normal.' It became like a mantra for us: don't be frightened of your words, even if they are good words; they are not going to make them 'better', and if you get it wrong, say you have. Say I'm sorry, I shouldn't have said that. I remember one time early on when I got it wrong. There was a dad who was particularly upset, and I put my arm round him and said, 'She's in your heart now,' and he said, 'I don't want her in my f**king heart, I want her here now.' And I realised then I was trying to fix him, when that wasn't comforting him at all. So I said, 'I'm really sorry, I won't say that again. I won't say it to anyone again; I realise that it was the wrong thing.' So I owned up to it immediately. I should have just said 'I'm really sorry' and allowed him his grief and feelings.

Those things you get wrong are the greatest lessons, the things you learn the most from.

One time, on Christmas Eve, I was waving colleagues goodbye in the car park, saying 'Happy Christmas!' when a couple arrived to see me. Christmas Eve was the first anniversary of their son dying, and they were returning to Helen House. My first words to them were 'Happy Christmas!' My shock at what I had said made me feel that I wanted to run away from them, but I didn't. I apologised, saying that I wished I could take it back, that it was an awful thing I had said. The couple were very gracious, but I could also see their shock. I know that evening, during their visit, I feel I said 'sorry' too many times, and the dad said, very nicely, 'That's enough, Marie, we know you are sorry.' My learning was that if you overdo it, the family is now supporting you, which is totally the wrong way round.

For parents at Helen House, their grief starts on the diagnosis of their child, so it was always important that we supported their grief alongside caring for their child and the whole family. Grief support didn't just start when their child died, it was continuous from when they came through the doors. It was important not to distance ourselves from those difficult conversations, however daunting that might be when you first start.

The last ten years of my work at Helen House was primarily with couples. I can see the absolute benefit of couples working together because although they are grieving for the same child, their grief is individual. They won't grieve in the same way, and it is about learning not to judge each other's way of grieving, even if it is abhorrent to you. One might go to visit the grave and find it comforting, while the other can't, they find it too painful. They need to hear each other, otherwise silence develops. It is so important.

Many bereaved dads find it hard to express their grief. They grieve just as much, but the opportunity to express grief is often harder. Once they start talking, they go into great depth just as the mums do. The groups we run have been groundbreaking for fathers. The groups are so beneficial because they are hearing others tell their story and how they are feeling, mirroring each other. The Dads' Groups just blow me away. We have dads who have been coming for eleven years and some people think we are holding them back, that it should have a time limit! I totally disagree: parental grief doesn't last just a couple of years, it's ongoing and I know you never get over the loss. You walk alongside it and take it with you wherever you are. You manage it and grow resilience.

The dads that are still coming after eleven years, they are in turn helping the newly bereaved dads. It's a two-way flow. Community is everything. It's hard, particularly in the early days, when friends, the people you feel could help you most, aren't always there for you and often turn away through their own feelings of inadequacy or fear, or their own difficulties. That's something that the Dads' Group can help each other with. Coming to the groups and having permission to share your memories, not having to think you are boring people, or you need to keep quiet with people who haven't been through it. It's not just hearing about the grief, we also hear about their children; it gives them permission to speak. One of them said, 'We really like talking about our children and not just about our pain.' It's a safe space where they can talk. I believe nobody can help a bereaved parent like another bereaved parent.

The continuing bond with your loved one is so important, bringing their memory with you.

In looking back over more than thirty years of being alongside the grieving, my overall feeling if you are supporting someone is:

Just be there for them. That's it. Keep inviting them. Keep saying 'Shall we have a coffee?' No matter how many times they turn you down, one day they will say yes. Just be there at their pace and don't try to fix things; let them say what they feel and if they are telling you their feelings, you are doing the best thing for them. You can't do more than that. Allow their feelings without judging or fixing. We can think of solutions, but it doesn't mean that solution works for them. Just let them talk.

We walk alongside and we pick up the conversation as it's flowing. We don't go back and unpick the last one again, we talk about today, how they are today and what they are feeling as grief ebbs and flows. We talk about what is current. Sometimes you may meet up with them and they may not want to talk about their feelings, they may just want to chat or even silence. Without formality, conversation-based work can allow for that.

Information on Dads.care: www.dads.care

Rachel Griffith

Rennie Grove Hospice Care and Hospice at Home, clinical nurse specialist and, more recently, practice educator

Two of Rachel and Pete's daughters, Misha and Natalie, died a year apart through Batten disease. They are mentioned earlier in this book, since we met at Helen House and Rachel went on to nurse at Douglas House, the part of the hospice for young adults. We met as parents using the hospice, became friends, and later became connected by both our work and our personal experiences. At the time of interview, Rachel had recently suffered the death of her father, during Covid.

ॐ

I'm never very good at the introduction bit because I think I blotted a lot of it out.

When our eldest daughter Misha was four, she started fitting and had treatment for epilepsy. But following investigation, CT scans showed she had a small brain for her age and perhaps her development was being affected. It turned out she had Batten disease, which is a neurodegenerative, untreatable (at the time) condition which is inherited. Both Pete and I carried the recessive gene for it. We had just had our third daughter Sophie at that point, so we had to have our middle daughter Natalie (two) and youngest Sophie (ten days old) tested after Misha's diagnosis. There was a one-in-four chance that all our girls could have the condition and die from it.

Our second daughter Natalie had a very normal development, so we felt somehow that she might be less likely to have it; she was born a good weight and was developing well. But she was found to have it while Sophie was clear.

There is a 50 per cent chance that Sophie could be a carrier but I somehow blotted that out. Later, I had prenatal testing for our fourth child Zak, and he was found to be fine. I remember the radiographer testing Zak in vitro, saying, 'This baby looks healthy,' but in my mind I knew it made no difference. I didn't know whether I could go through another pregnancy if he did have the condition. It was very traumatic during pregnancy – there were already losses.

Things degenerated pretty fast. Misha was only seven when she died in 2002 (the same year Zak was born) and Natalie died a year later. I can't even tell you what dates they died, the dates of the funerals; I don't want to think about it. I have always celebrated their birthdays – I like to make birthday cakes for them, involving Sophie and Zak in that. We have cake and balloons and visit the girls' graves, which are in our village.

The graves being there was a big decision. As a teenager I found graveyards strangely comforting, that feeling of history. So we wanted the girls to be buried here where we were living so that when Sophie and Zak were teenagers, they could visit independently to have that headspace with their sisters. It's a beautiful graveyard in the countryside; we are very privileged in that way. Some people think that grief rituals are bad things, but I don't feel that. Our rituals in grief and death give great comfort whatever religion you are.

It's been challenging at work recently, during Covid, to support families with their rituals, for instance supporting Muslim families, being involved in washing their loved one's body. Covid has changed our abilities to connect with some of those rituals.

My dad died recently and we were unable to visit him due to Covid. But one of the healthcare assistants was able to help Dad use WhatsApp video and message us individually – we could see him waving at us. He could talk on WhatsApp, but he was profoundly deaf and couldn't hear us. I recently shared with a nurse I was teaching how much that meant to us as a family and how we could look back with grateful hearts for that moment when we couldn't be with him. He wanted to give us comfort.

On nursing:

I always wanted to be a nurse or a teacher and I've been very privileged to do both.

I started nursing at eighteen and I was twenty-five when Misha was born. I continued working when the girls were poorly because in a way it was my lifeline to work, just one or two shifts a week, to think about and be with other people. It was an incredibly isolating and lonely experience to have four children in nappies and two with profound needs, so going to work was a gift to me.

After the girls died, I gradually increased my work, but I applied for a job at Douglas House in the young adult hospice, which was a separate building to the one the girls had died in. I didn't want to be known as a mother applying for the job but a professional in my own right, so needed that separation within the organisation.

I wrote a diary piece and presented it at a conference, reflecting on how difficult it was as a mother to deal with the seventeen different professionals involved with us for the girls. It was so hard to know who to approach with our questions, who was the right person at the right moment. I continued in palliative care and it has given me great insight. I've completed my palliative care degree now in the hope that I might be able to support research and a knowledge base for other families.

The care we were given was excellent and I believe that from excellent care is generated the strength and resource to help others.

I did have the deepest and darkest days; my experience of the madness of grief is that I had a flash of thought when Natalie, our second daughter, was diagnosed, that I should drive into a lake, so we could all be together and wouldn't have to go through the process ahead. Just before Misha died I had an image of driving into a wall. So it was evidence of considerable depression, but with reflection, I feel that it was mainly based on sleep deprivation.

For my dissertation, I looked at anticipatory grief and I published that piece of work in a palliative journal for nursing, in the hope that I could give people an insight into how grief affects us before death, especially in these long conditions which have a great burden of care.

It's really affected me this summer, the insight in knowing what it's like to be a carer, knowing that people can't get enough care due to Covid, and I think the burden of that, alongside my dad's death, has been too much to bear. I wasn't sleeping, I had physical symptoms of overwhelm in my health and then Dad died; it was all a bit too close to home. I think going through so many losses does allow you learning, being able to recognise symptoms of not coping. I know you have explored your grief with counselling and I've done the same. I so often tell my students and colleagues that seeking help when you're not coping is a sign of strength, not weakness.

I recognise some of the repeated physical symptoms. After Misha died, I just had to keep going to look after our three remaining children. I had tonsillitis repeatedly. This time it's been night-time waking, thinking about my patients and then heart and chest pain, which had to be investigated. But it made me realise it was time to change direction for a little while.

What has helped you over the years?

During the girls' lives, during our living grief, regular respite care helped, but was also challenging. When I used to pick up the girls, the burden felt heavier in a way and I would recognise the losses. The degenerative changes in walking, talking, eating, smiling – those things were evident and you had to explain the changes since you had last been for respite care.

Since then, it's been friends who have stayed in touch during the isolation of grief, walking and nature. Sometimes if I had a particularly difficult shift at Douglas House I would stop on the way home and just stand in a field and ground myself. So often I would see something that would seem special to me, a butterfly which would land nearby. One time a barn owl flew alongside the car beside me; it was just breathtaking. On an early shift, I was often up early enough to watch a special sunrise.

Sometimes I would get up in the night and make a cup of tea and just read, nothing heavy, just to switch off. Music has always been a real outlet too. There was a young man I worked with at Douglas House, and his brother wanted to visit one of the chapels for evensong, a way of them being together. We managed to get him there – we suctioned him, dressed him up and there we were at evensong. I suddenly found myself with tears pouring down my face; it was the acoustics and the moment of being there with him. He was fairly close to death at that point and died a short time later. It was so special for him. Music allows me to revisit grief. There's something about the mathematics in music, the repetitions, the fact it's part of a piece and it will start and finish and you will get to the end. You can deliberately visit music when you want to revisit grief, although sometimes it can catch you unawares!

I used to find it comforting to hear that people felt the same about their grief twenty years later, but you want to know that it won't be the same every day. I tell people that in anticipatory grief, we go through gradual losses in the approach to death, monthly, weekly then daily, but after a death, we have to reverse it and manage our time minute by minute, hour by hour, week by week. I wonder whether grief has circadian rhythms – perhaps that will be discovered in years to come?

I struggle at the moment with not feeling like I'm doing enough. I still find it hard to balance it all. What we went through was so difficult that nothing is ever going to be as difficult as some of those moments. So however hard work is, or things are now, they are never as crippling as they were then. So it's hard to know how much of myself to give. How to make a difference.

What advice do you have for anyone supporting a bereaved person or someone caring for the dying?

Offer the practical – that's what I always remember. Those who helped me to keep up with the washing, or delivered food. The fact that I would see someone made me feel less isolated. It's those small acts of very practical help. You are touching their space by showing up with something. I will never forget those people who came alongside us in our darkest place. Usually it's the people who have suffered themselves who will do it, or those who have seen their parents do it. So take your children along with you!

Pete Griffith

Professional photographer and chaplain (UK Board of Healthcare Chaplaincy), dad to Misha and Natalie, Sophie and Zak, husband to Rachel (previous interview)

I have four children, and that's as true today as it ever was. Rach doesn't do dates, but I can tell you exactly, sadly. Misha died 27th November 2002, and Nat died 8th December 2003. So seventeen and eighteen years ago.

As a professional photographer, one of the charities I came across a few years ago was Remember My Baby. They are a charity who offer photography for families whose children have died. Sometimes I might be called in immediately following the death, or sometimes just before the child has died. Some of the most precious moments of my photography career have been shared with parents, with their dead baby in their arms, with that deep connection of love there. To be invited in on what may be the last hours with their baby or child is profoundly affecting; we cry together, we laugh together and we talk about loss, life, dashed hopes while taking photos.

I think there is that element of grief that isn't discussed very much, the loss of hope. For me as a dad, not being able to walk Misha and Nat up the aisle, not being able to chase a boyfriend off the drive! Not seeing them go to university, not getting drunk together – those silly things too. It's some of the little losses too during their lifetimes. I still remember watching Nat on the day she realised she couldn't play and join in any more. I think Sophie was playing in the garden and she looked out and burst into tears. It broke me. Chips too. I remember the therapist saying that Nat mustn't eat chips any more – how could we explain that to her? Nat loved McDonald's chips!

In some ways when their deaths came, they were almost the lesser griefs because grief had been constant since diagnosis. We had lost so much by that point, we knew they were going to die and we had grieved heavily for all those years before the final point of death. I remember at the funeral people saying 'How are you coping?' and I think grief has a weird way of allowing you to do stuff – I coped with that day. Even now, my brain can switch off from grief and I think, no, I can't do that today, I need to be doing this. Then there are days when I let grief in and allow the sadness, my 'duvet' days – when I can't function at all. I have to acknowledge it. All these years on, there are still days when I will sob like a baby.

It has gone so quickly. For me some days can still feel like the day I held them in my arms to say goodbye to them. All the smells, the feels, the horror of having to think of burying them. In that whole period, the hardest thing for me as a dad was that the final act I could do for them (and I did it for both Misha and Natalie) was lifting them into their coffins and closing the lid for the last time. It still breaks me thinking about that, but I didn't want anyone else to do it; the thought that somebody else would see my child for the last time.

The awful thing is we had a practice run. With Misha's funeral, like most people, we didn't know what to do, what was 'right' or 'wrong' when she died, so we had a standard white coffin and did everything by the book. Sister Frances's words ring true, that as long as it's legal, do whatever you want! So when Natalie died, we had a bright yellow coffin; we each put our handprints on the coffin, in different colours – Sophie chose pink glitter for hers – and the coffin came into church to the Tweenies theme tune. It certainly broke the tension of the moment!

I confessed to Pete that I had funeral envy at both funerals – I wished we had carried out Harry's less by the book. Our self-imposed, traditional book.

Here we are, twenty years on, still talking about *all* our children, watching out for each other, laughing, and there are others who have walked this grief journey with us. Talking to you just weeks after Harry died, I witnessed you still able to laugh and breathe. You hadn't died, externally anyway, because at that stage for me I felt the biggest grief we could ever face might actually kill us. It nearly does. But talking together and knowing other bereaved parents is the greatest gift.

We also have a support group we have set up at our church, called Good Grief. It has helped me as well as the people who come along to it. It's open to anyone who is grieving and wants to come along. It's not rocket science really, is it? It's just allowing people to share their stories and to realise that they are not alone in it.

At the point of diagnosis you immediately feel very isolated and think nobody knows what you are going through, and then you identify with all the others walking that journey. So I feel very connected to my grief family or tribe.

It's hard not being overprotective parents for our surviving children. I've found that difficult, although Rach being a nurse always grounds me.

On male grief:

I think women are sometimes better able to deal with grief in some ways; they have stronger friendships and community. The Dads' Group set up by Marie and Tim, originally at Helen & Douglas House, has been really important, even if I can't always attend due to photography work at weekends. I've been able to more recently on their Zoom calls, due to Covid. I get the opportunity to talk about Misha and Nat in a safe space without anyone trying to move the conversation on because they find it uncomfortable. It's not easy, but we still want to bring our children back into the room and this is the one place I can do it freely. I see more male emotion there than I do anywhere else. It's not something I can talk about generally with my mates too much. I still remember those very early days when the girls had died, being in the pub and it was typical lads' chat – footie, TV, bravado talk. Testosterone in the room, and me thinking, *Hang on, my daughters have just died.* Church has felt lonely too. Sometimes the words will just get to me and I can't cope.

Running has helped me massively. I trained to do a marathon at the age of forty-five for Helen & Douglas House, but since the last one in 2016, I now run for me. I have had health challenges, but come through them. Getting outside is a big tick box for my mental health, especially going out at sunrise. But first and foremost, as long as I have my family, I can get through the days. That has been a weird gift of Covid, having my family around.

On the depth of sorrow and the height of joy:

I have struggled with depression quite a lot. I swing from high to low and perhaps that's part of being creative as well? I was bullied at school and when I left school I left that behind and started life again. But then the girls were diagnosed. I love to travel, to seize opportunities, to embrace life and fun, but then I can be in the car and a wave of grief and sadness will come over me and I'll end up sobbing. That's the weird dichotomy, isn't it? Extremes of joy and sorrow.

I watch my surviving kids and Rach, and celebrate in their successes, yet there is always sorrow too.

I just tell it as it is – if I'm having a bad day, people will know it. I try not to be negative, but I have to be open, yet I could never truly say how I feel; in some ways it's indescribable!

On further life changes:

In June 2019 I did the Three Peaks Challenge for charity with friends. Our van broke down and I had to see if anyone could help us out financially – we were trying to raise money for charity and this had happened! A dear friend said she would support us and at the same time said to me that she felt God telling her to give me a certain amount of money, but she didn't know what it was for. It turned out that the theology course I wanted to do was that exact amount of money.

So a complete change for me, from being a photographer to being a hospital chaplain. We all have pastoral needs which basically means 'looking after' – spiritual guidance. Sharing hearts and journeys. I couldn't preach in church but I can walk the journey with people, as you and I have done. From a Christian perspective it feels like a real calling.

Remember My Baby: www.remembermybaby.org

Hebe Campbell

Journalist

Hebe became friends with Cam when they were fourteen. They were never at school together but discovered that they were both bereaved siblings and had actually met when they were younger at Helen House. Hebe's sister Polly died in 2003 at the age of eight, a month before her ninth birthday, from an asthma attack. Hebe was six.

৯১

We were at a barbecue at a friend's house on a very hot day. Polly suffered an asthma attack at the barbecue and we only had an old inhaler. The ambulance got lost en route and she died. My brothers Otto and Hugo were there as well; Otto must have been two or three and Hugo early teens.

From that period I remember a huge amount of attention surrounding our family; at school, friends, our extended family. I remember missing school the day we were due back from the summer holidays because they were going to make an announcement about Polly's death (she was at the same school) and it was better we weren't there.

I look back and I think I was suffering from post-traumatic stress, and it lasted a long time, but I don't think it was ever really identified. I remember having severe anxiety every time my mum or dad left me, especially my dad, to the point where if they went out to the theatre I would chase them out of the house, I was so petrified of them not coming home. So every day, going to school was tough.

I don't think PTSD and anxiety were taken as seriously as they are now. Everyone wanted to find a new normal so it went unnoticed. Everyone pays a lot of attention but no one pays real attention. They are focusing on their route out of it and their own way of grieving.

I don't think I started to grieve at that age. After that day, I didn't feel the effects of sadness and the gravity until years later, maybe ten years later, in my teens.

Hebe and I talked about the fact that there really is no pattern to grief. There are so many factors: how other people around you are coping; that family life is quite fast paced, with school, friends, homework, brothers; all the things that were busy before carry on and suddenly you can find years later there is this life-changing event that has never really been unpicked.

Yes, and my parents separated very soon after, which distracted and occupied us all. So suddenly we were living between parents.

When it really hit me I was in sixth form. I remember reading 5,742 *Days*, the Anne-Marie Cockburn grief diary about the death of her daughter, and reading about grief made me realise that I had been through something similar and it hit me like a bus, all at once.

I hate pity. I feel embarrassed and don't ever want anyone to know that I'm upset. My parents are both quite emotional and I think I worry about them so much that I would never offload anything emotional to my family. I feel uncomfortable speaking to friends about it. I have friends I have known for a couple of years and they don't even know about Polly.

I've found a way round it; it's the way I can cope. I now watch documentaries on grief and that's how I've taught myself about it. I can be very affected by films, especially where a child dies. I read a lot too. In my work I'm very drawn to stories involving loss. I don't think this is unhealthy for me; I come across as an extrovert but really I'm an introvert and for me this way of coping works.

As a family we've dealt with it in different ways. My dad is the most vocal and will talk about Polly; he has photos everywhere. He has probably dealt with it the most. My mum is very emotional about it and will talk to anyone about it with her heart on her sleeve. I don't know how my brothers have coped. I'm really close with them but we don't talk about it. It plays on my mind how my older brother particularly has dealt with it; he had four more years with Polly than we did.

Hebe's advice for any family going through a similar bereavement:

I would say don't rush it. Especially with young children who were our age. Don't feel pressured. To the parents I would say – look at your children's behavioural patterns. Notice if your children are acting out. My behaviour was so obvious and I wish I could have been diagnosed and had help. I don't blame anyone, because parents are going through it as well. It doesn't have to be the parent helping, but there are organisations that will and I think it would have been good if my brothers and I could have gone to something together. It would have helped us to talk about it rather than us never talking about it. It feels like a taboo after a while. We feel too uncomfortable.

It seems so silly because it's so much easier when you unload it on someone. Everyone's sitting round the table who has been through the same thing and no one's helping each other. It's free counselling in a way and you've all been through it; we're all in the same boat so let's talk about it!

I talked to Hebe about how The Good Grief Project found on their Active Grief Retreats that it was often better not to have parents and siblings in on discussions together because the surviving children (of any age) will always protect their parents. Something Helen House discovered too, hence the need for The Elephant Club for bereaved children.

If there's a group of people with one thing in common, you usually talk about it, but somehow with grief you don't, or often don't.

Cam is probably the person I spoke to most; he's so good at talking about it and he would never be embarrassed to voice our connection. He pushed me to talk about it and it was something we bonded over. We have a lot of loyalty and good will to each other because we are both bereaved siblings.

I remember school having two memorial services after Polly died and planting a tree which is still there. And teachers took me under their wing. I developed a bond with Polly's friends at school and outside and I still feel that bond. I wish school had realised how anxious I was.

There are goals going forward that I would like to aim for and one is feeling less embarrassed about talking more openly.

There are positives you have to take from this that you put into everyday life. I try to seize the moment, really appreciate what's around. I'm grateful for health, for my family, for every day.

What I always refer back to is that on that day when Polly died, what triggered her attack was possibly sitting on a blanket that cats had been on before. We were both asthmatic, we were both allergic to cats and I sat on that blanket with her. So every day I think that could have been me. So I need to enjoy life and do it for Polly – it really could have been me.

It gives you empathy for other people. Every time I hear someone saying something nasty about someone else, I think there must be a reason behind it. They could be grieving; you never know what's happened. I'm here and each day has to be fun, my job is my life, but I would never do a job I didn't enjoy. You have to take something positive from this, otherwise this grief was for nothing. Small things don't bother me. That's what I want to keep working on as well, every day, to set my mind to be grateful for my day.

I would like to talk to my brothers about what we have positively taken forward each day. Hugo and Otto and I would not be where we are now, all of us so independent, if it wasn't for what happened.

Grief is so different for everyone and there is no linear pattern whatsoever.

Sister Frances Dominica OBE, DL, FRCN

Founder of the children's hospice movement worldwide

In founding Helen House in Oxford, the world's first children's hospice, Sister Frances created a blueprint used by many others throughout the UK and the world. Like so many other families, we can never thank her enough for the care we were given there before, during and after Harry's death.

෯

I realise that I encountered grief when I was very young. I was born in Inverness where my father was stationed in 1942. When I was three weeks old my father had to return to his regiment and my mother took me to Greenock where her parents lived, claiming that she didn't know one end of a baby from another. Tragically her mother died suddenly and unexpectedly of a strangulated hiatus hernia two weeks later. I suppose that was when I first encountered grief.

One of the results of this tragedy was that my grandfather and I had a very special relationship until he died aged ninety-six. He was a man of few words, a lawyer and an elder of the Church of Scotland. He rarely talked about God or his faith, he just lived it. It was infectious.

In later years my mother used to recount how occasionally she would go out with friends to see a film, having tucked me up in my cot for the night. On her return she would often find me on my grandfather's knee, with him singing Scottish lullabies to me. She would say, 'Oh dear, did she wake up?' to which he would reply, 'No, but I thought she might.' Perhaps he was working through the grief he had lived with for many years since the death of his little daughter, also named Frances. She had been a late addition to the family, adored by all. When she was three years old, she contracted a virus and died three days later. Since her death my grandfather had visited her grave every Sunday. Once I was born, he only went to the grave at Christmas. Perhaps our relationship had healed his grief in some way. We were very close for the rest of his life. He was a very wonderful person. I was three when my father was demobbed, and we moved south. I grieved for my grandfather and counted the days until his next visit to us.

When I was five my brother was born. He was a very sick baby and had pneumonia three times before he was a year old. I lived with the intense anxiety and grief of my parents. My mother was resident with him at the hospital for sick children, Great Ormond Street. I had already decided I was going to be a nurse so, when my brother was at home, I practised my nursing skills on him. He survived!

Eventually I was accepted for nurse training at the hospital where my brother had been a patient. During my training I witnessed much grief. This was a hospital to which very sick children were flown from all over the world for specialist care. Many of them recovered and went home to great rejoicing, but tragically some didn't, so I was sometimes alongside grieving parents. Sixty years later I am still in touch with a few of them.

When I qualified, I shocked family and friends by joining an Anglican religious community, the Society of All Saints Sisters of the Poor. I loved it! I worked in a little children's home for which we were responsible and witnessed the behaviour of those children who, for one reason or another, were not able to live with their families. We did our best and we had a lot of fun, but they lived with their own grief and sometimes acted out accordingly.

In 1977, eleven years after I joined our community, I was elected as Mother Superior General, ultimately responsible for sixty sisters. In 1978 I had a telephone call from the mother of a very sick child called Helen. Following six months in hospital and accepting that she was not going to recover, her parents took her home. She needed twenty-four-hour care and she had a new baby sister. I offered to have Helen to stay for short breaks to give her parents a chance to relax and to focus on their new baby. I learned so much from Helen's mother, who was very articulate about her grief.

So, with the help of Helen's inspirational mother – she had first-hand experience of long-drawn-out grief, whereas I was an onlooker – we created Helen House. We set out to offer hospice care for children with life-shortening conditions. It was imperative that the care was not just for the sick child but for the whole family. It was the first of its kind in the world. We were on a very steep learning curve and it was the families who taught us.

Each family who came taught us more – no two were the same. Many times, I was privileged to be alongside a family as their child's condition gradually deteriorated. And it wasn't just from the parents we learned; it was from the siblings too. Often while they were playing, they would express amazing thoughts and observations. Friendships developed quickly and went very deep.

Helen House opened in 1982 and to this day, especially at times like Christmas, I hear from families who came to Helen House many years ago, families who offered me the privilege of being alongside them at the most painful of times, without any answers, without much at all to say, just walking alongside them in their grief.

The Little Room:

We knew that all the children had progressive or life-shortening conditions and that some of them would die in Helen House, some in hospital and some at home. If the child was not in Helen House when they died, some of the families would bring their child back to us after they had died until the funeral.

We had eight children's bedrooms, each with a window seat which could be made into a comfortable bed for a family member or friend to sleep on. We also became adept at putting down mattresses on the floor! Families were offered self-contained flats upstairs. We created a ninth bedroom on the ground floor, furnished much like the other bedrooms but it could be kept at a very cold temperature. This gave any family whose child had just died the opportunity to make it their own. When one little girl died her parents dressed her in a white Victorian embroidered dress, very delicate and beautiful. Others were into Superman! We assured parents that there was no hurry. When they were ready, they could carry their child to the Little Room and spend time there, day or night. One mother wrapped herself in duvets and spent the night beside her child. If the family wanted music, there would be music. Brothers and sisters were free to come and go; some took their friends into the Little Room.

With each succeeding day the parents would see a physical change in their child. When it came to three, four, five or even seven days parents would realise that it was time for the next stage. Often, they would lift their child into the coffin. If they wanted help, we were on hand to help them to create a funeral service appropriate for their unique, beloved child.

It went on from there really; they knew that there would always be a welcome for them at Helen House. For many it became like having an extended family. It was so important that the well children in the family knew they would be welcome to come back and see us. A teenage brother cycled all the way from Northampton to see us some months after his brother had died in Helen House. He had been a right little tearaway when his brother was sick but he wanted to come back to see us and to say thank you.

We went on to create Douglas House in the same grounds because so many young people were living much longer than they would once have done. These young adults up to the age of thirty-five were often very articulate, bringing with them issues like loud music, sexuality, alcohol, partying. One young person described it as a decent hotel.

Looking back, I realise how privileged I was to enter a world of grief, to share it, in however small a way, with families. It created friendships like no other. Their grief was not just in the first year of bereavement, sometimes the second year was even worse, and I soon learned that you never 'get over it'.

It is too easy to compartmentalise the process of grief. Everyone is unique, even when it comes to grief.

I left Helen & Douglas House in 2013 and was invited to help out at The Porch, a project which had begun at our convent front door nearly thirty-five years previously. Sometimes our porch got so crowded with wayfarers and homeless people that it was difficult to get in or out! Visiting VIPs risked getting given an enamel mug of tea! The Porch has moved to improved accommodation on our property twice and may move again as more and more people use what is offered.

Listening to the stories of some who come to The Porch I recognise that loss and grief come in many different shapes and forms. The people begging on the pavement as we pass by have stories to tell, though they are seldom invited to tell them. Rejection, addiction, crime, prison, homelessness – so much grief manifested in a variety of ways.

A dear friend whose wife died recently sent me a beautiful card which says:

In the darkest of skies, a sea of starlight.

The card is on a blue background. Blue is the colour of hope.

Frances ended by reading me a beautiful poem, written by poet, author and psychiatrist Averil Stedeford, whom Frances knew when Averil worked at Sir Michael Sobell House, the adult hospice in Oxford.

The Heavy Stone

My grief was a heavy stone, rough and sharp,
Grasping to pick it up, my hands were cut.
Afraid to let it go I carried it.
While I had my grief you were not lost.

The rain of my tears, smoothed it.
The wind of my rage weathered it,
making it round and small.

The cuts in my hands have healed.
Now in my palm it rests,
sometimes almost beautiful,
sometimes almost you.

Francie Clarkson

Founder patron of Help for Heroes

At the time of this interview, December 2020, Francie was training for her tenth Ironman; she has completed nine Help for Heroes Big Battlefield Bike Rides (400 miles each) and the Race Across America with Team True Spirit (comprising injured servicemen). Francie suffered the death of her father, Major Robert Cain, a month before her thirteenth birthday; her sister Helly, who died at the age of forty; and the painful end of her marriage, with the additional challenge of being in the public eye. She has also endured the deaths of some very close friends.

Never shying away from her own grief or the grief of her friends, Francie is fearless, determined and independent, yet able to gently and unassumingly come alongside anyone in any situation. I have witnessed this many times. I rode horses as a child and teenager, and it was Francie who almost forced me back into riding again after Harry died. On her sturdy Icelandic horses we (still) relive our teens! They are typical of her, feisty yet sure-footed and down to earth with a soft side. Often the laughing stock of the smart-horse set, we love nothing more than meeting people on their immaculate steeds while we have been covered in mud when the small horses (never called ponies in Iceland) have their shaggy winter coats. Francie has been there for me every step of the way and particularly through Harry's death and my divorce. I was interested to know what she feels has enabled her to find the strength to go forward and thrive, quietly with her head down, away from the press.

Francie's family lived on the Isle of Man when her father was ill. Her father was in the Westminster Hospital in London and she took the phone call on her own to say he had died. She was thirteen.

۶۸

The awful event that happens when you're a child is your norm. You don't know anything else. I was pretty much on my own; Mum wasn't coping after my father died, and as a teenager I had a tricky few years, but although it's not ideal it's not 'woe is me', it was just all I knew. I was very alone but it was a different era. No one spoke to me about it; I went to school and nobody said a word. The other children had been told my father had died but nobody would speak to me or look at me; it was as though I had the plague.

You know this with Harry: there are those who want to be part of the journey you are on, and those who turn their backs. When my sister Helly was diagnosed with a brain tumour (she was five years older and my best friend) all her friends fell away. When she became sick her good friends were nowhere to be seen. One of them even told me later that she didn't go to visit because she 'didn't think it would be nice to see her like that and didn't know what to say'. She just wanted the good times and didn't want to be friends with a dying person. The karma was that a few years later I was on a press trip for a car company and was told one of the women, Carol, had just been diagnosed with cancer. I took Carol's phone number and phoned her afterwards. I didn't know her but just let her know I was sorry and that I was always there if she wanted to talk. I felt that, being an outsider, it might be easier for her. I phoned her quite regularly and we would talk. She told me things she couldn't share with anybody else: her fears for what would happen to her husband and the boys when she was gone, the fact she was slowly but surely replacing all the plants in the conservatory with plastic ones to save watering them.

I wondered whether Francie feels her work as a founder patron of Help for Heroes, tireless participant in their fundraising events and friend to many veterans of all ages, is linked to her father who was awarded the Victoria Cross, the highest award for bravery.

The military 'keep to themselves' – they don't share with civilians, and I am very much a civilian, but perhaps because of my dad I have a special pass. I don't talk to many of them about the people they have lost, but I do talk to them about what *they* have lost. It's a great loss, not just an arm or a leg that's gone. It's the camaraderie, their career, their way of life. For many, going into the military was about finding a family that perhaps they didn't have before, and they lose that all over again. They don't readily accept counselling; it's hard.

We talked about Francie's many losses, especially Helly and some of her closest friends who died, Annie, Fi and Caro. Francie showed me a beautiful necklace she always wears, bearing Fi's fingerprint, which her daughter had imprinted at the suggestion of the hospice where she died, so that it can be recreated in different ways.

Francie wears it close to her heart. This struck me as a wonderful memento, and one that can be reproduced if it is lost.

We discussed the Diana effect – how although Francie didn't feel strongly about Princess Diana, the grief of the nation after her death in August 1997, the outpouring, allowed her to howl for her sister and father. It felt as though the floodgates opened.

And, finally, the break-up of her family following her divorce from husband Jeremy Clarkson – a marriage where fame increasingly cut her off from her friends.

It was the difficulty of being watched and holding together a family of young children. Suffering a terminally ill marriage, so that when the death of the marriage happened, there was relief. The shock was terrible, but the suffering was over and, unlike a death, I could be reborn. It was like having a very heavy piece of furniture lifted off my chest so I could start to breathe again. The grief was for everything I had dreamt of; we imagined a life of all the hope and the joy of what was to come, but actually I realised how little joy was there, so it was grief, but before it happened. I lost the person I fell in love with a long time before that.

Francie's grief toolkit:

It is literally one foot in front of the other: find something to keep you walking on. Something outside of you. For me, helping other people helps me, and stops me wallowing with my own problems. Working with Help for Heroes, for instance – yes, I've had a marriage breakdown, but I haven't lost my legs and what a lovely bunch of people they are. Everyone who supports that group has great heart and motivation.

At thirteen I had no toolkit; I lacked confidence and went off the rails slightly as a teenager, but I very quickly learned to be practical and look after myself – paid bills, taxed the car, wired plugs, cooked. I'm not very good when people use being from a broken home as an excuse for their behaviour – we have a choice! My work ethic helped into my twenties; people needed me and I liked helping others.

Francie's divorce toolkit:

I needed a different channel for my energy, something I had never tried before. I was involved with Help for Heroes from the beginning and the co-founder Bryn Parry was organising a bike ride to Arnhem. He said, 'You have to come!' I found that having targets and goals was important. I had felt so powerless and small for so long that to stand up in my own right felt good. I regained *me*. I stood up tall again through exercise. I was a successful career person when I met Jeremy and somewhere along the line I lost myself. Now

I've just signed up to Ironman Estonia, which will be my tenth Ironman and I'll be sixty. I've just been asked to go with veterans to cycle down to Gibraltar, for a charity for homeless veterans, so I'll probably do that as well!

I was forty-nine when I started from scratch with the cycle ride. It's never too late – my first Ironman was when I was fifty-one. It doesn't matter what you do, or what level. My eldest daughter Em has started an online group called the Have a Gos (HAGS) on Facebook and @thehaveagos on Instagram. The group was set up to take the fear out of participating in sport and making it fun; exercising not to win, but to release endorphins. It's about using physical exercise to support mental health.

Horses have been a major part of my recovery, the connection on a horse and talking to friends on horseback so we're not looking at each other. On the cycle rides we also share things we would never share if we were sitting face to face. It frees us up.

I did have therapy for a few sessions and in the first one I cried for the entire session for over an hour; so much so, she was concerned as to how I would get home. After that I had a few more sessions, but that was enough.

The initial grief for whatever it is can be the big explosion, but after that it's the months and months of scarring that's left behind; that's when you need a holding hand, the talking. Everybody's situation is different. You never forget and you never stop living with it, but the devastation of the event will change.

Francie's book recommendation:

The Choice by Edith Eger, Holocaust survivor and psychologist, who teaches that we have a choice to be happy, to survive well, whatever our situation. '*When we grieve, it's not just over what happened – we grieve for what didn't happen.*'

Tom Skelton

Director and founder of House & Carriage, Charlbury

In December 1989, at the age of fifteen, Tom experienced the death of his father aged fifty-two. It was a tragically sudden death with no warning. His father came back from an evening out, was sick, which afterwards the family learned can be a precursor to a heart attack, went to bed and that was it: he was gone.

I asked Tom how he feels, how that experience at a young age has influenced the rest of his life.

૨ટ

It's not hard to answer that question, but it's hard to know how I would have lived my life differently because I have no idea what choices would have been changed without it.

After the emptiness, the crying, feeling hollow inside, I realised that the person who had died was part of me, part of my makeup. The character traits that I have now, the physical likeness, are all part of that makeup. How I love, how I feel, problem solve, socialise, my humour, are all in part thanks to him. That is so comforting. Something tangible that I remember is how he never looked down on children – he talked to them on the same level; he made people feel at ease. I'm not sure if this is nature or nurture, but I am the same – that's the good stuff!

So there he is: he is present in everything I do. Having this conversation takes me back to that time. Circumstantially, due to the physical force of the grief that you feel when someone so vital in your life dies, you don't realise until much later, but your actions at the time are instinctive. Mine were to start cooking, cleaning, doing jobs like putting up the Christmas tree (Dad died just before Christmas and it was something that I always did with him). These are all practical tasks that help keep everyone going, and I have continued to do these things throughout my life. Whether or not I would have become a 'doer' if he had remained alive, I will never know.

As a child experiencing the death of a parent, you grow up overnight, in the flick of a switch. You go from being a child to being an adult. It's almost like when you are driving and an animal crosses your path and suddenly you are wide awake and present! It's a shock that wakes you up, and as a child I distinctly remember that feeling of 'you have to be the man now'. Was that learned behaviour, or instinct? I remember some of my parents' friends voicing, 'It's up to you to step up now.' All said in a caring way, but without really thinking who they were saying it to. They were standing in front of a fifteen-year-old boy.

In 2018, Tom finally felt able to come out to his friends and family about his sexuality. He had voiced to me at the time that he felt he had become stuck when his father died, unable to move on, and not knowing who to talk to about his teenage feelings.

With grief, if there's something you don't want to tell the world, you can hide behind that grief and bury yourself. It possibly gives you a way to change how people perceive you, and hide what you don't want to talk about. And there is that element, in my case at least, that I felt the need to step into a pair of (heterosexual) shoes. I don't remember talking about sex or sexuality in our house. Combine the confusion of knowing that I was gay, with the notion, learned from those around me (and the decade: it was the late 1980s), that this was wrong; mix that with grief and you get one very confused teenager. I think that children, and this particularly pertains to grief, pick up on an awful lot more than adults give them credit for, which is ridiculous because we were all children once, so we know that. Children should be allowed to form their own views; I see so many parents inflicting their own beliefs and ideas on their children and not letting them find their own way.

The expression 'going mad with grief' is interesting. I remember my mum – not long after Dad died – staying in bed and saying that 'there is nothing to get up for any more'. Is that mad, or just shutting down with grief? I went to register my father's death, and I was the one to break the news to my grandmother that her son had died. She couldn't comprehend it on any level, it was the wrong order – she did go mad.

How we react to death in our society differs hugely from other countries. Is wailing in public alongside the coffin the right answer, or our British stiff-upper-lip approach? The truth is there is no right or wrong answer with grief, but our culture and society certainly affect how we behave.

I witnessed the silence around grief. Most people don't know how to deal with it, especially children, or in my case other teenagers. It isn't anyone's fault, but often people say the wrong thing; they find it hard to empathise, perhaps hide behind a sympathy card, or compare something that happened to them to what you're going through – never a good idea.

I do remember one of my parents' friends, Lynda, who is my unofficial godmother, writing to my brother and me individually, and one other person, out of around two hundred people that wrote cards and letters, did the same. I still have those two letters to this day.

Lynda wrote to me saying, 'Your father was the sort of friend that you can count on one hand and he will never be forgotten.' That's someone who knew how to deal with grief because she had her own grief. Others took the line, 'It's time for you to step up, work hard, go to university, make a success of your life,' almost encouraging you to suppress your own grief rather than talk about it... rather than talk about the person who has died. It reminds me of that line 'talk to me in the old familiar way' – I've been chatting to my dad for years! We all need to learn more about how to be around grief.

There's still an embarrassment around grief and crying, particularly for men. And in those days if anyone was going to have counselling it was the spouse, not the children. I remember wanting to go and see my father's body in the morgue, but I wasn't given the option, which upset me – I wanted to say goodbye. Looking back, it didn't seem fair; it felt like I was being shielded from death, that it wasn't about me and my feelings.

Tom had recently fallen in love and was feeling very emotional. Supremely happy, in fact. A great example of how the depth of sorrow can also be accompanied by the height of joy. We talked about how it had made him cry more recently through opening up, but happy tears, and how we are all who we are through our experiences, both good and bad.

Something people don't often talk about with grief is how it can make you a better person for those around you. Initially of course, if you were given one wish, it would be to have that person back; it's always the genie in the bottle. But when you get further down the line, and life has moved forward as it inevitably has to, the genie doesn't exist, but you realise perhaps that you are the person others go to because you have experienced something that might have shaped you in a certain way. I remember at university, on the 'getting-to-know-you day' the first three people I bonded with – all three had lost a parent within the last five years. We didn't know it at the time but discovered it as time went on; perhaps that's why we were drawn to each other.

People deal with grief in very different ways, and even though each person's loss is their own, it's important to show up for grief. It may help if you're an empath, but everyone can do something to help. Just being there alongside the person who is grieving, even without saying very much, just to listen, that's better than staying away. I've done it on numerous occasions and I think that it always helps. Just as we are there for our friends and family in life, it's important to be there at the tough end too. It's going to happen to us all one day, and although it's terrifying, grief makes you realise how short life can be and it's important that we look after ourselves and others.

Tom's grief tip:

Think of the children when a parent has died. Write to them individually, treat them as adults and include them. It takes a special person to be able to do that. Just because someone is small or quiet or shy, don't think that they are too young to understand. Stay in touch over the years to come. The nicest messages are those on anniversaries five, ten years on. 'Thinking of you' is enough; even better, mark other occasions or life achievements – say the person who has died would be proud (a driving test, A-levels, a relationship, a new job). Show up for them, and continue to do so.

Camilla Engberg

Naturopath, foster mother

Camilla and I live in neighbouring villages and became friends some years ago, drawn closer by our life experiences. We share a love of music festivals!

৶

My parents divorced when I was three and we moved from the UK to Holland when my mother married a Dutchman. I grew up as a Dutch girl, cycling and skating to school in the winter and loving the Dutch way of working hard but being laid back too. By the age of twelve I was doing the equivalent of nine A-levels due to the baccalaureate system, with ambitions to become a doctor – that was my dream. I was an academic.

My mother became ill with breast cancer, but she was such a positive person that she would always say 'everything's fine' even during high-dose chemo and radiation; she covered it up to protect us. So, when she died when I was thirteen, it was a real shock. We believed her when she had said she would get better – we even saw her the day before in hospital; she'd made the effort to put on makeup, to look as normal as possible and was still saying she was fine. So, we had no idea that she was going to die. It was traumatic. I later found out that she was euthanised, yet I was not given a chance to say goodbye to her. This started my mistrust in people telling me the truth.

I remember going back to school immediately after Mum died and all my friends turning their backs because they didn't know what to say to me. It was such a shock. I just wanted a hug and to be told they were sorry. It was devastating and I felt even more alone. I needed my friends.

Even being with me in silence would have been fine, but just walking away was so painful.

Our stepfather decided he couldn't cope with having two young teenagers to look after, so friends of my mother hired a private detective and found my father in London, whom we had never met. He reluctantly took us back to the UK and put us into boarding school. The school was a multi-national school because we had only just started learning to read and write in English back at home in Holland. Looking back, I think that I had started to believe that being abandoned was what would always happen to me. My mother, my father, stepfather, family, friends and grandmother had all left me and so I made sure I integrated into my school like a chameleon. I was able to be part of all the different circles. Each of the different ethnic groups would say, 'Camilla, you're one of us!' I think I just needed to belong.

Due to all the upheaval and change, my academic performance suffered. I was unable to focus on my studies any more and quite quickly my dreams of being a doctor and going to Oxford faded.

Later, at sixth-form boarding school in Bath, I fell in with a great-fun but badly behaved group of friends, but I was happy there. We were rebellious, sneaking out, drinking and smoking weed. Obviously, it meant I had found a group I belonged to but was so distracted I could not concentrate on my studies at all. I still didn't feel grounded either at home or school. Going 'home' to London in the holidays, I didn't feel wanted and I would wander around in a daze, feeling like I was floating outside of my body, wondering where I was. I was lacking parents, family and any emotional support. My father wasn't interested in us – when I was fourteen, he moved my sister and me into a house, alone, in Notting Hill during school holidays, so we wouldn't interfere with his life in Sloane Square. We had no friends there; it was a very unsettling time.

Grief is definitely not just about dying. In my twenties and thirties I was drawn towards people who had experienced trauma in some way, the people who wanted to stay out late dancing and partying. I lived my life believing I would never get past forty-two, the age Mum was when she died, so why put down roots?

I wanted to get every second out of life, always the last to leave the party, and I met others like me. My body was irrelevant because I wanted to get the most out of it and I crammed as much into life as I could. In my twenties I became a high-level PA/event organiser, working in the City for the chairmen of several huge companies. I came across as confident, capable and fearless and could pick and choose who I would work for. On the surface, my life must have looked perfect. I had a great job, an incredible social life: sailing holidays in Antigua, skiing in Verbier, partying in Ibiza. And yet underneath my life still felt empty.

Not looking after myself came with that lifestyle too. Many of my friends had addiction issues due to their traumas. Looking back, many of us were highly functioning addicts who were hiding from our past, our inner emptiness. It's so interesting how people become extreme athletes, party animals, alcoholics, workaholics, cold-water swimmers (who must cool themselves down in order to feel something) – all those extremes just to numb the pain. Distraction from busy minds. Highly functioning 'busy' people can be the same: they can't stop or relax for a second, becoming high achievers or helicopter parents.

I realised in my late twenties that I didn't want to live that life any more, and I volunteered for Raleigh International in Africa helping underprivileged young adults. It was an incredibly humbling and awakening experience and I realised how fortunate we are and what we take for granted in our lives. I became ill out there with bilharzia (a parasite which destroys your liver and other organs) and this was what made me finally slow down.

Bilharzia left me with ME and suffering from chronic fatigue. My body gave me a major intervention and said 'stop!' I was back in London and went back to my previous life – the only one I knew. After a few years a friend took me to a Tony Robbins UPW (Unleash the Power Within) self-development weekend, which gave me the courage to follow my life-long dream, and I chucked everything in to travel around the world solo.

On my travels I went to a detox sanctuary in Thailand, where I had a life-changing conversation with a stranger who asked what I did. She said she was confused that I was working in the City as she thought I was a healer. Following an incredible health shift as a result of following a juice fast, I realised I had found my true vocation. I enrolled at Westminster University for a degree in Natural Medicine, earning a BSc Hons in 2010 in Naturopathy. I realised I wanted to help others to achieve their optimum health goals and deal with their chronic health issues too.

I had to shed and mourn my old lifestyle in order to do that and grow.

Through doing the work on myself, consistent learning and finding my true purpose, I have finally found inner calm and peace. It's been hard work and some of it has been forced on me by my body, having to slow down. But I'm now so grateful for my life. I drive down the road and will stop for a sunset, feeling so grateful to be here right now and be alive. For my friends and family and the beauty around me. It's a very personal journey and I want to help other people get there too.

I remember waking up in London with a hangover in my thirties and just wanting to be in the countryside and find peace, but I didn't know how to get there. It was still so ingrained in me from a young age that I wouldn't survive beyond forty-two, that I wouldn't marry, have children or survive. It was a self-perpetuating lifestyle. I was so unhappy underneath. I would never tell anyone my age because I was trying to reverse it. The mind is so powerful, it was my reality.

I eventually met my husband Adam in 2009 when I was thirty-six. He was the only person I had ever cried with. In all those years I had never cried. I came off the pill to try and get pregnant and the floodgates opened! Poor Adam took the brunt of the unleashing of my trauma. Out it came. Now I only cry fully maybe once a year with a real meltdown, but during that time I have no idea how he stuck with me. We eventually took advice about having IVF, but it was so complex – emotionally, financially, physically – after all we had been through, that we wrote a big pros and cons list and decided not to go ahead. We considered adoption or fostering at that stage, but life somehow got in the way.

I think I'm good at dealing with grief now that the pain of not having biological children has dissipated gradually. I had a session with a brilliant naturopath friend which helped, but in general I think I've protected myself by telling myself that I didn't need children. I changed my mindset to look for what I am grateful for in my life. For me it was about finding a different, more positive, attitude. That's how I found peace and calm, so I don't have triggers any more. When people ask if I have children, I can simply say, 'No, none of my own.'

Camilla's toolkit:

Travelling solo around the world and doing the detox was a major turning point and realising how amazing you can feel after doing a ten-day juice fast. My passion to help other people feel that way too started me on the path to doing my naturopathy degree for four years. Treating patients and seeing them transform was very empowering and helped me to believe in the work I am doing.

I had a patient with such chronic fatigue she couldn't even get out of bed, and had lost all her friends and her high-powered job, being forced back home to live with her parents in her forties – and within six months of treatment she was back to her previous life. Some patients reflect my own experience, like a mirror, so helping people overcome major traumas helps me learn more too. Learning how grief is set in the lungs, anger in the liver, unspoken truths can lead to throat problems: those weaknesses are related to unresolved emotions or previous traumas. It is important to have remedies to release these issues from the body, so they are not allowed to fester there and create worse conditions in the future. Naturopaths believe that illness can benefit health because it shows the body is strong and vital enough to get rid of something, to detox naturally. A cold is good because it's the body actively rejecting the virus, instead of it festering in the body and creating worse illnesses down the line.

All this really made me realise how out of my body I was for so many years. Everything came together: the awareness of the power of the body to heal itself, when you know the body–mind connection; how vital nutrition is, a healthy gut and the importance of positive thoughts to feel alive.

On fostering:

It's wanting to give something back, realising how significant it is to have a loving and caring home with proper boundaries and a sense of belonging; to give you a solid foundation on which to go out in the world. Giving a child a safe space when the whole world is falling apart around them. It's another personal achievement for me to be able to get to a position now where I can offer this for vulnerable children; mentally, emotionally, physically.

I'm so grateful that Adam and I have such a strong relationship to be able to do this. Fostering is tough but all the training really helps, especially how to be a therapeutic parent. I'm able to give love and kindness but with strong boundaries to help the children feel safe. It's been an amazing learning curve. It's so lovely seeing how calm the children are after a few weeks of being here. I wish all parents and teachers had the training we have been given to produce well-rounded, emotionally secure children.

What would you say to an adult supporting a teenager whose mother has just died?

Ask them how they are feeling. Tell them it's OK to feel sad, to cry, to feel mad, to get their emotions out; that it's not their fault. Talk to them, don't turn away. Go into their heads before their heads make up stories like mine did. Tell them the truth. They need support and love – not just for one weekend or for a while, they won't just snap out of it; it takes years. I buried my feelings so that I wouldn't have to confront it, which led to some very skewed behaviour over the years. It would have been so much better if I had someone to talk to about it, to share it with. Having a community and family is so important.

Camilla's top tips:

The Landmark Forum has really helped me find inner peace by explaining that all thoughts are either triggers or strong suits from the past. It comes with years of practice – none of this is a one-off session – but I find it more helpful than counselling, where you might go over and over the old stuff.

Eckhart Tolle's teachings and his book *The Power of Now* – about being in the present, not sweating the small stuff. I'm grateful to have come across Tony Robbins' UPW (Unleash the Power Within), Bruce Lipton's *The Biology of Belief* and hundreds of other books and medical research papers on healing the body.

Accept people for who they are – we never know what they've been through in the past.

Contact Camilla at: www.naturalhealth.doctor
The Landmark Forum: www.landmarkworldwide.com
Eckhart Tolle: www.eckharttolle.com
Tony Robbins: www.tonyrobbins.com
Bruce Lipton: www.brucelipton.com

Georgie Payne

Interior designer, Cruse bereavement support volunteer and mindfulness teacher

Georgie and I met through friends at Glastonbury music festival and bonded immediately. As our friendship has grown, she has shared her beloved brother Gordie with me.

❧

My brother Gordon [Gordie] died twenty-two years ago [in 2000] by suicide. He was the profile we hear about: young man [aged thirty-two], working in London, successful, professional, fun, everything to live for – and now we know that this age group of men are the ones who are most likely to take their own lives. My grief was a type of devastation, where my life became suspended. I was thirty at the time and my eldest brother, Charlie, was thirty-four.

I knew Gordie was quite heartbroken and he was going abroad. I had this gut feeling, this strong sense that he shouldn't be away from us. It was Christmas time and I felt he shouldn't be on his own. I didn't know that there had been an event years before, and probably if I had known about that (with enormous hindsight), I might have acted more forcefully – or gently – but with more knowledge.

I felt like I was in a big, brittle, glass bubble. My work didn't really know much about it, other than my brother had died. They gave me a month off, which was good, but looking back, I don't think I knew what was going on; I was in deep traumatic shock. It felt like a strange limbo. I couldn't really have meaningful conversations with anyone; it was exhausting and I was trying to survive it. My brother's circumstances were so complicated because he wasn't in the UK, and it was just much more than our brains could cope with.

I was an adult, but my parents were worrying about me, and I was worrying about them. It was a strange, unrealistic time. I remember it as a real suspension of reality. It was a long time that I felt like that.

We didn't really have support. I remember going to my GP and I was referred to counselling, but I realised she was a trainee and I felt uncomfortable and didn't pursue it. HR at work didn't really have anything in place. There was no manual, or even common-sense compassionate blueprint for support.

Gordon also worked for a big corporation and I often wonder whether he had the chance to talk to anyone at work, or if that would have made a difference. There are so many questions I have now – did anyone know at work, or his GP, his manager? I've now worked as a bereavement counsellor and trained in suicide awareness and so much can boil down to a gut feeling of *Do I need to ask that uncomfortable question?* I guess that's what my instinct was when I had that gut feeling over my brother going away. The uncomfortable question that needed to be asked was 'Are you having suicidal thoughts? Is what you are saying to me that you feel hopeless?' You can frame it in different ways, but you have to ask the question that needs to be asked. A common worry is that by asking this question you are planting the idea; however, research shows that it is the opposite. There is relief in airing it, a relief in being asked it, getting it out into the open.

I don't think my grief changed very much until ten years ago. It's a long time, isn't it? I was looking at your questions earlier and now I realise that there are great chunks of my life missing. I think I was functioning, I was living; I had a great job and career. I don't know what it's like to have to live a different life – it's all that I know. But I was living it at a pace and on reflection, I wonder if some of the partying hard was a bit of numbing of grief. I don't know. People who didn't know about what had happened wouldn't have guessed.

My shift in life came when I worked with a coach and committed to run the marathon to raise money for a charity for suicide awareness. It was a huge deal; I remember going off on my first run and thinking, *I'm doing it*. So much of my life has changed from that point, including my job.

There's so much of my work that relates to my brother: my mindfulness teaching, training, being a Cruse bereavement counsellor, my interest in people and who they really are; trying to understand them is very positive and I'm very thankful for it.

I feel as though I've come through a very noisy and messy tunnel and the break in the tunnel was marathon training, wellness and wellbeing. And now the Cruse and mindfulness training has made me realise that looking back I wasn't completely bonkers – I can look back and see things more clearly.

I think there is a huge overwhelm with grief, but I now know I don't have to get over it: I can embrace it in a way that I want to with continuing bonds and the Tonkin model of grief.

Tonkin's model shows that, over time, your grief will stay much the same, but your life will begin to grow around it.

What makes me happy now is that I know that I can choose to keep the continuing bonds and embrace my grief fully in my life. Now that I can make sense of that there is relief. There is no other need or expectation of what is supposed to happen. So now I actively make time for me, for me and my brother. I walk a lot on my own, I need solitary time, and for me that's when my connection with my brother happens – when I have time to think and to be outside. When I don't have that time, that's when I start to feel out of balance. I was due to walk with friends the other morning and I soon realised I couldn't do the talking part on that day, so I just explained I needed some quiet time and I walked on my own and had the most amazing morning. Crunchy ice at six or seven in the morning and at some stage the sun broke through, with me on my own on the South Downs, and that meant everything, really. Those moments when I feel connected to my brother, I need them.

I constantly find my situation is changing and that the more I talk about what's happened to me, the more other people will talk about their stuff. Suicide is different: it is still a taboo; it is a complicated and traumatic grief. However, the more brave and courageous we can be, the more you find that there are people around you that are similar or the same. For many, many years I couldn't talk about it to anyone other than my closest friends. I would hint, leave breadcrumb trails in conversation; I knew I was doing it, but I just couldn't talk. There's a taboo, and shock, and I didn't want to deal with other people's reactions. I just want to be able to say it and it's a fact that has landed. I don't want to be the shock factor and fielding other people's reactions to what I have said. That's why I love the Cruse organisation – you really just need people to sit with you, shoulder to shoulder, to hear you, to listen without judgement but with kindness. To be honest and help in a frank way. We tend to think it's so old-fashioned to wear a sign that you are mourning, a patch on your arm, as in Victorian days, but now I find myself thinking what a great idea that was! At least you knew to handle the person with care. You should be able to have that mourning period.

I find it very hard to talk to my mum about her grief, but I find it easier if I talk to her about my own. The child–parent relationship is very hard, who is responsible for who, and it's an area for people to get good support.

There needs to be such a shift in attitude to death and grief. It's hidden. And the way we deal with it makes people feel out of control. It's something that everyone grapples with, but it would be so much easier if we could be more open.

My mindfulness training is showing me that there can be a repairing nature to this practice, in being aware and gently focusing on grief. That's the most amazing thing; it's incredible that we can choose to be brave and look forward and back. To witness it and come away differently. You don't have to feel you haven't said what you wanted to say, because you can still say it now. Whether it's in a physical way outside, or a more meditative way, it doesn't have to be the end. You can help yourself, repair and keep on holding something and growing it as you grow in your life with your loved one who has died.

My advice to everyone going through grief is find a way to talk. Not straight away but when you are able, usually around the three-month time. Find someone you can talk to. It's never ever too late to talk. It's great to be able to talk to friends and family, but there is also a lot of worth in talking in an anonymous and confidential way as well. Find the right thing to suit you.

I remember that for the longest time I did not want to be in this new landscape that I found myself in, not just of death but suicide. I didn't belong there, I didn't want it to be happening to me and I didn't know what to do. But gradually, over time, I met others, like the people at Sibling Link, who all had similar experiences to me; it made such an enormous difference. And that was only a few years ago!

Georgie's top tip:

Talk as openly as you can. Keep on talking and find a support group of people with the same experiences.

I know it's all very personal and individual, but I really believe there is hope and growth that can happen after death.

Grassroots Suicide Prevention: www.prevent-suicide.org.uk
Cruse Bereavement Support: www.cruse.org.uk
Sibling Link: www.siblinglink.co.uk

Sally Magnusson

Broadcaster, journalist, author and founder of Playlist for Life,
a charity enabling people to have access to the soundtrack of
their lives, which is beneficial to their healing and can help
them through the process of dementia

Sally and I met through her brother, Jon, who was Harry's
godfather. Our families have shared a deep friendship for
more than three decades.

>å·

I was seventeen when Siggy died. The day that he had
his accident, towards the end of May, I was swotting for
a German exam, for what is now Advanced Highers in
Scotland. So I was at home and my little brother Jon (eight
at the time) was also there. I was ready to go to university
the following October. So I was revising when my mother
took the phone call to say that Siggy, my other brother,
who was eleven, had had a road accident. I remember my
mother saying, 'I have to go off to the hospital, could you
look after Jon?' and she said, 'It will be all right. He's hurt
his leg, that's all we know.'

Siggy died a couple of days later from an arterial
embolism. I had gone to the hospital that day with my
parents to visit him, buoyed up by what seemed to be their
optimism that he was pulling through. Certainly their talk
as we travelled to the hospital in the car was very much
about what was going to happen when Siggy came home.
I remember them saying he was going to be hurt for a very
long time, he might never walk again but we would get
through that together. I remember my father talking about
him maybe being in a wheelchair. Now, with hindsight, I
see that they were desperately hanging on to hope, trying to

be positive and optimistic for us. I don't know to this day exactly what they had been told to expect. But I do know it was a terrible shock, to them as well as to me, when we arrived at the hospital and an older man – the consultant, I suppose – came in and said he would like to talk to my parents alone. And that was to tell them that he had died.

My next memory is of the three of us driving home that day and arriving at home, Blairskaith, and my siblings Margaret, Topsy and Jon looking out of the living-room window as we drove in, and that awful feeling of how are we going to tell them? How will we do this? I don't know if it was at that moment, but at some stage my father said to my mother, 'These children have lost a brother, don't let them lose a mother as well.'

I remember Sally's mother Mamie Magnusson telling me, when Harry died, that she always wanted to put on a brave face to the family. She told me that she would find time to go up to the top bedroom and lie on the floor between the twin beds and howl, then go downstairs and carry on. I used to do the same after Harry died: I would go to the furthest room after the children were asleep. But of course, children are aware and Sally's brother Jon once told me that he always knew when his mother had been crying.

It's nearly fifty years ago now and memories change. They are also affected by what you then live through yourself and my own experience as a mother now. My memories of the time are filtered through my mother; both what I observed of her and the agony I sensed, yet never fully accessed because she was always trying to keep it from us. Not in a paranoid way, but she was always holding back, even when she leant on me. So in a way I had the vicarious grief of a mother, even though I was a sibling. What I have experienced since being a mother to my five children has enabled me to realise more what she went through.

My childhood ended that day. I went on to university a few months later and I felt I was so much more grown up than most other students. I'm sure it made me quite dull in many ways because so many of the natural, normal preoccupations of teenagers just seemed so petty and banal after what had happened to us. I was so deeply concerned with the meaning of life and what it was all about, the position of faith and all these things that you might not think about until you are older. It deeply affected my whole life after what happened; the whole foundation of existence was shaken. The assumption that you have as a child or young person that by and large the world has been organised to make you as happy as possible, that you will be all right!

I was very conscious that I had a very special mother. I used to pinch myself as a child and think, why was I so fortunate to get her? She just seemed so wonderful to me in every way. And suddenly it all goes just like that. What it did for me then was it showed me that really bad stuff can happen to people. And instead of going through life thinking that bad things happen to other folk, it happened to me early. So it gave me a somewhat pessimistic outlook on life, born of the worst thing having happened. And the danger is that you become someone who expects the worst. I don't think I have ever lost that, so I have had to really struggle not to become the clawing mother who doesn't let her children out of her sight.

I was the person who drove Siggy that morning and gave him a lift. I said goodbye to him and I never saw him again. Every time I say goodbye to my children I know I might not see them again; my siblings, I might not see them again. That gives you a profound sense of value and perspective, which is good, but also I think there is an underlying throb of anxiety that can transmit itself to other people and make them anxious about life, about seizing opportunities and about doing risky things which you have to do in life.

So I feel that the aftershocks from the earthquake in my life at seventeen, they go on and on, and make me who I am. It's a constant balancing act and in some ways it gets worse as I get older and possibly get more fearful.

A couple of times I've met people who were Siggy's peers at school and it's given me a flash of insight into how he might look now. I heard from one of them who had been in his class and he is a doctor, a consultant in vascular medicine. He said how they had all been so traumatised by Siggy's death. He has thought about him since because of his work and knowing it was a blood clot in the damaged leg that killed Siggy. He said that with the advances they have now, it is likely they could have saved Siggy. It was such a strange feeling to know that he had also lived with this grief as a friend. He too had been making sense of it in his own way; there are these ripples.

On the anticipatory grief of Alzheimer's (Sally wrote about her mother Mamie and the challenges she faced through Alzheimer's in her book Where Memories Go*):*

It's a very different thing, but I do think that what we went through with Siggy and what we learned from it helped the process we went through with our mother. It was this strength that came from the family, from going through it together and understanding that we knew what mattered now. That we had a sense that nothing was worth fighting about, nothing was as important as having each other, loving each other and appreciating what we had when we had it, because we might lose it at any point.

That did carry us through with Mamie, who was diagnosed in her seventies. You begin to lose somebody but in a way that's not a final death, or shock, it's this bleeding away of something that is substantial.

My reaction was – how do I hold on to what is good, while we have it? That came directly from the experience with Siggy and it was the genesis of my book, to hold on to my mother with words. At the end of every day coming back and describing what we had. When life is so fast you don't always have time to appreciate it and the writing helped me to experience it and focus. It gave me a basis for remembering, a way of valuing what I had. I wrote that in the book and so many people got in touch to say that, wherever they were in the dementia journey themselves, it helped them appreciate what they had, because they might have less of it the next day.

It was Siggy's legacy in a way.

I was talking with my sister the other day and we were discussing the fact that even though you become an orphan at fifty or sixty, you are still an orphan; that was a revelation for me. You might as well strip fifty years away; you feel like a child again. You are feeling the same things.

I asked Sally about music. The Magnusson family are great singers and performers, through all the generations, and I have stood among them over the years, as we laugh and cry in equal measures while exercising our lungs and hearts!

Music has always been a huge part of our lives. With the exception of my brother Jon, there isn't a musician among us, but it's all in the joyous music-making together, the creating, in the doing of it – creating rituals and traditions.

When Siggy died, our mother and father insisted on that first Christmas that we celebrate it, by carrying out the traditions that bind a family together. You do them, even if you feel completely hollow and nobody feels like it, but by doing them and honouring them, one day there will be happiness in there again. It's a bit like the plastering of a smile on your face: you put it on and one day you find it has come naturally again. What music has always done for our family is to provide that ritual; to sing when your heart is breaking is a really important thing we discovered.

It was incredible to find gradually that this singing and music-making, these songs and daft ditties that we had enjoyed so much over the years, were actually a pathway through the horrors of dementia to help my mother in the first instance, and then others through the charity. It helped them feel better and more able to connect with themselves. It was just wonderful, somehow fitting and right. Life-enhancing. It has helped me to feel that my mother is still singing for people all round the country. Another legacy.

On how to treat people who are in grief:

I think we all agree that you don't want to be shunned when you are grieving, but I hear people being interviewed and saying 'people crossed the road' and 'if only they would speak'. But in the next breath they will say, 'Someone said time will heal and I was so hurt that they could say such a thing.' And I think – that's why people don't speak!

We all reach for clichés because they are all that is available to us, because there are no words *ever* in the whole earth that could compensate anyone or deeply make a person feel better. Words can't do it! Sometimes you can't even hug a person or make the food for their doorstep, so sometimes you have to reach for words and they *will* be inadequate. But I beg people who are hurting and grieving to be kind: even if somebody says something stupid, it is still well meant.

There is no perfect way of dealing with it. Some people will do it better than others, especially those who have been there themselves, but others will say the wrong thing and even when we know time will never heal, we must understand that they are just trying to do something rather than nothing.

To find more about Sally's work and books, both fiction and non-fiction: sallymagnusson.com

And her dementia support charity Playlist for Life
www.playlistforlife.org.uk

Ann Sinfield

*Retired teacher, shop owner, baker, proud Yorkshirewoman
and Scrabble fiend*

Ann's son Tim died from leukaemia thirty-five years ago,
aged eleven.

    We met Ann and her husband Brian (gallery owner and
co-designer of the Cotswold Wildlife Park) when we moved
next door to them all those years ago, when Harry was two
and a half and Cam one. I soon learned that Brian and Ann
had already walked the path we were on: their son Tim
had died when he was eleven years old. We quickly became
firm friends and it was actually thanks to Ann that we had
our daughter, Emilie. She encouraged us to try for a third
child since she had always shared my thoughts that they
couldn't cope with care needs, hospital visits, etc. for Tim,
look after his older sister Liz, and introduce another child.
It was something she had regretted since Tim's death, and
she promised she would help me with that care if we did
have another baby. She was, as always, true to her promise
when our daughter Emilie was born and is her much-adored
godmother. They are not just friends: Brian, Ann and Liz
will always be family to us all. Our connection runs deep.

≥♣

Tim was almost three when he was diagnosed. He hadn't
been well for some time; he wasn't his usual self. He had
already had mumps and the doctor said it sometimes took
a long time to get over it. But then he started having pain
in his leg, behind his knee, which is often where leukaemia
cells gather, so after that he was diagnosed. A devastating
and unexpected diagnosis, which left us feeling completely
numb.

I couldn't really go back to teaching at that point: he had hospital visits for treatment almost every week and I needed to be around for Tim and our daughter Elizabeth. We didn't know what the future held and how he would react to it all. Treatment went on for two years and he wasn't too ill during that time. Then he went into remission for nearly five years at which point you begin to think that's a turning point and he might be fine. But the leukaemia came back and he had some very strong treatment which resulted in his immunity becoming extremely low. A few days later he developed an infection and it was so severe his heart gave in and he died. It was a huge shock – we had no idea it was going to happen.

There had been a terrible uncertainty about leukaemia, but I'm a very positive person and from that perspective I never thought he wasn't going to get better. We always had hope. When you have two years of harsh treatment and then five years of being fine, gradually you start to believe that things are OK.

At that last stage, we didn't have time to anticipate what was going to happen; it came so quickly. A week before he died, he was playing rugby for Burford School.

I have always been very aware of the incredible treatment we had with all the bereavement care we received thanks to Helen House and the difference between Brian and Ann having to leave the John Radcliffe Hospital in Oxford that day with Tim's things, their son in the morgue.

Friends came to collect us and bring us home early in the morning and that was it. I think Liz was with them, but it's a bit of a blur. Tim was eleven and Elizabeth was twelve.

Initially, the thought that we had to go on for Tim's sake helped me get through the days. He was the most generous, kind-spirited boy and he wouldn't have wanted us to be miserable. I remember once at school, I asked his teacher how he was doing and she said, 'Oh you never need to worry about Tim, he has so many friends. When he comes into a room everyone wants to talk to him; he's the most popular boy.' So that also helped me to move forward and cope.

Also for Elizabeth's sake. She had a tough eight years because of Tim's illness and needs. There had been that underlying feeling that we had to watch out for him. It's never quite normal. So I wanted to devote time to her to make sure she was all right. I feel so much for people who lose their only child, or two children; I don't know how they cope. Liz has been amazing. Losing your brother is such a terrible thing, but over the years she has always been an unwavering support and constant joy to us. She now has three children who bring us great happiness; their closeness to us is such a bonus and we feel extremely lucky to have them in our lives.

I found it hard with friends. I'm a tearful soul and I think I made it difficult for them because I cried so easily and it helped me, but I don't know how they coped with it! A friend's husband was recently diagnosed with cancer and I phoned her the minute I heard about it and said I'm so sad for you. She said, 'It's so lovely to hear from you because nobody talks about it; they walk on the other side of the street because they just don't know what to say.'

It means so much when you are suffering that somebody rings you. I had to protect friends from my tears a bit! Unless you have been through it, nobody has any idea really – friends think they can empathise, but really it's impossible to have any idea. I used to get really upset seeing parents shouting at their children in supermarkets – they have no idea how lucky they are! If only they knew.

There's always this feeling of what would he be doing now, would he be married? Would he have children? What would he look like? I feel very lucky that my grandson Jago looks very like Tim and that's a comfort; all my grandchildren are.

I adapted my working life following Tim's death. I knew I couldn't teach any more, so I had already opened a wholefood shop in Stow-on-the-Wold with a friend, Pat. Because of Tim and hospital visits I didn't feel confident to do it on my own. It was a really successful place and it made enough to make it worthwhile for the two of us. When Tim died, I thought I would open another shop. So without any research I opened one in Faringdon. I was in the slightly mad stage of grief and needed to keep busy. I didn't want to sit at home and wallow in grief, I wanted to move forward. Really it was the wrong time for a wholefood shop in that location, so I opened up part of it as a coffee shop and did all the baking myself, and from that moment on it took off! I wasn't sleeping anyway, so I would get up and take things out of the oven throughout the night and early morning. It was one way I could get through it and keep busy – it was completely mad really! Cooking is a good therapeutic way forward.

At that time thirty-five years ago, nobody offered us any help. Tim died early in the morning and we left – that was it really, we were on our own. It may have been that there was help, but I didn't know about it – but I also believed that we had to face it ourselves. I just assumed that we would get through somehow. Our families were incredible and really couldn't have done more for us. We are a very close family.

Ultimately I think we were so lucky to have had Tim for eleven years. You talk to people who don't have children and we were just so lucky. You learn to appreciate the small things in life and make the most of every moment.

Brian has cancer now, but we are older and maybe our experience with Tim has helped us to be resilient and accepting of the diagnosis. If it had happened thirty years ago I don't know how I would have coped, but we have a very philosophical approach to it. I do believe stress and worry are terrible for everybody, so I think this approach helps us to carry on. We have had some wonderful experiences and a wonderful life together and we don't want them to stop, but on the other hand we can count our lucky stars that we have done so much.

We each grieved very differently over Tim. I respect that Brian hasn't wanted to talk about it in the past, although he does now. He couldn't have been a more loving father and it hit him very hard, but you wouldn't have known in the same way. I knew he was suffering just as much as I was. It can bring you closer together and for some people the opposite; we are all different and you have to respect that.

I have a wonderful card in my kitchen which was sent to me by a friend whose husband has cancer and it says, 'Ignore the rain, look for the rainbow.' I look at it and I think yes, that's the best thing possible. It's easy to get bogged down in the rain, but keep going and the sun will come out!

When Tim first died I was in a world of my own. We had his funeral, but I couldn't think about anything, I just wanted to get through it. The shock was too much. But that changes very slowly and you come round to more positive thoughts and you want people to be there.

My advice for anyone going through bereavement is get together, cry together and you never forget the people that are there for you. However upsetting it is, just be there. Even if you don't appear welcome at first, everyone appreciates those who stand by them. Keep trying.

Nothing can ever take away the pain and sadness of losing a son, but we have found it possible to lead a full and happy life in the knowledge that Tim had eleven wonderful years as part of our loving family.

Jane Harris

Psychotherapist, bereavement specialist and supervisor with twenty-five years of professional experience and a special interest in grief. She also produces films for the charity sector with her partner, Jimmy Edmonds (also interviewed), including Gerry's Legacy *(for Alzheimer's Society, 2013),* Say Their Name *(for* The Compassionate Friends, *2014) and* Beyond Goodbye *(about the funeral they created for their son Joshua).*

After the sudden death of Josh, aged twenty-two, in 2011, Jane and Jimmy co-founded the charity The Good Grief Project to share their experience of grief. In 2018 they co-directed the award-winning feature documentary *A Love That Never Dies.* They also run regular Active Grief Retreats for bereaved families using photography, film and creative writing as well as physical exercise.

❧

When Josh died, he was at a time in his life where everything was going really well. He had realised his dream and was working as a young producer at the Ministry of Sound. He was so happy, and travelling was his treat. We felt we had done our job as parents; we had given him love, roots and wings and let him go. I wasn't worried. I was so relieved as a mother that nothing had gone wrong and we were at this stage of life; he was independent, free and happy. After the police gave us the news, we collapsed in on ourselves as a family. We literally huddled in the sitting room like little animals. We couldn't let each other out of sight in case anything happened to anyone else. This is the nature of shock and trauma.

We had to plan the funeral – and as every bereaved parent knows, you never think you are going to plan your own child's funeral. We did that with the help of our community. We made a film out of it, *Beyond Goodbye*. So, really, we lost our way and we had to rebuild, and it started with that life celebration and everyone coming together. It was a turning point.

I was very preoccupied with Josh's sister Rosa, who was eighteen at the time, and his stepbrother Joe, who was ten years older. I was terribly aware of wanting to protect them, but I also needed to find space to let off steam on my own. I would force myself to go running, which helped enormously, particularly when I felt least motivated to do it and would sometimes end up in a field crying in disbelief that my son was dead.

I think after the funeral people expect you to go back to how you were in some way, but of course that doesn't happen. We are still not who we were and I'm glad about that. Some friends became frustrated after a few years and turned away. They probably couldn't bear the pain, and in a way, who could blame them? Our eyes are the windows to our hearts, and the pain never leaves your eyes. How do friends deal with that?

I started to learn how lonely grief was. I knew that as a therapist, but when you experience it from the inside out, it's very different. It's agonising.

What helped me was going back to work. I was stunned that people thought I wouldn't work again, or that it was too soon, but I could already feel that because of my years of training and my theoretical knowledge, I could actually compartmentalise it. I could healthily grieve, and work. So, when I went to work it was almost like a respite in some way. I could focus even more than I had before on other people and their stories, and it didn't get in the way. I had more insight and I wasn't afraid of anything to do with death any more. In terms of other people, I was more able to absorb their pain.

As a therapist you are trained *not* to make it better. Of

course, we all want to 'make it better' but we also know for sure that it's not fixable. Grief is not for mending. So, I became better and better at doing that. Bearing witness is what people need; they just want to be listened to. We just want to be listened to.

Clichés, with the best will in the world, don't help. They possibly help the person who is coming out with them, but it doesn't help the person who is struggling with their grief. In fact, it can be almost offensive, but you can't respond because it's a bit like when somebody gives you that present you really don't want, the polystyrene rabbit! You can't say, 'I really don't want that.' You have to thank them.

So, I think as a bereaved mother and a therapist I have become better at knowing where to put my energy, so I don't have to use language or words which are meaningless. I also choose who I spend my time with.

In the initial stages of grief, we wear a metaphorical mask to protect others; we become 'high performance mask-wearers'. We make others feel better and hide our pain. After you lose your child it almost becomes essential to put it on to go out into the world. People seem to find the bereaved so baffling!

I remember on one occasion in London, meeting someone whose child had gone to school with Josh (when they were much younger), and we just bumped into each other on the street. It wasn't long after he died and she said, 'How's Josh?' I said, 'He's fine.' I just couldn't face stopping and saying what had happened. I knew they would be so upset, and I didn't have the wherewithal to pick them up or to put them back together again. It was to protect them, in order to protect me from having to save them from the shock.

Metaphorical mask-wearing can be fundamental to going forward, but at times we have to work to find a better balance. There are good days and bad days and it's about constantly assessing the situation to see what you can deal with.

The competitive nature of grief is a question that comes up. We often get asked which is worse: a sudden death like Josh, or the anticipation through an illness like Harry. I can't imagine one of our children going through a life-limiting illness and witnessing their pain, but then people have said that they were so glad they had time to prepare for their child's death and that extra anticipatory grieving. For us, it was very much he was here, and he was gone. So, trauma sets in intensely. I try not to think of a hierarchy of grief but when I think of an only child dying, that has to be worse. For me, my children and grandchildren are there. And with suicide there is the terrible confusion, discomfort, shame and stigma amplified around external judgement.

With sudden death, you lose your belief in the world and you lose hope. I think that's something that is really complicated to deal with.

My history with being Jewish is relevant. I think I always knew I was at a cellular level, but it wasn't confirmed until later on. So, this really surfaced in my grief: not only had I been thrown into confusion about the world, but I was also confused about my ethnic identity. It then opens up other grief which you haven't had a chance to explore.

Then my parents died, and I didn't have time to grieve for them because I was so preoccupied with Josh. Everything surfaces eventually but it takes a lot of hard work to process it. Unless you do the work, it won't go away by itself and it will manifest. So, you have to be really careful of that.

You can't turn your back on grief – it will get you, especially physically. It's no surprise that you and I have both been through issues connected to our gut, lung and breathing since our sons died. But why doesn't the medical profession join up the dots? If your heart is hurting badly and you don't know what to do with that pain, what are you going to do with it? There's almost a denial about the impact of grief by the medical profession and yet there are some amazing practitioners out there who will ask, 'What's been happening in your life?'

It's worth doing the work on yourself. I have to remind myself every day to make space to do the work. Right now, I have my running kit underneath these clothes. But we can still block it and forget to do it. So physical exercise for me has been a lifesaver. I used to journal my running thoughts by voice-recording them. I would start out thinking I knew nothing and come back from running with these nuggets and ideas. Nuggets of realisation and hope that I could survive it. Articulating it is so important. It's dangerous not to.

Jane and Jimmy are about to move house, so are going through huge potential change.

Josh died ten years ago almost to the day, and we moved into this house ten years before that, so twenty years ago. We had ten years here with him. We know that we take those memories with us, but in the 'doing' it's really hard. You have to pack them somewhere, contain them, and that's really unsettling.

Following trauma, you look for stability. In many ways you want to put something down, whether roots, or something solid, or in our case starting the charity. But personally, it's about wanting to keep things the same, yet craving change too, so there's a real contradiction in there. So moving house represents a terrifying paradox. I have to dig into the attic, both literally and metaphorically. I've decided not to do that for now because it's too difficult. It's a deep unconscious process. Moving house and change, it gives hope, but also despair. A total mix.

I listen to Jessica's song [professional singer Jessica Carmody Nathan, who was Josh's close friend, wrote a song in memory of him called 'Joshua's Song'] and see the imagery of the tree in the film, and his young friends; it is bittersweet. It's more sweet than bitter, but it's excruciating.

I tend to think of that pain as helpful, but when you're in the midst of it you almost want to step away from it.

That helps to understand the distance and denial that we suffer as bereaved people. I have to stop myself and say, 'It's OK, just stay with it.' We have to use these feelings to understand why people do what they do, and that can leave us feeling so isolated. It's really hard. My temptation this year was not to mark Josh's tenth anniversary. I wanted to shut down everything – social media, shut the charity, shut the 'shop'! Yet the following day, because we had been surrounded by such openness through messages, such support and love, I wondered how I could have felt so desperate and alone yesterday and so different the next day. And that illustrates what grief is! That's the impossibility of grief and it's why it torments us and makes us mad.

My own therapist would say, and I sometimes say to my own clients, 'Sometimes you have to have your back against the wall before you can move forward.' That's true. So, when things are desperately bad you have to remind yourself that you can find it really is possible to move forward, and that can happen ten years on, and for you, twenty years on. When I hear people in their early grief, I know they don't realise they will get through it, but ten years on I'm fairly certain I'm going to be OK; never completely certain, but fairly sure.

Something that's hugely comforting is Josh's friends sending us postcards, and they are still doing it ten years on. It started when he died. Josh's friends tell us that they are grateful we put pressure on them to be included and part of Josh's celebration of his life. That if we hadn't done that, they probably wouldn't have done what they have done since. They might have felt it was an intrusion. If we as bereaved parents can be robust enough to invite our young folk in, then it's shared. If you read the words on these beautiful postcards, you can't help but cry. They say that we gave them permission to bring Josh's death into the present tense and it's made it a more comfortable place for them as his friends. The postcards land on the doorstep, or online messages; it's very therapeutic for them and for us in the way we can all talk about him.

They had never really thought about death at their age (in their twenties at the time) because on the whole you hope you don't have to. Josh's friends say it strengthened them and gave them the ability to put words around it. It's so touching that now, some of them are in their thirties and are parents themselves. Not only does it make them treasure their own children even more, but they've actually integrated death into their lives comfortably in some way.

My stepson Joe married Josh's best friend Hollie and they now have our wonderful grandchildren Elsie and Martha, who are three and one. They talk a lot about Uncle Josh and on the anniversary they made a shrine, so not only is that lovely for us, but it's lovely for them to know him in some way. To carry him forward. They express it so beautifully and comfortably, openly. It's not hidden or uncomfortable. They can talk about him.

When we made our cinema documentary *A Love That Never Dies*, we made an additional short film on the Mexican Day of the Dead. We wondered if we would find that culturally Mexican people were more comfortable with death in some way. What we discovered was that they are not more comfortable with death, but they are comfortable with colourful rituals! There was still the same fear and isolation among the bereaved, but the rituals are a vivid celebration of life. Their children come back and they feel them in the room. The families embraced us and said, 'Can you feel Josh in the room?' We said we weren't quite sure. But they replied that it didn't matter, he's here! There was a real sense of inclusion and hope. There are two days, one for the children and one for the adults, with trails of flowers, marigolds, copal burning so they can find their way back and their favourite food is put out.

We have a lot to learn from other cultures. When we were making our film, our daughter Rosa said, 'There's an awful lot of room for death in Vietnam.' It's true; it's so lovely to be in a country where it's comfortable and it doesn't feel strange to be remembering someone. In a way death is everywhere there in a comfortable way.

Meanwhile in England, when Josh died somebody said to me, 'Everything happens for a reason.' I thought a) I'm Jewish, so did the Holocaust happen for a reason? and b) how could you say that to a parent about the death of their child? It's well intentioned, but illustrative of the discomfort that people feel here. Just to be able to say 'I don't know what to say, but I'm here for you' would have helped me at that moment at the beginning of my grieving.

On setting up The Good Grief Project:

Very early on as a family, we realised we needed to be active and creative to navigate our way through grief. Jimmy immersed himself in photography and I immersed myself in running, but together we also carried on making films (we had met at film school originally).

Setting up the charity seemed to be a fusion of all of that. It was about creating a space to find a more comfortable language and way of communicating grief that wasn't so isolating and lonely.

It has become a real lifeline for a lot of people because doing and being creative is something a lot of people think they can't do, but actually it's something we can all do. Whether it's creating photographs, being active, attending a retreat. It's a way of coming together.

The Active Grief Retreats are residential retreats in a beautiful, comfortable place. We offer bursaries so they are very accessible to everyone. In principle, it's about allowing yourself a weekend to take that metaphorical mask off and be with others whose children (of any age) have died.

What often happens is people arrive there and say they can't even come in through the door! We had a call from one person from halfway down the motorway saying they were going home; they had made a big mistake. We encouraged them to come. But they all arrive and it's about the comfort of being able to be themselves freely and to be with other people that helps. Over the course of the weekend, people's body language changes. They laugh, they cry, there's music, there's dancing, there's photography, boxing. Our kids are at the heart of the retreat. Rosa produces home-cooked food; she takes time out of her film work. As a bereaved sibling, she wants to honour her brother. Joe heads up the active side because boxing and physicality got him through his depression when his brother died.

In summary, people often think they can't survive, but they come on a retreat, decide to give it a try and they are given hope. They find they can create photographs, they can write stories and they can dig into their broken hearts and come out stronger.

So people leave the retreats very differently to how they arrived. They hang onto the positives. A quarter of the people who come are parents bereaved by suicide. Some are parents who were bereaved many years ago, some just a year ago, but many have never shared anything to do with their grief.

It's never too late to grieve, to allow yourself to grieve.

I believe one of the most important parts of grieving and learning, and one of the things that offends me the most, is this idea of closure, the dirty C word. That you will be who you were before. I know that will never happen and I'm OK with that. What we seek is openings and that is so gratifying to be able to recognise.

So, what I would say to anyone who is reading this is please allow people the space to change and adapt, but don't put pressure on them to find closure. They won't ever find that or be who they were before but that doesn't mean they won't be stronger, more robust people. In a way you have to get over yourself and be alongside them.

The anger issue too. We're not allowed to be angry so that can be a massive problem for people. It has nowhere to go. So, if people want to support the bereaved, you have to understand that there is anger and it shouldn't be hidden. We're told a bereaved person who is doing well is 'dignified, silent, brave, strong, robust, good-humoured'. It's never 'angry, confused, erratic'! We don't make allowances because it's too uncomfortable and difficult. And that's where the masks go on!

Full circle.

All information about Jane Harris's and Jimmy Edmonds' films and Active Grief Retreats can be found on The Good Grief Project website www.thegoodgriefproject.co.uk. For information about their films, including *A Love That Never Dies*, go to thegoodgriefproject.co.uk/our-films. Their book *When Words Are Not Enough: Creative Responses to Grief* is available via www.quickthornbooks. com/title-list/when-words-are-not-enough

Jimmy Edmonds

Documentary film editor with over 100 TV credits, including the BAFTA award-winning Chosen *for Channel 4 and his own personal film,* Breaking the Silence, *for BBC1, on the abuse he and his brothers suffered at school*

Following the death of his son Josh, Jimmy co-founded The Good Grief Project charity with his partner, psychotherapist Jane Harris (previous interview), whom he originally met at film school. Together they have also made films on grief including *A Love That Never Dies, Say Their Name, Lessons in Grief: The Mexican Day of the Dead, Beyond Goodbye* (about Josh's funeral) and *Beyond the Mask.* Jimmy runs the photography element of their Active Grief Retreats for bereaved parents.

⤫

I think it's true that men don't talk about their feelings in the same way as women. Perhaps we don't have the same sort of empathy or connection with other men? I found myself withdrawing after Josh died. I found it easier in the first instance to hide away from feelings rather than exploring them with other people. I found I could explore those feelings more easily with female friends than male friends. That might just be me because of my history of child abuse and my distrust of the male authority figure. That may be built into my psyche.

But it's also true that I found it difficult to maintain any sort of ongoing 'normal' relationship with the men in my Gloucestershire village after Josh died. This might be the same for men and women, but it's hard carrying the baggage of friendship past a bereavement, when you have very little else to talk about (or feel) in the early stages of grief. Your friends can't join in with that, but it's not their fault. But I have found new friendships with other bereaved dads and it's much easier to talk with them. I've found that those relationships can grow and develop.

At the beginning, after Josh died, the more I heard other people's stories, I felt it diminished my own pain. It diminished the story I had in my head about Josh, and that was unique, special and much more important than anyone else's story to me. So if I started hearing about other parents whose children had died in possibly similar circumstances, there was an element for me in protecting Josh's memory and what we were going through.

I guess that after a while it became inescapable that his death is one of many and that I had to face it rather than running away from it. So at that point other people's stories became fodder for my own grief. I could recognise that other people's experiences helped to validate what we were going through.

Jimmy and I talked about the intensity and purity of the memories we want to hold onto in the early stages of grief, the not wanting to let go of them and the worry that they will fade. I shared with Jimmy that I started my memoir twenty-two years ago, then revisited it and edited it in 2015 but still didn't want to share it. Now, I finally feel ready because of the work I am doing in listening to other grieving people's stories.

You need to hold onto the pain as well, you need to know that it's a real feeling. It's only by holding onto the pain that you can really feel properly. Otherwise if you dull the pain, by drinking, smoking, whatever, you are escaping the reality.

When I was twenty-one, so a similar age to Josh when he died, I was in a bad car accident in what was then Yugoslavia, just south of Sarajevo. There were four of us in the car including my girlfriend at the time, Jill.

We had been together around eighteen months and were travelling around Europe. The car crashed into a fast-flowing river and three of us managed to get out, but Jill's body tragically wasn't found for two weeks. We were picked up and taken to the nearest town, the police put us up in a hotel and at that point the British Consul came from Belgrade to help. The first thing he did was open a bottle of whisky. So there I was, at twenty-one, completely green, I didn't understand anything that was going on, and there was this guy thinking the best thing to do is to numb the pain with whisky! It just illustrates a male approach to dismiss the deeper feelings.

I wasn't offered any support at the time, my family were just pleased to see me alive, and I went back to London. There, most of my friends didn't know how to deal with it. There was one older friend who was a bit like an older brother and he was more open and had arms to put around me. He supported me but there was nothing else. Sadly he was killed ten years later in an air accident.

How does it feel now, when you see people open up and share their stories on The Good Grief Project retreats?

It makes me feel proud. The image I have is of people on the Saturday night dancing and laughing. We have had the solemn part where we raise a glass to our children, but there is community. It's people coming together, that mass of humanity that feels good when we have all shared similar grief and feelings and found the business of linking arms and hugging. It's food for the soul; it makes it a lot better.

It took me a good couple of years to accept that there were networks around like The Compassionate Friends who could offer us support. Jane had tried it first and I went eventually. I still really prefer to be behind a screen or a camera and it takes me a while to engage and trust. I occasionally went to the men's groups, but on the whole

I'm not that keen on gender-only groups. Everyone's grief is individual and others might get more out of it than I have.

On open-water swimming:

There's a camaraderie with the other swimmers, with dunking yourself in freezing-cold water, but ultimately for me it's also about being alone. There's an edge to swimming away from the shore, out of your depth in slightly dodgy water (especially if out at sea); it can feel like leaving one reality behind and entering another one. There's something about the fact that water can be buoyant but also drown you. You are physically in touch with that life-death moment. And the colder it is, the more intensely you feel that. I have also found that rhythmically, as you get into the stroke, there is a mindful element, you get into a buzzy mood, and at that point I consciously turn my thoughts to Josh. Even to the extent that when the sun is relatively low and it's very bright and you're swimming, there can be a strobe effect as your arm comes over. I remember at one point I thought he was sitting on my shoulder, he felt that close. It allows the imagination to become quite vibrant and you don't have to answer to anybody out there. It makes you feel closer to death and that's part of the deal I think. I would never do it, but at sea you could just keep swimming.

I asked Jimmy about his views on cumulative grief, where we can be triggered massively by the pile-up of grief on grief, and where his thoughts on being abused as a child and the car accident he experienced sit with his grief over Josh. Had they accumulated, or did they sit entirely separately and differently?

I think they sit in a similar place. I wish I could have learned more from those experiences earlier in my life, and used them more productively than I have been able to with grief over

Josh. Similar sorts of feelings are generated. For instance, with child abuse there is a lot of secrecy, shame, guilt and a lot of 'I don't know what's going on' involved. Lack of trust in the world and individuals. Never knowing whether someone is really going to be your friend, or whether they are going to abuse you in some way further down the line. That goes for everybody that I meet. When trauma happens, some of those responses are enacted again, especially if the world doesn't engage with you in a particularly empathetic way. So, for instance when Jill died, I didn't get any real sense of my family being there with me. They didn't know what to say; they didn't have a clue what I was going through.

If you are suffering some kind of abuse at school, you don't know how to deal with it and I very much pushed it away. After Jill died I also didn't know how to deal with it; I had nobody helping me or showing me a way forward emotionally so I pushed it away.

What helped was meeting Jane. She was the first person that I ever told about my childhood abuse and that was twenty years down the line. Grief gives huge insecurity and in my case it was on top of a foundation of child abuse.

I didn't know whether it was right that I felt so bad, so sad, that I felt so guilty, that I couldn't love in the way my family required. So you have to find ways of dealing with it, of learning how to go forward, but the trust issue doesn't help.

After Josh died, we had come to a point where we had learned so much more and I found a way to navigate around other people's feelings – to say 'that's your stuff, I don't need to deal with it' – and it gave me the tools to cope with other aspects, because I had more security from knowledge.

On film and creativity as a response to grief:

Twenty years after I first told Jane about the abuse and subsequently had therapy, I made two films. One was my personal story called *Breaking the Silence* (2006) and one was *Chosen*, which I edited and which won a BAFTA.

For me film is a bit like diarying or journaling, by recording. With the abuse films, there came a moment in time when I felt it was OK to do something like that. That project came to fruition forty years down the line. *Breaking the Silence* was really difficult because it was our own story of abuse at school (with my brothers).

In documenting in this way, we are not only looking at our own stories, but telling the stories of others, which in turn validates our own feelings in some way. The motivation is to hear from other people in order to help me feel more secure in what I'm thinking and feeling.

After Josh died we made *A Love That Never Dies*, and interviewed other bereaved parents and siblings on our journey through America. It was a cinema documentary and has now been shown globally, often with Jane and I doing a Q&A. It has opened up a conversation about grief and our own story is intertwined.

Each film we make helps us to ground ourselves in a new reality. We feel less alone. For me it's slightly easier to be behind the camera or in front of the screen, editing. That's where I'm comfortable.

Breaking the Silence: vimeo.com/53945691
Chosen: www.truevisiontv.com/films/chosen

Jeannette Waterman

Jeannette's son Tom died suddenly in a drowning accident seventeen months before our interview, at the age of twenty-eight. Jeannette attended one of The Good Grief Project's Active Grief Retreats.

Our interview took place just before Christmas 2020.

❧

It's a hard thing to be able to describe who I am, because when you go through huge loss, you lose your identity and where you fit in the world and how other people perceive you. The healing process is about being reborn into a new era, painful as it is without the person that you've lost. In the past I might have said 'I'm this, that or the other', but actually I don't know who I am any more. I am adrift and at sea.

On time healing:

Until you have that personal experience of losing someone who you love so much and who was an integral part of your life, you tend to think that after a year you may get back to some sort of normal, but the reality is, it's a life sentence. I try to think that every day I haven't seen Tom, I'm a day closer to seeing him again when we will be reunited. I try to look at it like that, but the void and the pain never goes away.

My daughter is in Australia and I am divorced, so we had the grief of losing the family unit before Tom died. Being 12,000 miles away it's both a physical and emotional separation.

I will be on my own this Christmas, so I am volunteering at the Caring in Bristol shelter where Tom used to help out. I know it will be a gruelling time and it will bring up painful memories. I did it last year and people said to me 'oh you're so good' but it's not that, it's quite selfish in a way; it's my way of filling the day but doing it in a meaningful way with a tribute to Tom. It's an honour and it gives me comfort to know that he would be proud of me. But also a huge sense of sadness because I just wish he was here to do it in person with me. Tom lived in Bristol so it was pertinent to do it there.

The traditions of Christmas can be rather superficial and based on materialistic consumerism and overindulgence. I think that Covid is giving us a rethink on many facets of our lives and on what is important now and I hope that as the 'new normal' emerges, it will give us an opportunity to do things differently. Volunteering feels authentic and intrinsically right in my heart. It's meaningful and comforts me to think that I may be helping people that do not have the luxury of a family unit.

It's about humanity really. Loss really does make you reassess and re-evaluate what your priorities are and hopefully you come through it so that you can be more compassionate and more caring.

Seventeen months on, I look back at the early days after Tom died and there was certainly a complete manicness to begin with, almost like a denial. The shock at the start. Organising his 'leaving party' for three weeks after he died focused me. I called it a leaving party because I hate the F word! I don't like 'funeral'; it's too final. It was an amazing celebration of the authentic Tom. It was gutsy and not sugar-coated in any way. It confronted his struggles; it was honest, true and absolutely right for him.

I had a complete instinct of knowing what was the right thing to honour him. It needed to be a natural burial, a humanist celebration, a portrayal of the true Tom. We had music, films of him being a complete comedian, tributes from his friends and from his father and his sister. We all took a different facet of him and did him justice. We read his poem which was to do with mental health, we hired a wood-fired pizza van. It was very informal and from the heart. Looking back it's all a complete blur, but it got me through.

I went ahead with an (already planned) two-month trip to Australia and it became an extraordinary pilgrimage. I went to places Tom had loved, his childhood home, beaches, and had my bee tattoo done. It reconnected me to him and to people who he and I had loved and who shared that grief.

I wanted to talk to Jeannette about her time during Covid, spending the year entirely alone under lockdown, work and social life stopping and how she has coped with her family being so far away. I had been inspired by her daily Facebook posts about her allotment and often lone walks in the Cotswold countryside – her honesty displayed her exposed heartbreak even when it was a bad day, but she always countered it with a thing of beauty or positivity in her photography. Her creativity, cooking with allotment produce, painting, writing, volunteering and taking a day at a time with absolute authenticity. Her raw explanations of her grief, illustrated by the seasons and nature.

It was almost a relief when Covid hit to have permission to stop. People had been so concerned and compassionate about me being OK, but I felt more recently that I had to put on a metaphorical mask and pretend I was. Tom suffered with attention deficit disorder and I too have a busy brain, so where some people with depression will sleep and go under the covers, my brain doesn't let me do that. My way of coping is to be active. Everything else was shut down but my way was to walk and take care of my allotment. The allotment was somewhere Tom and I had spent time together and there were shelves in the shed he had put up. It was too painful at first, I had no sense of purpose, but lockdown changed that.

I had ordered a tonne of manure and it was dumped in a great pile, so I had to do something with it! Once I set myself a task, something triggered and I had to get going. I'm a perfectionist, so internally that was the motivation for me to start. The allotment and walking gradually became my daily activity. If I had walked and done nothing else, I felt satisfied that I had achieved something that day. Tom was a huge photographer as well, and I found myself starting to take photos of things that caught my eye. Social media (for all its faults) became a way of me posting photos each day with thoughts. You wake each morning on your own and there is a dread each day of a renewed sense of loss, and by putting that photo up, something of beauty or to be grateful for, it became really important for me in a mindful way. A way of being thankful and facing the day.

I was dealing with loneliness. I have an amazing group of friends, but twenty-three hours out of twenty-four I have to cope with being on my own. I don't have anyone to care for at home, so my way of getting through was to be creative.

On Tom's birthday I made his favourite vegan cake and delivered pieces with a hand-painted card of a bee to my friends – a way of remembering Tom and connecting people. On his death day I drove down to Bristol to the pool where he left us and I met with two of his friends and then gathered for a picnic and it felt like a ritualistic honouring of him. I ended up at his graveside with other friends in the evening and we shared stories about him over a few beers. It felt right.

In my family, we have all dealt with our grief in our own ways. I feel I have confronted my grief head on. If I have needed to howl, I have. I haven't buried it; I've acknowledged it and sometimes it's bloody!

They say at some stage you might be comforted by the happy memories. Seventeen months on I'm not quite there yet. Of course you go through the anger at being in the club you don't want to be in. Tom had struggled with mental health issues and was coming through them with meditation and creativity, helping others. I live by the acronym WWTD – What Would Thomas Do? In some ways that has helped me through my grief; I'm living this for him.

People say 'Tom would want you to be happy' – but that somehow undermines the depth of the loss and the pain of losing someone you love so much. It's a line people bandy about, and while there is an element of logistical pertinence, it's not really very helpful. So I try to emulate his goodness, his compassion. I follow his steps. I want him to be proud of me.

I had to give up my job; I just couldn't do it after Tom died, but I still needed money, purpose and structure. I'm still not sure what my purpose is, but I'm exploring. I'm not at the stage where I have much idea of a future, so I volunteered because it didn't matter to me if I got Covid and died, but I needed purpose. I wasn't scared, as to me the worst had already happened. It wasn't an irresponsible attitude, it was just the headspace I was in.

Jeannette's toolkit:

Physical mementoes:
My tattoo. I have one that Tom designed and had on his wrist, in memory of a very special friend of his who tragically died in 2017. I now have the same tattoo, drawn by the same girl in Australia who did Tom's.

You need some physical remembrance, so they are ever present in your life and close to you. The tattoo is a constant reminder of my love for Tom, and being in the place that it is on my wrist, when I have been in very dark places (which I have since his death), Tom's father pointed out that it would remind me not to take my own life. So it feels like a protection against a knife, a protective guardian for me. It's funny because Tom would be having a good laugh because I was so anti-tattoos in the past!

Rituals:

There is a tree Tom loved. He painted it and I have that in my home. I don't pass the tree every morning, but I often detour that way and acknowledge him in my heart, hold him close and look up to the sky. That's my ritual, my way of connecting with him. I see it through all the seasons and it's about finding hope again, renewal and rebirth.

Book:

Healing After Loss: Daily Meditations for Working through Grief by Martha Whitmore Hickman.

It was spot-on for me – and reading other grief books. Understanding that it's OK not to be OK. Validation that you're not going mad.

Tom's friends:

One of the most comforting things has been being in touch with Tom's friends. Feeling their love and support has meant so much. I hope it's a reciprocal thing in some way, but feeling that connection is important and keeps him alive for all of us. It will get easier to remember the happier times, but they have been so solid on keeping me strong. One very special friend of his, Livvie, sent me a sunflower necklace with 'Keep Fxxxxxx Going' written inside it, which makes me smile. When I run now it jangles and it reminds me to do just that. It makes me think Tom is looking after me, running by my side.

Active Grief Retreat residential weekend for bereaved families with The Good Grief Project:

I found this so helpful – the creativity, the connection, the realisation that you're not alone, the love of the group and its facilitators and that it was OK to show your grief openly. There were wonderful touches that happened that connected us with our loved ones. Each session brought out a different aspect. It was daunting to go there but an extraordinary experience. When you have been through grief you feel the grief of others keenly. It was incredibly sad to hear of all the young people who had died. Each segment had been carefully thought through and brought out a unique way to remember your child. It comprised creative writing, photography and a fitness regime, including an introduction to boxing, something I never thought I would find myself doing. But it was about being brave, facing the fear and the comfort of making a tribute to your lost child in a meaningful and creative way; it was very therapeutic and comforting. It will stay with me for a very long time. There was camaraderie, finding a tribe who could give comfort and love. Jimmy and Jane and their family are extraordinary in what they have set up. You forget that they are going through their own grief over their son Josh. It was a beautiful transition through the weekend, from arriving feeling so vulnerable, fearful and shy to seeing it unleash into friendship and bonding with people who can truly understand your loss.

Friendships:
These can be severely tested. Some people cannot cope with the grief and are unable to deal with the raw emotions that are unleashed. Some actively avoid you. Some people hit the mark spot on and the acts of kindness that emerge, sometimes from people that you barely know, are a true blessing. It really is a challenging minefield. But the overriding fact is that people are not deliberately trying to be hurtful and there is an inclination from some to try and 'fix the problem' but of course death is not something you can fix. I love the analogy of someone walking beside you on this journey... and will be forever grateful for those random acts of kindness. Some people manage to say all the wrong things, but it is important to remember that they are saying them for all the right reasons; they care and love you and are anguished at seeing your pain.

Creativity:
I performed Tom's poem in Bristol. I wanted to honour him, to have his poem acknowledged and let the world know I was so proud of him.

To watch the short film of Jeannette delivering Tom's poem, enter 'Are You OK? A Poem For Mental Illness by Thomas Waterman' in your search engine or YouTube. You will also find a second version made by his close friend Colin McCord, featuring friends and family.

A Poem for Mental Illness
By Thomas Waterman – April, 2017

Ready your seats, be uncomfortably shifted
For unpleasant insight I have been gifted.
Underestimated is the power of talking
Many whose speech comes easy as walking
Endlessly chirping, in comfort we sit
Though come certain subjects, like birds we flit.
In conversation unwittingly choosing
The shape of the world with the words that we're using.
Familiar topics of weather and snow
However like plants need manure to grow
An unpleasant feeling, on eggshells we tread
But by pushing through it, awareness is spread.
Sometimes we call out, safe ear hard to find
Isolation's toxic, to those sick of mind.
Under carpets we're swept where we wither and rot
We get on with 'normal' yet we feel we've been shot.
So much shame and such guilt felt in our depression
But problems not shared become our obsession.
Thoughts swirling forever never find clarity
Readily accepted as just a part of me
Eating through your armour with no clemency
Existential cobwebs entangle identity.

So rarely in banter this snake gets a mention
But his is a venom that needs more attention.
This anguish retention
Of secret extension
An unknown dimension
Of infinite tension
A lethal intention
Beyond comprehension
So why the contention
On suicide prevention

But let me assure you with new-found elation
Between me and my illness there is separation.
Mental illness can blur lines of sickness and health
Burrows right into your own sense of self.
It's so unaccepted to show signs of weakness
But sharing out loud is a strength not a meekness.
We keep all our garbage in bags in our homes
But everyone has garbage and you're not alone.
Acknowledge you're sick and it is not benign
Just like smoking will kill you if given the time.
How serious is it? You're about to be shown
Less people die of war violence alone
Kills more humans than most kinds of cancer
The good news is we're all part of the answer
There's no silver bullet nor a magical cure
The key's conversations, of that I'm sure.

Take time to stray from safe subjects like football
Show courage and talk about something more fruitful
I tell you, it's easy, now here's what you say
My friend let me ask you – are you REALLY OK?

Luke Ashworth

Founder of Adviser.ai

Luke's son Harvey died aged eleven. Luke and I met when he interviewed me on stage at COVER Mental Health & Wellbeing Summit in London, just before the first UK lockdown in March 2020.

❧

Harvey was a happy, healthy boy, and we were in Greece, on the first day of our summer holiday with my wife (who was not Harvey's mother).

It was the first morning of the holiday and, unusually, Harvey had not woken up early. My wife went to check on him in the adjoining bedroom and I heard the most god-almighty, terrifying scream. I ran in and Harvey was lying face down on the pillow and the first thing I noticed was that he was black and blue on his back with bruising. When I rolled him over he was warm on his front so I automatically went into 'save' mode thinking he was alive. I tried to resuscitate him but rigor mortis had already set in so I couldn't open his jaw. Because of the warmth, I couldn't compute the reality, so I was just fighting for him to survive; I couldn't begin to understand that he was already dead. I have no idea of the timeline, but suddenly there were people around, there was a defibrillator and that didn't work. I was told to say goodbye.

It was like a reverse bungee jump to the moon – being dragged away from everything in an instant. It was all so quick. They shepherded me outside and I remember my skin was on fire. Nobody could touch me; my nerve endings felt like somebody had put me in flames. It was a physical traumatic response. I don't know how long that lasted. My body was trying to compute everything, these levels of shock. The speed of waking up feeling 'thank God we're on holiday' to 'my son's dead'. It was too much to process.

I like looking back at how my body was processing things straight away. The first twenty-four hours were weird, but thankfully the holiday and insurance companies were amazing. I watched Harvey's body being taken away; I then had to go to a police station to be interviewed by three Greek police officers. We were taken back to a different part of the hotel (obviously we couldn't go back to the room), but there were kids playing everywhere. That should have been us! We didn't sleep at all and then we were out on a flight the very next morning – but without Harvey, because there had to be an autopsy. All of this within forty-eight hours of leaving home.

Back in the UK, we had no sleep. Friends were amazing and also my ex-wife's family. We would watch terrible films until the early hours (because I couldn't watch anything with any emotional depth), so I would get two hours' sleep. In this sleep-deprived state I would wake up and think Harvey was alive and that I'd had a bad dream that he died. I would go downstairs and bang, reality would kick in – the dream was that he was alive. It was my body trying to catch up with everything. Traumatic shock and sleep deprivation: not a great mix.

Interestingly I was immediately strict with myself to regain some control. I would allow myself a small glass of wine each evening but no more, even when friends were drinking around me. I knew that grief was bad enough, but waking up to grief and a hangover would have been horrific, so I was already looking after my mind and body to survive. Self-protection had kicked in.

The rate of learning this sends you on is just extraordinary. I was about to tell you how long I was in the grief waiting room for, but my learning just carries on and I feel I have changed even since Christmas a month ago! The things that come up in this never-ending, recurring cycle are questions like 'Was I content enough last year, in the context of what happened to me?' and the answer is 'Yes, *at the time*'. But then this Christmas made me hit a really dark period and I was nowhere near happy or content. Right now I would say 'Yes, absolutely!' And that's been happening in a recurring way with improvements where I think I'm doing well, and almost immediately setbacks. Which is why I get up every day and think, right, what's next then?

I think the difficulty with grief is that the rest of life can mask you from being able to look at your grief effectively and make the right decisions. The issue for me wasn't necessarily the grief, although that was tough enough, but as a result of what happened, within six months my Australian wife, who was younger than me, wanted to go back to Australia, so we divorced, sadly. I lost my son, my marriage, my home, my dogs.

I put someone in place to run my 100-person business because I couldn't function properly, especially in a highly pressurised environment owning one of the UK's largest online and telephony life-insurance brokers. Three to four years later I lost the business (having picked the wrong guy) and all my money. Perhaps it wasn't a cycle but a domino effect. When one bad thing happens, unfortunately it can mean you then make poor decisions because you're not in a balanced place. You go further and further down. You would have thought the worst year was the year Harvey died, but it accumulated after that. What do you do? Do you collapse? Do you fight? If you try too hard, it might not be realistic, but if you don't move forward at all you will never get out of bed in the morning. That accumulation for me, when the business went in February 2016, that was when the dam broke. I had lost everything.

I had no answers to the normal social questions people ask like 'What do you do for a living?', 'Are you married?', 'Do you have kids?' The cool thing now, and it's why occasionally it's good to look back and see how far you have come, is that if someone asks the 'Do you have kids?' question, I just say 'No.' I let it land; I don't feel a need to tell my story.

It's interesting with dating, because now I don't always tell my story straight away, and I can see dates wondering why I'm single at forty-two. Am I a playboy? What's my story? I just say, 'I'll tell you when I know you better.'

Nowadays, I'm not aiming for anything huge, I'm not aiming for some giant take-over-the-world business – that's what Harvey has given me. I've made a lot of money in my time, and lost it. I've also, due to the financial crash, lived with financial insecurity for many years, even before Harvey died.

I want to live. Whether it's dog-sledding in the Arctic Circle, the diving I've done, snowboarding, going to Burning Man – all of these things are amazing – but it's also about balance. I'm forty-two, I would love a family at some stage (even if not my biological kids), and if I'm going to have young children in my life, I'm not going to be working all hours – it's not going to happen. I want to be there, savouring every moment and LIVING. Of course I need to be realistic and have enough money, so I'm trying to achieve more balance for the first time, thanks to Harvey. For now there are more lessons for me to learn and places to explore. I have this urge to walk the Dingle Way in Ireland and explore Antarctica!

One of the things I used to do when I was low or struggling with grief was to reach out. But I've come to a point now where I look in. I find space on my own and I allow space and time and know I will be OK. The ability to do that fixes things faster. But I don't think you can learn that overnight: you have to have pushed for so long or to have been very low before you really learn that.

Christmas was a low point again this year, but I came home to my mum's, where we've since been in lockdown together, and I just couldn't get off the sofa. The thing with the cyclical nature of grief is that I am better at dealing with the lows. I know they will pass and I now know what to do. I know I will be OK – it might be that I just need to sit there and wait.

Grief can either be my Achilles heel or my superpower and that will probably always change. But to make it my superpower, it takes energy. I have a responsibility to myself and those that care about me to keep fit, healthy and in a good headspace.

Social media is an interesting one; I started writing posts describing my inner emotions and it felt good to get the dopamine hit when I would get a good response. I liked inspiring other people and, when I was in a lonely place, it helped me too. I would always put a positive bent on it and writing it positively meant I was applying it to myself. So I was shaping and controlling my own reality through writing. It was almost like public journaling. When I felt bad I wouldn't say anything.

I have heard it said that 'alone' is an amalgamation of 'all-in-one', i.e. everything is right here; there's no need to be lonely. At my age, my friends are married with kids; they are still close friends, but their time is taken up. So I have to find my own inner resources. The locus of control and judgement can fall out when we look at the lives of others. For people isolated in a dysfunctional or unhappy relationship it can be the loneliest place, so you have to keep perspective and look inside.

Making the switch to look inside is so important. I can now be more open with people and just say, 'I'm finding it a bit tough at the moment; I'm going to take a little time. Don't worry about me, I'll do some meditation and sort myself out.' It gives me the ability to take control, rather than defining myself with 'By the way, I lost a kid.' It gives me a quieter confidence in the expression of where I'm at. It's a subtle difference. I don't want Harvey's death to define me from the outside, only from the inside. I would rather people get to know me and then find out. Internally, of course I'm that dad whose son died; I accept that internal definition. That's how the superpower might grow.

I like the definition that we humans are more thoughtful and intelligent inside than we are able to communicate. I could never begin to describe to anyone all the processes I've been through internally.

I love being with older people and hearing what they say. The small comments they make are the sort of lines you hear from people in their thirties doing huge amounts of spiritual work but they don't fully know what it means. It's not a lived experience. An older person knows life well and has real experience of the challenges. It's not the fun bits that define them, it is the hardships they have lived through. We have been forced into that learning, insight and wisdom earlier and perhaps we have the opportunity to make decisions sooner as a result.

It's what we do with it that counts. I've had some 'fake awakenings' when I thought I had recovered and come through grief! It's almost like a false summit; you climb the grief mountain, think you're 'there', have a burst of energy that you totally misuse. So looking inside and being grounded is so important. I think 'there' is actually 'here'. I get it every morning, the moments when there are no thoughts and then suddenly your brain floods with them, but there's a gap just before you wake fully. That is what being 'here' is about.

I've had to become more discerning through grief. Actually looking at whether decisions are good or not, from a balanced perspective. But I can only do that now with what I have learned from my mistakes. You don't want to dilute yourself or take away the passion, but you have to be discerning.

Luke's toolkit:

These days I have a journal. It has various helpful and interesting action points – a recent one was to call someone you have been meaning to. So I called up an old school friend and we had a great chat. Examples of the daily actions are: *Name three things you are grateful for. What would make today great? Give a daily affirmation.* I've been doing it most days, but I don't worry if I don't feel like it and miss it for a couple of days. But it's nice to return to it, particularly during lockdown. This style of journaling is accessible and not challenging. It's bite-sized entries and an easier approach. It will also help me to see how I progress and move forward.

I heard the spoken introduction (below) to a song just after Harvey died, and one of the biggest things I have tried to do is to genuinely apply these rules to my life in building my life back up. For example, I have deliberately built my new business to give me the freedom to enjoy my relationships and explore the world around me, as opposed to the ever-consuming businesses that so many entrepreneurs build. It might mean no supercars and boats again, but it will bring me a lot more contentment!

'Ta Moko' by Whirimako Black: 'Some people wander around interviewing dying patients, and not one person said they regretted not making more money, or working harder. They all seemed to say their regrets were not spending time with the people they loved, not travelling more and relating more to the world and the planet.'

Russ Kane

Writer and broadcaster, co-founder of Women's Radio Station and Men's Radio Station, the Flying Eye on Capital Radio for twenty years

In April 2004 Russ's wife Sally Kane died, aged forty-three, from breast cancer. They had five-year-old twin boys. Before their cancer experience, the family had suffered other major traumas when the twins were born very prematurely. Sally was left in a coma for a week following the birth (having lost seventy-one pints of blood) and Russ was in a car accident, resulting in all of them being in different hospitals at the same time (the full story is available in *Shout at the Moon*, co-written with Sally).

❧

Sally had beaten her breast cancer originally and, as a former model, she became a media spokesperson for Breast Cancer Care. When it came back again, it went to her lungs, liver and brain so we knew it was game over at that point. I sought counselling during that time; I knew I had to be prepared in advance of her death.

The worst thing for me, and I don't think I've really talked about this before because it's a hard thing to revisit, but the worst thing was having to tell the twins. People say to me now, 'You don't seem very nervous going on stage in Los Angeles,' for instance, and I'll think, well, compared to telling your children that they are never going to see their mother again, it's nothing! It was ghastly. She had been so ill for so long and absent because she had been in hospital so much. They are twenty-two now, huge achievers who leave me in their wake!

On grief:

I went to a grief counsellor for a while but it didn't really help me. The advice they gave me on the appropriate time to grieve was 'One day is too short and a lifetime is too long.' That's partly true, but you never stop grieving. One of the great myths is 'time is a great healer'. What time does, if you allow it, is it can give you coping mechanisms. You just learn to cope and adjust. I would say to people who look from the outside and think that eventually you will be fine, no you won't – you'll be different. You'll be coping, you'll be living, but you will be different. There's always a fraction of you which will be dead. When Sally died, part of me died, but that's OK. I accept that.

Grief mustn't define you and it mustn't destroy you. You mustn't live in the past. You can't change it, you can learn from it, but you can't go back in a time machine and change anything. So, if you live in the past you are doomed; your life will be a waste. I live in the present and I look to the future. I was so lucky to meet an amazing woman who took on the Herculean task of being with me and being Mummy to the twins. It was incredibly brave of her and her role cannot be overstated. Not many people have the courage to take on such a challenge, so I count myself very fortunate.

Life is a complicated business. There's no one-size-fits-all approach and everyone has to adjust to what suits them. One of the main problems with grief is mourning the past; she's not coming back, life won't be reversed, so you have to look at what you have and enjoy and embrace it!

I was very angry for a while. Public Image Ltd's song 'Rise' describes anger as an energy, and that is so true. You can either let anger destroy you or it can propel you, and I just harnessed it! I harnessed it in my work; it empowered me. I recognised that I was angry and that's OK, if it gets you through.

In January 2018 we started Women's Radio Station and, in 2019, Men's Radio Station. It was due to reading about the suicide statistics in Britain. I was shocked to learn that it was 80 per cent men and 20 per cent women at the time. An absolute chasm. Women are better at talking – men bottle things up. Those phrases: man up, grow a pair, big boys don't cry. Those feelings get so bottled up and it can lead to depression and ultimately suicide. Both stations have taken off. We don't play music; it's speech-based radio and of course during lockdown the figures have gone through the roof.

When a major life event like this happens, you think what am I going to do with the rest of my life? I think, had I not had the twins, I might have checked out. I really might have done. Not because I was depressed, I just felt I had done all I wanted to do. But I had the twins and they were my priority. Now they are twenty-two and just finishing university, my job's kind of done. I'll always be Dad, and I miss them hugely, but it gives you an extra level of thinking about how to address some of the bad stuff out there.

I've learned more from Men's Radio than I could have imagined, especially when we talk to people who have survived suicide attempts. They have all said, without exception, that the moment they started their act of suicide, whatever it might have been, they instantly regretted it. They are grateful it didn't succeed.

We cover huge topics. I don't do soundbites – we engage in deep conversation. We let people speak at their own speed. This is the problem with so much of life: if you don't have some degree of empathy it divides society and there's no middle ground.

At Men's Radio, we talk to ordinary members of the public and see that the human response to adversity is just so impressive.

I loathe that expression 'these things are meant to happen'. Someone behind the till in a chemist said to Sally when she had cancer, 'You know Jesus wants you for a sunbeam, don't you?' I happened to bump into her at a fete and I went absolutely nuts! How dare she.

What illness and bereavement do is define which people are there for you and which people head for the hills. We would be walking down the street and people we thought were friends would literally cross the road to avoid us. They would say 'well, we didn't know what to say' years later and then expect to be friends. Someone wrote to me and said 'it was a misunderstanding'. What part of cancer and dying did you not understand? People were either appalling or absolutely incredible. You're not asking people for a miracle or to cure someone, you're just asking for their friendship at a time you need support. There are the ones that leave food on our doorstep, when you know they live miles away – you never forget those kindnesses, but you also don't forget the ones who walk away. It causes a lot of friction and it says more about them that they can't face these things.

What is the worst that's going to happen? You can't catch cancer or grief! Just say – are you OK? Is there anything I can do? Shall we have a coffee? You feel very alone in grief. Just talk, just be there. It's not going to be a bundle of laughs, but it's not going to be so horrific either. Just be kind. It's a universal thing, this silence and fear.

Keep trying. Grief evolves and everyone experiences it in their own individual way and pace. The tiny gestures are everything. You don't want anything else. Silence is the worst thing and I found it unforgivable.

And as a survivor, don't keep beating yourself up. Don't look for reasons – you will go mad! If you look for logic you will go mad. These are random acts. I never said 'Why me?' and Sally didn't either. The question is 'Why *not* me?' It's a lottery, completely random, and if you can accept that, it's helpful. There is no logic to this. It weakens you if you question it too much. It's not constructive.

ح&

When Sally died, we launched a rose in her name, the 'Sally Kane Rose'. The proceeds of the sales went to the Royal Marsden. I can't say enough good things about the Royal Marsden Hospital in Fulham, London – they were absolutely magnificent, sensationally good. People bought the Sally Kane Rose all over the world. It was beautiful, life-affirming and it made thousands of pounds for the hospital. I didn't want to build shrines to Sally. When someone dies you have so much mundane stuff to deal with, but it has to be done when the time is right. She was a model and designer, so boy she had clothes! But they were just clothes; Sally was in my heart and mind, not in the clothes. You have to let go. But only when you're ready to do so.

I think people feel too guilty that they are around and their loved one isn't, so they must live in purgatory. I live my life to the max every single day because I enjoy it; it's life-affirming and we're only here once. Life is short, so have a good time. I think that's what Sally would have wanted. Remember and cherish the great times you had and whatever way you can, embrace life. It might not be in five minutes or five years – there's no timescale.

There's that great story of someone in New York, and they want to be pointed north. They get to Canada and ask to be pointed north. Eventually they get to the North Pole and say, 'Can you point me north?' 'No, that's it! You're as north as you can get.' There is no answer to grief; it's unanswerable. So don't question too much.

In some ways you always think of the person as they were, they are ageless; Sally is still the model! But I have had to block out how Sally looked at the end. You are with someone you love, they are dying, they look terrible. It's not like the movies; they become somebody quite different and in the end it can be a mercy, but I have chosen not to dwell on that. By then she had gone and I now think of her as the stunning woman with the fiery temper. I look older and older and look like my dad and she remains young!

Our strapline for Men's Radio is 'Where Men Really Talk' and somebody years ago gave me a great analogy for grief and mental health issues. If you buy a lovely fresh chicken, and you put it in a drawer so that's it out of the way and you don't pay it attention, the smell from that chicken is going to permeate EVERYWHERE. If you bottle things up, they will affect everything in the end. There's a direct correlation between mental health and your physical health.

There is no statute of limitation on grief. It will take as long as it takes. Give yourself that permission to grieve and move forward from there when you can.

For current Russ Kane information: www.russkane.com
Men's Radio Station: mensradiostation.com
Women's Radio Station: womensradiostation.com

Sasha Bates

Psychotherapist and author of Languages of Loss

Sasha was widowed three years before our interview at the age of forty-nine, when her husband (and best friend) Bill died unexpectedly of a heart attack.

Sasha's book is one of the books I most often recommend to clients. When she asked me if I would read it pre-publication, my feedback included 'you have knocked C. S. Lewis off his pedestal' – before that his *A Grief Observed* had been my go-to grief memoir.

৵

When Bill died, it was so catastrophic and so tumultuous since his death came out of the blue that I realised the only way I could a) get some of these feelings out from where they were torturing me and b) start to make sense of something that wasn't easy to express, was somehow vomiting my feelings down onto the page, just scrawling my stream of consciousness. It gave me something to do, it gave me an outlet and a route through. I started writing early on, within a couple of weeks. I didn't think anyone else would read it; it was for me, wanting to remember as well and wanting to give shape to it.

It's hard to remember much about that first year and writing the book to be honest. It grew out of also responding to so many emails and letters, trying to expand on my feelings and also having written the eulogy. It grew from there into a bigger body of work.

It made me feel I was being heard, even though it was only me doing the hearing at the time. I don't think I'm very good at telling other people how I feel, but somehow I was able to do it on the page. It felt like an organic process.

I asked Sasha if being a psychotherapist had given her any tools to deal with her own grief.

I think it is very helpful being a psychotherapist. I don't think it takes the pain away, because nothing can, but it enables you to step into a slightly different space and understand more objectively why you're feeling like you do, even if you can't change that. It became apparent as I was writing. I could feel that shift as I could hear a different voice coming in, as though I was commenting – almost being my own therapist. For instance, thinking *oh that's what they mean by anger*, or *I can see what's happening there*. I almost split into two selves and they were able to help each other because even when my therapist self was helping to normalise and understand, my grieving self was saying 'this is what it's actually like'. Theory is all very well, but it doesn't change the screaming inside! It was an organic process of these two selves, helping each other to learn from the other side.

Coming alongside someone who is grieving is everything. People underestimate the power of just witnessing and sharing the pain and showing you that they love you and you're not alone. What you want on one day can be so different on another and friends need to be OK with that. It can be really frightening being with somebody who is in that level of distress and pain and you can't do anything to take it away from them. So it leaves the non-grieving person feeling very helpless, which is never a good place to be in. It is confronting, and it is their own helplessness and fear and inability to change things that they run away from. I don't think they are running away from you; they are running away from what it brings up in them about their powerlessness.

It can be so annoying when people say 'time heals' because it really doesn't and all they are showing is their own desperation to be able to see progress. Partly because they don't want to see their friend in pain, but partly because they want to believe that if and when it happens to them that they would be able to 'get over it'. Which of course isn't the case: you are able to manage, but you don't get over it.

I voiced to Sasha that friends sometimes expect you to be the 'old you', as you were before the loss or losses happened. We can't be the same people but that's not always a bad thing – perhaps we are more courageous, and stronger in some way. Friends can find it hard to adjust to our new landscape and who we have become through our grief.

They do find it hard, because they like to believe that you can slot back into their lives, that you are not going to change irrevocably, but I agree, some of those changes are important, powerful, useful and life-affirming. It's the same when people have a terminal illness – sometimes life can become more vivid. That's a hard thing to acknowledge because no one wants to believe that something good has come out of something so awful, but on the other hand, how can you live the rest of your life without thinking that you have something to balance the scales? Yes, you have lost, and yes, you are in pain, but you are possibly given these other things alongside them.

I still feel guilty if I say something positive or joyful – and back it up with 'I still wish he was here.' It's so silly because of course everyone knows that and I know that, but I still feel I have to articulate it!

It's really hard to describe how life-changing grief is and how much pain you can go through and still survive.

I asked Sasha what her perspective is now, three years after Bill's death.

The pain is definitely less acute, it's now more spread and diffuse. I still get the acute moments and I still get very low lows. And sometimes around the anniversary it still feels as though it's only happened yesterday, so those moments are still there. But most of the time I feel I have absorbed it and it's no longer an arrow to the heart, it's spread throughout my whole body. It's part of me. Practically, I'm more used to him not being here; the missing him is still there emotionally, but it's not quite as all-pervasive just from the fact that you get used to the familiarity of not having him. The deep shock of the early days can be very comforting and can help you not confront it head on. It wraps you in cotton wool while you have the deep connection to the person. You feel they are still there.

I think the whole first year and with the writing of the book I was in a slightly altered state and alongside the numbing and the shock, I think there is adrenalin which gets you through. I was slightly manic. I set up a scholarship, wrote a book, charged around the country seeing people and did all sorts of things as though I was on speed! It's very clever, the adrenalin, just like if you have a physical accident or lose a leg, the adrenalin is there to keep you alive.

So in some ways the second year was worse as the adrenalin dissipated and the wrap was no longer around me. Everything felt very dull, grey and painful and it was more of a chronic pain rather than an acute pain. I was just so depressed and flat and couldn't hide any more behind the sort of tale I had been telling myself that 'if you just keep busy enough and power on through it will be OK'. That salve stops working.

I think by the third year, somehow you find an uneasy truce with it. You learn to live with it in a less extreme way.

I asked Sasha what helped her through the second and third years. That shift of gears as grief moves forward and changes.

Yoga has been massive for me, all aspects of yoga: the philosophy, the breathing, the meditation, even the yogic community – the teachers have been massively helpful. Other aspects too: my friends, my work, finding ways of commemorating Bill – the setting up of the theatrical scholarship, planting trees.

I have found that if I talk about Bill, it gives other people permission to do so and feel OK about it. Otherwise I feel they are holding their breath and not knowing whether to or not. It takes the pressure off. The onus falls on us, the bereaved, and as a therapist I'm used to being open, so I'm not squeamish about that, but for others who are more private and haven't been trained to talk or to hear about other people's pain, that can be a really difficult thing. It does feel like it should be the other way.

When you find a tribe there is an ease that brings, when you all have knowledge of grief. It's so important to open up this conversation as we are both doing with our work.

Sasha and I discussed the expression 'going mad with grief' and how it resonated with both of us.

Well, I absolutely thought I was going mad. I couldn't believe how my life could just do a complete 180-degree shift overnight. It was too big a shift from the life I thought I had and the person I thought was going to be with me in that life, and I felt completely deranged! Plus you have all your emotions flying all over the place, your thoughts; you start thinking mad things like 'if only we had done this' and 'when he comes back I'll tell him this' and you go in and out of it. It seemed crazy that I could even function normally, like when people would come to the hospital when he was in a coma and I would just be chatting away. I would go and get a prescription, normal things, but I couldn't understand that. I certainly felt I was going mad. It was something I didn't really understand before that.

I shared with Sasha that in the early years after Harry's death I actually took an online dementia test because I thought I was on that path. Memory loss, brain fog, etc. but it was grief. With good self-care it eventually cleared. The same post-divorce. It can be so shocking if you don't know. I felt as though I was losing my mind.

Yes, you lose basic skills. A bit of leeway is needed, both with yourself and others: knowledge that you won't be functioning properly; you will be a bit doolally. I mean – how can you *not* be? It makes complete sense when you think about it!

With the physical effects of grief, having been a yogi for thirty years, it definitely gave me a sense of what was going on. In the early days I had heart, gut and lung reactions but I think for me the way it manifested was just feeling different in my body. Everything felt heavy, that sense of feeling burdened, lumpen and lethargic. I had no sense of vitality (from the word 'vita', to live) and I had lost the will to live. Not in terms of wanting to kill myself, but the life had gone out of me and my body reflected that. Everything was solid, slow and heavy; there was no life force, no spark, no energy. I was just dragging my body around. That was my biggest physical symptom.

Three years on and at my age, I find it hard to know what is grief and what is menopause. There is a loss about menopause anyway – your youth, the body you once had, all of which mirrors the grief, so when they are happening alongside each other it's very hard to know which is which. So I'm very different physically than I was when Bill died, but I'm fifty-two now. Maybe some of those things would have happened anyway? It's impossible to know, but it all feeds in.

There's no point in saying 'if I didn't have the grief it might be like this', because you do have the grief and it is part of your life; it is what it is. There's no straight line to getting 'better'.

Sasha's toolkit:

Kindness to yourself is essential. Using your friends and being open about what you need from them. Take each day as it comes and do what feels right to you and don't be told what to do. Try things out. Understand that what you feel one day may feel very different on another and friends need to try and accommodate that.

Alongside yoga practice, my knowledge as a therapist of knowing where you are TODAY, and being compassionate to yourself has been important. So for instance, I knew I couldn't go running (which I love), but I knew that was OK. And only a very gentle yoga practice. Understanding that there is a reason you can't be as athletic, there's a reason I didn't want to go out running. You are bearing that weight.

It doesn't make it easy when you think, after a year or two, when am I ever going to get back to how I was? Not just physically, but how I felt. The enjoyment of running and how it felt. I still felt after six months, *Oh for heaven's sake, when am I going to run a 10k?* and of course you can't!

On anniversaries:

The first two years I got together with Bill's friends; the first year I did a quiz about his life and the second year I did 'Billy Bingo' with phrases and charts that he used. The third one was during lockdown and I was on my own. I didn't do anything other than sit and think about him, walk and just remember him. Part of me might have done that anyway because, much as it was lovely to be with other people, it also required a superhuman effort. For all that I gained from the others, it also took a lot from me too. I was able to be alone with my weeping. It reflects how grief is different all the time. It's a dynamic, fluid process.

For links to Sasha's writing and psychotherapy practice visit her website: www.sashabates.co.uk

Instagram, Twitter and Facebook: @sashbates

Languages of Loss, A Grief Companion and her latest book, *Yoga Saved my Life*, are available in bookshops and online via www.hive.co.uk

Although the following interviews form the basis for an entirely different book, I feel very strongly that they should be included here. In my grief community so far we have covered grief for parents, children, siblings, partners, divorce, not being able to have children and the views of grief professionals. But through two friends, I have closely witnessed racial and historic grief plus grief for identity, community and family, which became increasingly evident during 2020. Oumou and Ismail have generously helped me to understand more about their experiences.

Oumou Longley

Researcher, journalist and podcaster

Oumou and I met through Cam and our families are now close friends. Oumou spent the first lockdown in 2020 with us at the time of George Floyd's death. She has a BSc in Population Health Sciences from UCL, and a Master's degree in Gender Studies with a specialism in Race, Black British Feminism and Archives from the London School of Economics (LSE). She is studying for a PhD at the LSE Department of Gender Studies, with further archive research into 'Presence', looking at what happens when histories are deleted and loss is experienced by Black women. When absence becomes so loud, it almost becomes 'presence' because it is so obvious.

࿎

Until I came to your talk, I hadn't spent much time thinking about grief in relation to my own life; despite going through various forms of loss, I had never theorised it as grief. But maybe I just didn't know how to put that into words? I know I carry a lot of it within me and it comes up in various ways and I recognise that it's connecting to something much bigger. So it resonated with me to learn what those feelings were. I didn't feel I had much understanding of it before and it really does play out in so many aspects of my own life.

The physical aspects of grief definitely made sense as I've often had issues with my skin and sometimes it's aggravated when I'm stressed, including during lockdown when I've had eczema for the first time since I was a child. It was maybe three or four days after the London Black Lives Matter protests started, and after the first protest I attended in June 2020, I developed eczema all over my face, and that continued on and off until October. I do wonder about that, because when the protests started that was such a deeply intense and emotional time, so it can't have been a coincidence that during that time I started to have those struggles that hadn't arisen for years. I think the space that lockdown created allowed for this under-the-surface racial suffering to really become unavoidable. There was nothing else to do but to face up to that reality, and it was intense!

I've always kept on moving, kept busy – I struggle to deal with not having stuff to do. I don't know whether that's avoiding having time to stop and think too much. This is probably one of the first periods of my life when I've had to stop. Since I was a kid, we have been on the move. We left my dad and moved all around the world, and since then we have kept on moving, living in different places, so sitting still has never been normal to me.

On archives, Black history and racial grief:

As a Black person, when things happen in the world like the death of George Floyd or Breonna Taylor, it always feels very personal because it's about the colour of your skin. It's about something that's inherent within you, that you can't change, and you don't have power over it. It's interesting to watch how that suffering spreads so quickly, especially because we have the internet so grief spreads at a rate that's so much faster because it's laid out on Instagram for us all to partake in. I wonder if that's a good thing or a bad thing because it desensitises others to our pain, like our trauma almost becomes a commodity or something to use for social media clout. I have personally found that very hard. It's very sad because every time you see somebody suffering you think, *That could have been me.* It connects to such a long journey in the way you have been treated and it's triggering.

To grow up in an environment where you are constantly beaten down and devalued means that you carry it all on the surface, literally in the colour of your skin, but it's very much under the surface of your entire existence, so when something like George Floyd's death happens it can be very overwhelming because it connects to years of trauma, not just for me but for other people around me too. It's personal and generational.

Whether it's something that directly happened to you or not, it affects you deeply. There are some theories around intergenerational loss and grief surrounding racial bodies. So, for instance, Black people experience grief as their history has been erased, as their identities are policed, as they literally die at the hand of white society, but they are not allowed to mourn and move on from that grief, because society doesn't let us resolve it.

So if I think of myself as a Black British person and I want to go to school and I want to learn about Black British history, I'm often taught essentially that 'Black British people didn't exist', which is simply not the case – we're just not in the curriculum. It's just manufactured racial prejudice that denies the experience of a whole part of the population. So you feel a sense of loss there, but it is almost so normalised that it becomes accepted and unconscious, making it really hard to point out and resolve. So you're kind of stuck in this sense of mourning, but you can't resolve it because your mourning isn't legitimised. You're not seeing people accept your history, you're not seeing people agree and acknowledge your pain or erasure.

As a result I have spent my whole life feeling confused by a lingering grief which isn't necessarily attached to an individual so that makes it even harder to resolve. This grief is everywhere in terms of how we're being deleted and denied, yet I can't grab hold of it and move on.

At the same time, in the wrong hands, the stories can get misrepresented, so you want to air this grief, but when it's viewed from a white perspective, often all you are told is about suffering and how 'terrible' it is to be Black. We are taught that Black people were slaves and that's basically it! It's a really damaging narrative that maintains an oppressive hierarchy. At school there were even a few students who made 'a joke' out of referring to me as a slave. It's just not real; it denies your humanity in a way when you are told 'to be Black is to suffer' because it denies the complexity of what it is to be human. Sure we have suffered, but we have more of a complex experience of life than that.

In relation to my archive work, because Black people didn't historically have the means with which to put their histories into a European institution, you are left with Black histories that are told from the perspective of people who colonised them. So you get Black histories told as 'native people in undiscovered lands' or 'slaves on ships' as opposed to human beings with their own stories and experiences to be told, so it's very challenging when you go looking for those histories to find something that feels true to you.

On her PhD:

There are a huge amount of Black people trying to work with the archives to deal with this erasure, to try and document something that is more realistic. Whether that's taking the oral histories of Black communities, or bringing together stuff that's previously been ignored. Or coming up with creative ways of rereading histories and finding things that aren't there at first glance. So perhaps a photograph of someone who has been documented as a colonial purpose, or documented by an anthropologist in a dehumanising way. Instead of seeing this as a Black loss, an absence and a violence, it's looking again and actively connecting with their humanity. So looking for perhaps a clenched fist or an averted gaze, to return some of the humanity and resistance that existed, beyond the white lens. To make the history real. Otherwise that's why we end up in the situation where in the current climate Black suffering spreads across the internet without a thought and we're so desensitised to seeing these images of Black, dehumanised people dying. We need to address the histories to challenge the way we think of Black people in the present and challenge that sense of identity better.

I feel the battle of working within an institution which is historically violent to Black people. It's quite a hard environment to be in because it's not really designed for somebody like me. But using the facilities and I guess the finance that the institution can give me to challenge that same institution is a weird position to be in.

Within the institution I still experience a lot of denial of my experience – denial, erasure, loss – so I really grapple with it, having to put myself in an environment that has been hurtful to me.

While Oumou was staying with my family in the spring of 2020, we witnessed one example of exactly what she is talking about. I asked Oumou to share it here:

As someone who writes about race, you realise that all the people who have control over your work are white, so your work is edited in a certain way. It's very weird to have that filtered through a white editor and then put back into the world.

I had this exciting opportunity to work with a magazine run by two Black men, so I wrote an article. I did all the work for it, an interview on Black masculinity that I was commissioned to do (unpaid but with a credit). As a Black woman you are supposed to just be thankful to be given a seat at the table, you're not really valued for your time or work. It's 'oh I can use this person because she's so desperate to be here'. So I did the article and I checked multiple times that I was going to be credited with the work; there were a few different people involved, but I wrote it, did all the interviews, and handed in the final piece. They assured me that it would all be fine and then when the piece was published, I opened the magazine and they hadn't credited me. This was at the time of Black Lives Matter and it was just so demoralising.

Yet again it's someone thinking that you don't exist. They had taken my name out and put the name of the magazine as writing it plus the name of another person who had more credibility than me. I messaged that person and let her know of my confusion and she was confused too because she hadn't written it! I confronted the magazine and they basically gaslit me and said, 'Oh sorry you feel like that, we really value your input,' but they wouldn't change it.

It makes you feel that you are not valuable basically, that you don't exist. When someone puts you on a level down there, it's inhuman. It was two men as well using me for free labour.

They came back to me this year and asked me if I wanted to be involved with their magazine issue and it transpired that it's the same thing again. The answer was 'no'.

Within the context of loss and erasure, I had always felt like erasure was something out there, so what was more disturbing was to feel it happening directly to me. It's very different talking about erasure and then experiencing it actually happening to you. It's like screaming into a void and thinking, *Oh my God do I not exist any more?* It happens all the time to Black women: being erased from things.

On Olive Morris:

Olive was a South London community activist in the 1960s and 1970s who died of cancer aged twenty-seven. She was a big part of the squatters' movement and set up two really influential Black women's groups. She was a force within South London that people remembered and recognised.

Having gone through my degree at university, I was doing my Master's, and I had still really only heard this narrative of Black suffering and I felt that it was so weird; that it was not all there is to being Black. So I needed to figure out something more real for myself. It was making me feel bad. So I went to the archive and learned about the history of Olive Morris and I wrote about her, but I also wrote about the impact of how connecting with moments of Black history is so personal for Black people and how it can reconnect you to some parts of your own humanity. Just to experience that representation and to understand what went before; to better know why you are here in the present and how that influences you.

So it was very powerful, largely because I got to learn about the communities who remembered Olive. How outside of traditional institutions, Black histories were carried in memories and conversations, and that is passed down across generations in a non-traditional way and that is a really legitimate form of identity that should be recognised.

Olive Morris isn't alive any more, and we could learn about her at school, for instance, but we don't – we learn about the Tudors. What we do in the British education system is we learn about Martin Luther King, we learn about Rosa Parks and we ignore the fact that there are figures in Black British history that we could recognise. So what that does is generate the idea that blackness exists 'over there' in America and not the UK.

Just because institutions don't recognise and remember Olive, it doesn't mean that communities don't talk about her and value her, it just means we haven't looked at it. It's about creating new ways of seeing the past, so instead of looking back and seeing how little you are left with, instead we're allowed to look back and pull out something and bring a new interpretation to it, by writing, for instance, or a play inspired by a photograph. We can create a new representation.

History doesn't need to be static or past, it doesn't have to hold us back; we can take it and move forward with it in a way that feels more true to us, to how we live now and how we want to be remembered in the future. How we recognise our lives now, how we memorise and archive our lives so that future generations don't have to experience the loss that my generation and younger have felt, which includes recognising and celebrating Black history.

Remembering Olive Collective: olivemorris.org

Ismail Jaily

Originally from Darfur, Sudan

In 2018 my partner Jez and I met someone from whom we would learn so much. We had been to the theatre to see *The Jungle*, the play by Joe Murphy and Joe Robertson, two men who spent seven months running a theatre company called Good Chance in the Calais refugee camp. Afterwards we were lost for words at what we had witnessed and heard from this incredible immersive theatre piece (some of the actors were refugees) and Jez voiced that he would love to do something practical and regular to help. He contacted NGO HostNation, who would be able to match Jez with a refugee to befriend and mentor. There would be a three-month commitment to see how the match worked, and they would have support from the charity as and when they needed it. Six months later, on Valentine's Day, 14th February 2018, Ismail and Jez met and as their friendship built through their weekly get-togethers, Ismail soon became part of our family, coming to stay in the Cotswolds, meeting family and friends and educating us, his friendship enhancing our lives beyond measure.

I have often talked with Ismail about his journey to the UK, but every time I hear it, I am in awe. The strength of his spirit is beyond anything I can imagine, not just in his journey here, but how he has coped since. Ismail's loss is one of identity and home. He came to this country in just the clothes he was wearing; by then he had no possessions, no papers, no passport, no ability to speak English. He has suffered immense loss but has never given up hope.

In brief, his journey is this:

Ismail grew up in the countryside in the region of Darfur in Sudan; he is around thirty years old (his tribe don't register birthdays). Before the war in Darfur his family lived off the land with a few animals – sheep, cows, camels and horses for transport – and no electricity or water in his village. It was a 1.5 hour walk to the nearest well.

War took its toll on the region and he and his family were living in a refugee camp. Increasingly Ismail felt he should try and leave to find a safe and better life in order to help support his family financially. His father had died and he needed to look after his mother and brothers.

He left Sudan, heading for Libya. With three friends, he paid someone to get him by car from his village to Chad, which took three days. From there, he paid smugglers to take him on a lorry to Libya across the Sahara Desert. There were thirty people in the lorry for ten days. Ismail says it was very frightening, but they had no choice.

Ismail lived in Libya for eighteen months, managing to find building work, but there was danger from that country's civil war, plus racism and poor security. So this was a temporary stage, but allowed him to make a little money for his family and for the next part of the journey.

The next aim, in the hope of finding safety, was Europe, but to get there they had to cross the Mediterranean. Traffickers had to be paid and 300 people were packed onto the boat. Ismail says it was terrifying, but again, there was no choice. After three days, they were rescued by an aid organisation who put them into a larger boat. They were taken to Sicily and from there to Milan.

They were given food, drink and clothes and looked after at the refugee camp, but there was a rumour they could be sent back home, so soon Ismail and his three friends fled from the camp with the aim of getting to France or the UK.

Once more, with no papers or European language and only the clothes on their backs, they managed to board a train for Paris. Ismail managed to climb into the luggage rack to hide, but his friends, who were hiding elsewhere, were eventually arrested by the police. From that moment on he was on his own.

Ismail arrived in Paris not knowing anyone or where to go. He only had his tribal language, Zaghawa (which is not a written language), and some Arabic. He was walking down a street and he saw someone he could tell was probably Sudanese. He was also a refugee and he took Ismail to a railway tunnel under which homeless Sudanese people were living in tents.

From there, Ismail found out about Calais and journeyed there by train from Paris. At Calais, he tried to get a train to England, but was arrested and taken to a detention centre away from Calais for twenty-five days. He was taken from there back to Paris to the Sudanese Embassy, and by staying silent, they didn't know where to take him, so he was taken back to prison. After a few days he was released and managed to get back to Calais, still with no papers.

Ismail was in Calais for a week and one morning he decided to go back to the train station and try for England once more. He managed to get over a fence and hid in a train tunnel. A train moved slowly from the station, through the tunnel and, amazingly, stopped. It had lorries on it and Ismail managed to climb on to it and cling to the underside of a lorry through the Channel Tunnel.

In England, he arrived in Dover with just the clothes he wore.

Ismail says he was received with kindness; the authorities found an interpreter and he was taken to a hotel in Stockport, Manchester. He stayed there for twenty-five days, was given clothes, food and drink and treated with respect. He was given £5 a day spending money. He is not sure what the organisation was, but he felt welcomed.

He was moved to Liverpool for nine months, to a shared house with other refugees, and was granted political asylum with the right to stay for five years. A day he says he will 'never forget for the rest of my life'.

Ismail was able to get to London, where he lives now, five years on. He connected to a church who had volunteers teaching English and was supported by NGOs Breaking Barriers and HostNation. Crisis helped Ismail to contact the YMCA, who were able to give him accommodation, and he bought a laptop with money he had saved.

⁂

Most of my language I learned from YouTube. Most of the time I am alone in my room, so I have time to listen. I focus on YouTube and there are many YouTubers who share their lives. I love them and they teach me. It helps me to feel less alone, to watch these people. Otherwise I can feel alone and get anxiety and stress but they help me. I went to Breaking Barriers to learn basic IT skills, email and how to browse the internet, and they told me I could meet an English person through HostNation; that is how I met Jez and then you, Cam and Emilie, and became part of your family. So I had friends.

Note: Jez met Ismail three years after his arrival in the UK.

On bereavement (his father's death):

It is difficult to cope with being alone here and losing someone from my life. I have no choice but to accept. If you lose someone and can't get them back, there is no choice. I still feel lonely, but not like at the beginning.

In Sudan it is different from here when someone dies. We bury the person the same day they die. We wash the body carefully and wrap the body in a white cloth called a Kafan, we go to the cemetery and dig the grave and immediately we take the dead body there on a stretcher. We don't pay anyone to do all of this; there are always older people in the village who know what to do. We all help to wash the body. Only family members or people who are close will see the face of the person who has died.

When my father died, I wasn't there. I was away for twenty days bringing sheep from West Sudan and I knew my father was a little bit ill, but while I was away he died and was already buried. I couldn't say goodbye to him. I was shocked and felt very alone.

In my culture, you don't really talk about someone who has died. I didn't know about grief until I came to this country. For a few months or a year we remember them and talk about them, but after that it is behind us. We have a remembrance gathering after one year with food and drink to remember the person but not after that.

I still feel sad about my father, but not like at the beginning. I can't get him back so I have to overcome the sadness and anxiety.

On loss of identity, having to start again:

Sometimes I try to listen to music (sometimes from Sudan or from England) and if I feel sad or lonely that helps, or I go back to learning English on my laptop and it helps me. I look forward – I'm learning. Life here is very different. People here don't understand how difficult life is in Sudan.

I asked Ismail how he found the inner strength and courage to get here and to live life here now (which is still challenging).

It was a very difficult journey, almost impossible – but it wasn't impossible. I had to be motivated and not give up; I had to move forward. No one helped me to do this, I was just going forward to complete what I wanted to do. Even my family thought I was only going to Libya, a neighbouring country, not Europe and the UK. I couldn't phone them to let them know. I didn't have a phone and they didn't have a phone. I could eventually get a message to them through a relative in Al Fashir [in North Darfur] who had a phone. They took the message to my family to say I was OK.

What do you look forward to?

I just want to be motivated to educate myself. I didn't get enough education where I grew up in Sudan. It's not too late and I want to learn. The reason I came here from Sudan was because I want to help my family, change my life and live a better life with education. That's what I am looking for. I'm doing it now, but it is difficult on my own. Covid has not helped but we have to accept it and it will pass. We can find inner strength. I hope my interview will help someone to do what they want to do. Thank you for having me.

Part 5

Current Work and Resources

Grief Investigation

My main paid work these days is from speaking sessions for companies, educating staff about grief and helping people back to work following major life changes, from bereavement, to diagnosis, divorce and workplace change. I also produce podcasts for companies, sharing the stories of staff for good communication and mental health awareness. I am passionate about changing the landscape for people who have to face work when the rug has been pulled. With the knowledge that time doesn't heal, and that people can become stuck in addressing their grief, I help them to start conversations in their workplace, to understand the messy patterns and symptoms of grief and the importance of not judging each other. My firm belief is that if grief is faced and worked through gradually, if people are well supported, there is a rich seam of energy to be found from surviving it and possibly thriving.

My strange advantage in this work is the fact that I am *not* a therapist. I have had therapy and found it incredibly helpful, but what I gained most from Helen House was the fact that open conversation makes grief support accessible to all, especially those who might not want to unpick their lives too much, but want to find practical ways of moving forward, knowing how to help themselves. When I had bereavement support from the team at Helen House for many months after Harry died, it wasn't therapy; we were free to walk and talk. Sometimes Marie would dig the garden with me, we would take the children out and talk, and sometimes if I felt up to it we would sit down and discuss whatever had cropped up for me in the time in between sessions. I cried with Marie and I knew she had many years of experience being alongside grieving families, but she was free to guide me and respond to my needs on any given day. She could signpost me to what might help; it was incredible and it has given me the confidence to put this into action for other people, particularly those trying to go back to work, opening conversation with their teams and attempting to take the fear out of discussing death and other major life losses.

In my one-to-one grief guidance sessions I can help clients to build a grief toolkit and find ways of helping themselves. I help to provide a safety net as grief unfolds and changes in its messy way. With some of my clients I suggest creating memory boxes or memory books, journalling, meditation, yoga; sometimes we might discuss a grief podcast, film or book to aid our discussion. We are fearless and courageous in what we talk about and there is a great liberation in that. There are no limits and it is all led by the client and what they want. I am just the guide.

Redundancy – another form of loss

In my client work I am sometimes asked to talk to staff who have been made redundant. They are offered the chance to have coaching, or to talk to me about loss and change. I treat this work in the same way, helping them to acknowledge and feel their shock and grief, and then helping them to think about what they really want from life and how they might put it into action. I often discover that those who react particularly badly to the prospect of redundancy are also suffering from unresolved, cumulative grief. They might have had major losses already, in childhood perhaps, and redundancy can be a tipping point.

There is one element of my story I have purposely left out until now. It is the time I became completely stuck, because I didn't manage to get resolution on a situation.

That time was in 1990, at the height of my early career, when I worked for a successful small production company making corporate films. We had limitless budgets, travelled all over the world and had the best time! One day, when I had just completed a film for a client, I was at my flat in London. It was two weeks before my wedding and it was a Sunday night. There was a knock at our door and when I opened it the two directors of the company were there. They came into my flat for maybe twenty minutes and in that time handed me my P45 and told me they were having to make me redundant. I went into complete shock. I wasn't allowed back to the office; they had brought my things and there was little explanation. I had just signed my first mortgage with my husband-to-be based on both our salaries. I was absolutely devastated.

Looking back now, I can see how badly this was handled. I was cut off from my colleagues and I had thought the company was doing brilliantly. I now know that they had overspent, and in the coming months more people were made redundant and the company eventually collapsed. But that didn't stop my hurt at being first out. If they had explained that there were problems it would have helped, but nothing was said; they were not allowing themselves to be honest, vulnerable or empathetic.

I felt betrayed, angry, traumatised and hurt. My ego was bruised and I lost all confidence. Not just for weeks but for months to come. In fact it was the best thing that ever happened to me because I ended up soon afterwards at Channel 4, but that didn't help. For many years afterwards, I dreamt that I met my boss. I would go over and over what I would say to him, sometimes vindictive, sometimes in tears, and other times just pleading for my job back.

If only they had talked it through with me, clearly and bravely and faced it full on, maybe helped me with advice or coaching, I would have been fine; I would have had answers and resolution of some sort. Acknowledgement of the pain. But that hurt lasted for many years and with much confusion.

Isn't it strange that by dealing with my son's death I didn't become stuck, because I knew we had done all we could for him, but with that professional situation and a lack of openness and bad communication, I did.

Recently, all these years on, I was in touch with one of the company directors via Facebook. I mentioned the company and he said, 'Oh we didn't have a clue what we were doing, we were so young.' At last I felt some sort of resolution – for the first time I was finally able to truly let it go!

The grief of siblings

I feel siblings are often overlooked. I have watched the courage of my own children over many years as they have come to terms with the death of their brother. How they are now adept at answering the question 'Do you have siblings?' or 'How many siblings do you have?' – whether to say one, or 'I had a brother but he died. I now have...'

We all lead good lives, we are *so* lucky in many ways, but I know, like me, they have to live with the void that Harry left for the rest of their lives. It is well documented how important the early years of a child's life are, and for both my surviving children, those years involved a major seismic change in the dynamic of our family. However, I have also seen the positive impact of how they have dealt with that pain: their appreciation of life, of the smallest things and their lack of materialism, their love of friends and family and generosity of spirit. How they are always drawn to people needing help, fearless in their ability to talk about subjects from which many people shy away, how they value their own community. They have suffered, they are courageous and they are kind.

Divorce

In the aftermath of my separation from Hugo, I soon discovered that just as much as with the topic of death, people shy away from really talking deeply about divorce. There is still a massive taboo about it, little empathy from those who haven't been through it and a truly terrible blame culture, even though now 40 per cent of marriages end that way. I found that people just wanted to know 'who was to blame' when in truth it is always far more complex than that.

With my 'embracing change' work in companies I often start with a general talk on the effects of grief and ideas for how companies can support their staff. Following the talk, staff are offered 1:1 discussions, which can relate to death, divorce or workplace change. What I see is cumulative and generational grief, and many people, particularly men, coming forward to talk about divorce. They are often dislodged from home, they have lost community, they are working hard and they have nobody to talk to. No one at work understands or even asks. Just like grief over a death, there can be a phase early on when there is attention and a bit more support, but then nothing. And just like bereavement, it often hits hard in the years afterwards.

Personally, I am very happily in a relationship with my beloved Jez, an old friend from my teen years whom I re-met in 2017, thirty years after last seeing him! We have found a new way together; we don't share finances and we live side by side, but we are so well matched emotionally that we are strong together and apart. I found love again. And Hugo lives ten minutes away with Martha, whom I like very much. I can see they are also right for each other in this next phase of our lives. But it still hurts and, just as in our marriage, we both communicate and deal with this new phase differently.

So, I have ended up helping people suffering from the effects of divorce in the same way – we create similar continuing bonds: ways of bringing the good memories through, the good lessons learned and the positives. We look at how to open up conversation and take away the taboos, to normalise grief over divorce and educate others. We try to eliminate blame and look forward. We talk and open up with courage, and feel the pain. Divorce has taught me so much and I hope I can now help others with their grief.

Courage to talk

It takes great courage ('of the heart', from the Latin *cor* for heart) to face loss full on and that might not be possible in the early weeks, months or even years, but it is never too late to start talking about it and usually such a relief when you do. I often support and collaborate with The Good Grief Project, the charity set up by my friends Jane Harris and Jimmy Edmonds (see their interviews in Part 4) following the death of their twenty-two-year-old son Josh. I was with them when they were speaking at the Cheltenham Literary Festival and screening their film *A Love That Never Dies*, and during the Q&A a woman stood up to ask a question. She was standing next to her mother who was in her eighties and in a wheelchair. The daughter said, 'My sister died forty years ago and we have never been able to talk about her from that day, we don't mention her name – is it too late?' She was brilliantly and bravely illustrating the scale of the problem. Of course the answer from us was 'No, it is never too late.'

Physical effects of grief

If unaddressed, grief can cause serious physical effects. How many people do you know who are suffering from the symptoms of heart, lung and gut problems and taking medication? And how many have truly investigated where those problems originate? Many symptoms will be from stress or grief from events which may have been recent, or many years ago. So many people I meet have had a parent die too young, a sibling, a child, or have been through divorce. And years later these symptoms are treated with medication, but no one stops to ask 'Why?' Doctors perform scans and don't come up with answers because most often they relate to issues from years before, which if withheld will show physical symptoms eventually. Think of the expressions we often use: 'broken heart', 'gut reaction', 'lump in the throat', the irony that when we grieve we often stop breathing properly. A broken heart doesn't necessarily show up on a heart scan.

I now see a craniosacral therapist once or twice a year for deep healing of body and mind. The first time I visited her, she had been working on me for around thirty minutes, with her hands placed under my spine, when she said, 'Lizzie, when did you stop breathing fully?' I answered, 'Probably when my son died?' I had been very aware of holding my breath as Harry took his last, and even all these years on (this visit was probably fifteen years after his death), I had a tendency to hold my breath for unhealthy amounts of time. She explained to me how doing that was actually going to damage me at a cellular level, withholding oxygen and therefore starving my vital organs. Yoga and meditation have now helped this.

Conferences

I'm always pleased to be invited to speak about grief and, particularly, to speak at conferences for mental health in the workplace. Two of the best I have experienced are This Can Happen and the MAD World Summit. It is such a relief to know that grief is now being factored into the mental-health-at-work agenda and, although it's early days, I feel so happy to be a part of the conversation.

At the conference run by This Can Happen, I was invited to do an 'in conversation' piece on 'Understanding Grief' with Dr Chloe Paidoussis Mitchell. I have to admit that when we were initially put in touch with each other, I immediately had an attack of impostor syndrome when I saw the letters after Chloe's name and the academic side of her work – my default reaction! When we met, she gave me confidence in the fact that my two decades of grief investigation was 'lived' experience, through my own grief and being immersed in the children's hospice world for so long. We have become friends and are bound to collaborate many more times!

Chloe is a chartered counsellor, psychologist and coach, specialising in trauma and loss. Her personal motto is: 'We can't control what life throws at us, but we can control how we respond.' I asked Chloe to talk about her work with grief.

Chloe

I'm a Doctor of Counselling Psychology and my PhD was in Traumatic Loss.

For my PhD I interviewed people who had experienced a number of different, unexpected, often violent deaths and, like you, I was interested to see what the common themes, or common essence of the experience was. So I wanted to look at a variety of losses and the more I did that, the more I realised that there are so many common threads to a difficult grief.

What took me into my work was a series of events really. When I was young a friend's sister died very traumatically, and although I knew it wasn't my grief, it affected me profoundly. I was sixteen and the death felt a bit sanitised; there was little communication and I watched my dear friend unravel – that was what frightened me. It brought me face to face with the reality that sudden, horrific things can happen to really good people. I had lived in a little bubble of never having to think of anything like that before.

It affected me quite seriously at a time that was key for my own emotional development. I started withdrawing; I went through what I now know to be a repressed grief, bottling up a lot of big questions like how do you get over this, how do you adapt, what does it mean?

We were a very small community and everyone just clamped down. There was no counselling, advice, nothing. It just wasn't talked about and that was my biggest problem. I didn't have the emotional intelligence at the time to say 'we need to talk about this'. I was very young but I felt things very deeply so I was picking up a lot of negative fear around everybody. The image I have of my friend in a collapsed heap when she found out what had happened has stayed with me forever. It's always a source of sadness.

So that led me into thinking, *What does it mean to be human?*, *What is it to trust?*, *What is it to lose?* I eventually studied Psychology and loved it. I ended up working at the BBC within the news department, in coaching and development, and I was there when 9/11 happened. It was a time when awareness was building of what it means to survive trauma and PTSD, how some people cope and others don't. How some of our incredible journalists who survived Bosnia couldn't cope with the images coming in of 9/11. That really kickstarted my deeper interest in trauma.

I started working with the journalists on meaning-making through trauma and the rescuing that this can provide. After that I went on to do my clinical doctorate.

The physical effects of grief:

When I did my trainee psychologist practice in the NHS, I would get a lot of referrals who were diagnosed with many types of problems from addiction, to personality disorders, depression, panic attacks. With a little bit of history and fact-finding I realised that a huge number of these people had suffered a trauma and often a traumatic loss which they thought they had previously coped with. It showed that if you don't give yourself an opportunity to navigate through grief, it takes hold of the body and it finds another way to come out.

With over twenty years of experience now, I have definitely witnessed the physical embodiment of loss. Loss of any kind, not necessarily by death. The primary rule of all existence is to express itself and in order to do that it needs to feel like it is in balance. Whether it's our minds, our bodies, our nervous systems, they are always in pursuit of harmony and balance. So what science calls the law of homeostasis is really thrown out of balance when a difficult event happens. You can't orient yourself in the world any more; nothing quite makes sense; what you thought were your norms are no longer available and the body responds with that unconscious fight-or-flight response. It's almost as though the body responds before the brain has had a chance to catch up.

So often people will say, 'I know it has happened, but I just can't fathom that it has happened, I can't believe it.' But the body is already responding. No two people have the same experience, but there are some prevalent symptoms of grief and trauma: having an empty feeling in your stomach, feeling hollow, chest pains, having difficulty breathing, being dizzy, feeling sick, being sick, being very hot, being very cold, sweating, having difficulty concentrating, being noise intolerant, not remembering what people are saying or have said, not being able to focus, not being able to read a book, watch a film or listen to a conversation. Pronounced physical aspects – appetite, digestion, sleep patterns. Over-eating, under-eating – whatever the individual response is – but all of those are normal responses to grief.

I work with so many people who are worried that they are cracking up, that they are losing their minds, that they are doing something wrong. The other side is that the shock is so profound and paralysing that you go into that total freeze mode and you don't feel anything at all. You detach.

Is it ever too late to talk about grief?

No, it is never too late. I have a real issue with 'time heals' – it doesn't. It's about finding a way to have that turning point; time itself doesn't do the healing, and if you don't engage with your grief and use the feelings of grief as your compass to what happens next, in moving forward, then that grief will come out when you stop avoiding it. I think grief never stops; it comes back again and again. As the time expands from when you were last together, you discover a new layer to your grief, and you have to find your way with each stage and make peace with each one.

It's about normalising your grief, making friends with it, making time for it and processing it. There's a big difference between experiencing the feelings of grief and expressing them. What worked last year might not work now, so we need to tune in with what we need today.

We have pathologised suffering, we have medicalised it. I'm not suggesting that people shouldn't seek medical support if they need it, because sometimes they do need medication to stabilise, but it shouldn't take away from exploring where your heart and soul are with it.

The only thing that I think works to heal any form of loss is receiving empathy and compassion from within. Also being validated, being heard, being held and being connected on a human-to-human level. If you can do that to yourself and also have a few good people in your life, you can get through anything. That's why I feel sad when people start to pathologise their pain and see it as something they are never going to get beyond. People are frightened and think that's it. So, the key is to keep that dialogue going and keep doing the work. There is so much that can help.

I have no magic formula or cure; the only thing I can offer people is a space that is safe, open, non-judgemental, where they can meet themselves and be met by me, in a holding, loving way where we can really explore what it means to be them. Because when you lose a part of yourself, you lose an essential aspect of your life and you don't know who you are any more.

It's a problem of 'being', not necessarily 'doing'. So I get a lot of people coming to therapy saying 'Tell me what to do!', 'Fix me!' And I wish I could, but I can only help them to find out what it means to be them and what is meaningful, purposeful and joyful, and from there, we can go! So much energy is generated from that process, but it is all a shock to people that they need to engage and step into their pain. Everyone has their own unique journey.

Therapy is also helping people to discover self-love and what is going to make them happy.

On empathy:

I'm a huge believer in empathy and that with it we can adapt to anything. Human beings are social beings and we can receive sympathy, empathy and compassion.

Sympathy is important, but not validating; it's not holding. When you're in crisis and reconstructing your sense of who you are and how you're going to carry on facing life, in being functional and resilient, empathy is by far the biggest source of everything; of hope and growth. When you feel people are empathic with you, you feel safe, you feel seen and you matter. Your pain is understood. This can trigger compassion, which is the call to act, to do something. Not everyone can receive empathy, sometimes they shut down to it and shut it off, which is sad – that level of distress when they have disappeared as a way of surviving.

Empathy is like oxygen for the soul. Organisations need collective empathy more than ever now. This is why therapy works because the negative charge of that pain diminishes when you flood it with empathy, compassion and love.

www.dr-chloe.com

Lizzie's Tips For Supporting Someone Through Grief

- Get comfortable being alongside them in their grief. Don't try and have answers, just be there for them and respond to what they actually need.

- Check in with them. Grief is messy and the stages of grief (which *may* include, in no particular order, denial, anger, bargaining, depression, acceptance and meaning) might come in any order over any amount of time. This can be uncomfortable and confusing for those grieving and those alongside.

- Realise that time doesn't necessarily heal, but people can move forward (at their own pace). You may feel your friend, colleague or family member should be 'getting over it' by now, but sometimes it is harder to be further away from the person or loss and feel that time is creating a void. I found it harder, for instance, to say I had not seen Harry for six years than to say I hadn't seen him for six weeks. Yet I was able to move forward, *with* his memory.

- Don't expect 'closure'. This notion can really anger the bereaved, but do be prepared to witness healthy new beginnings. Support them in these when they appear. They won't be 'better now', but if well supported, they may begin to find hope in the new landscape in which they find themselves.

- Don't give up on them. You may receive a snappy reply one week, if they want to be left alone and don't want to talk – but sometime later they may be feeling isolated and need to talk about their loss incessantly. This is the hard part – so many times I have had people say to me that someone they are close to who is suffering is rude, unapproachable, difficult, challenging – but if you can manage to stay alongside them, they will come through. Navigate their grief with them.

- Having a grief ally at work is a wonderful thing. As a team, see if someone can be appointed to do the checking-in, or take it in turns. This should be in place over weeks, months and years potentially – but as time goes on it may be a case of checking in once or twice a year, ahead of an anniversary (in the case of bereavement) or birthday. Acknowledging it goes a long way in releasing stress for that person and making them feel less isolated with their thoughts.

- Don't be afraid of upsetting someone – it is better to say something than nothing at all. Silence can be deadly! The phrase 'don't mention the war' and the silence that ensued from soldiers, and for those to whom they were returning, resulted in many people still suffering during the 1980s, forty years on. This was illustrated in the book and film *The Railway Man* by Eric Lomax. I personally knew a man who was a prisoner of war in Burma and was sectioned due to PTSD in the 1980s, when the trauma finally, tragically caught up with him. As a result of witnessing this, I see tears as a good thing! If someone breaks down with you, don't worry that you have upset them – they were probably upset anyway and are just relieved that someone has been brave enough to mention their loss. Those tears will be helping to release stress, which otherwise could be stored at a cellular level. So I see tears as a gift and feel privileged if someone is relaxed enough to cry with me.

- Do investigate good support and find ways of signposting, either through your company (if it has provision) or by doing your own research. But always ask if that might be helpful first. Recommendations could include finding out about therapy, coaching, meditation, mindset work, sport, yoga, retreats, volunteering, fundraising or just a visit to the local pub! Ask what the person you are supporting wants and react to their needs. If they can't afford the costs of grief-guidance, perhaps friends can fundraise to help pay for the help they choose – if appropriate.

- Don't judge someone else's grief – everyone grieves differently and we don't always know what has gone before. It is easy to try and give grief hierarchy, so a pet or even a grandparent may be deemed less worthy of outpourings of grief than when a partner or child dies. But we don't always know the full story: someone grieving deeply over a pet may have suffered trauma in the past (the death of a parent or sibling, for instance) and that pet may have been their greatest source of comfort; a grandparent may have been their significant human, they may have brought them up. We just don't know, particularly in the workplace, and cumulative grief means that grief can accumulate over many years until something happens to tip the person off balance, the final straw. It isn't a competition!

- Small acts of kindness cannot be overestimated. Because so many people are fearful of the bereaved, you never forget those people who turn up – whether through just being alongside you through the discomfort and messiness of grief or delivering food during the low moments; those who still mention Harry's name in a card, text or phone call; and the ones you know will put down everything when you need them. I hear too many clients describing the loneliness of grief, their friends who have walked away, who can't get over their own fears.

What Has Helped Me Over the Years:
My Grief Toolkit (so far!)

Friends: the greatest comfort.

Community: my community has increased as I have worked with charities, volunteered and met so many bereaved people who are now my allies and friends in grief. I feel less alone with these people who have shared experience. We don't always need words: there is innate understanding.

Meditation: this is particularly good for the physical effects of grief and lack of sleep, heart-racing and shock. There are many free resources and subscription apps. I often meditate during the day; just five or ten minutes will calm your breathing, your mind and your headspace. It is so powerful at a cellular level.

Check out Headspace, Buddhify, The Mindfulness App, Calm, to name but a few.

Yoga: for good health, calm and deep breathing. Post-divorce, yoga really helped me.

Find a teacher near you (in the UK: www.bwy.org.uk).

There are also plenty of free online sessions which are brilliant for starting your day when you get out of bed! 'Yoga with Adriene' is particularly good; I like the fact you can search on her YouTube account by the amount of time, by a part of the body that needs attention, or by emotion. I often do twenty or thirty minutes each morning or at the end of my working day.

Craniosacral therapy: for balance and restoration. I go once or twice a year.

Mindset coaching/hypnotherapy: in my first session, I set an intention to be more present. That had a profound impact on my sleep; not looking too far forward or back helps reset the mind and stop the constant mind-whirring from trauma.

Check www.hypnotherapy-directory.org.uk for your nearest practitioner. Based in Oxfordshire, Nicola Ménage (www.nicolamenage.com), Mindset Coach, transformed my sleep and ability to be more present. She will work with you wherever you are in the world!

Life coaching: I keep checking in on where I want to be and how I want to do it. I consider it to be a gym workout for the mind.

Podcasts: there are interesting podcasts on grief and loss.

Audio books: if you don't feel like reading, it can be very calming to be read to and to mentally escape for a while.

Exercising outside: give yourself time to walk, run, or whatever is your favourite form of exercise.

Reading: through books, you can share the stories of others who have experienced grief and loss.

Music festivals: for me, gathering with friends outside and dancing to live music is the greatest thing to lift my spirits.

Reading and listening recommendations

Books

The titles here are listed in no particular order, but I match my clients to the books that may help them. These are often part of my recommendations.

Dr Edith Eger, *The Choice* and *The Gift*. Psychologist who survived concentration camps and still helps clients in her nineties. She shares her extraordinary story of hope and that we have a choice to live well. I have found both books so helpful. *The Gift* is shorter and easier, focusing on what you CAN do. She also has a superb fifteen-minute TED talk on grief.

Atul Gawande, *Being Mortal: Medicine and what matters in the end*

Paul Kalanithi, *When Breath Becomes Air: What makes life worth living in the face of death*

C. S. Lewis, *A Grief Observed*

Sasha Bates, *Languages of Loss: A psychotherapist's journey through grief*, *A Grief Companion: Practical support and a guiding hand through the darkness of loss* and *Yoga Saved My Life: Life lessons to take beyond the mat*

Brené Brown, *Braving the Wilderness: The quest for true belonging and the courage to stand alone* and *Daring Greatly: How the courage to be vulnerable transforms the way we live, love, parent and lead* (among many others)

Julia Samuel, *Grief Works: Stories of life, death and surviving*, *This Too Shall Pass: Stories of change, crisis and hopeful beginnings* and *Every Family Has a Story: How we inherit love and loss*

David Kessler, *Finding Meaning: The sixth stage of grief*

Kathryn Mannix, *With the End in Mind: Dying, death and wisdom in an age of denial* and *Listen: How to find the words for tender conversations*

Denise Riley, *Time Lived, Without Its Flow*

Eckhart Tolle. Everything! Writing, meditation, courses, podcasts with Oprah – he is wonderful and insightful.

Cheryl Strayed, *Wild: A journey from lost to found*

Clover Stroud, *The Wild Other: A memoir of love, adventure and how to be brave* and *The Red of My Blood: A death and life story*

Gary Andrews, *Finding Joy*

Bessel van der Kolk, *The Body Keeps the Score: Mind, brain and body in the transformation of trauma*

Gabor Maté, *When the Body Says No: The cost of hidden stress*

Matthew Walker, *Why We Sleep: The new science of sleep and dreams*

Dr Barbara Mariposa, *The Mindfulness Playbook: How to bring calm and happiness into your daily life*

Megan Devine, *It's OK That You're Not OK: Meeting grief and loss in a culture that doesn't understand*

Dr Joanne Cacciatore, *Bearing the Unbearable: Love, loss, and the heartbreaking path of grief*

Joan Didion, *The Year of Magical Thinking*

Elisabeth Kübler-Ross, *On Death and Dying: What the dying have to teach doctors, nurses, clergy & their own families*, *On Grief and Grieving: Finding the meaning of grief through the five stages of loss* and *Life Lessons: How our mortality can teach us about life and living*

Helen Macdonald, *H is for Hawk*

Anna Lyons and Louise Winter, *We All Know How This Ends: Lessons about life and living from working with death and dying*

Primo Levi, *If This Is a Man*

James Nestor, *Breath: The new science of a lost art*

Erica Buist, *This Party's Dead: Grief, joy and spilled rum at the world's death festivals*

Jane Harris and Jimmy Edmonds, *When Words Are Not Enough: Creative responses to grief*

Matt Haig, *The Midnight Library* (fiction)

Jodi Picoult, *The Book of Two Ways* (fiction)

Podcasts

Jess Mills, *Human*

Cariad Lloyd, *Griefcast*

Oprah Winfrey, *Oprah's Super Soul Conversations*

Brené Brown, *Unlocking Us* (including her interview with Dr Edith Eger) and *Dare to Lead*

Elizabeth Day, *How to Fail* – Julia Samuel's episode and others

Fearne Cotton, *Happy Place*

Some of my family's favourite grief films (for a good cry and life lessons)

Nomadland

About Time

Truly, Madly, Deeply

Up

Living

Wild

Manchester by the Sea

The Railway Man

Dead Poets Society

Pieces of a Woman

The Greatest

Good Will Hunting

The Bucket List

Extremely Loud & Incredibly Close

And the film *Let Me Go*, which I co-produced with director Polly Steele, now available on Amazon.

Other support recommendations (including their written materials which are accessible online):

The Good Grief Trust is a fantastic practical resource for help and recommendations. www.thegoodgrieftrust.org/

Cruse www.cruse.org.uk

Child Bereavement UK (CBUK) www.childbereavementuk. org

The Good Grief Project www.thegoodgriefproject.co.uk

Helen & Douglas House, Hospice for Children and Young Adults www.helenanddouglas.org.uk

The Compassionate Friends (US and UK) www.tcf.org.uk

Good Grief, A Virtual Festival of Love and Loss: includes speakers on many types of bereavement and online events for a subscription each year. goodgrieffest.com

Survivors of Bereavement by Suicide uksobs.org

There are of course many, many more grief charities and resources, far too many to list here.

Epilogue: The Rich Seam of Energy When Grief Is Survived Well

I have witnessed time and time again the amazing energy of those who have faced their grief head on. When Harry was diagnosed, I wanted to be informed, I wanted to survive my own pain and not put up a barrier, and I was inspired by people who had written about their grief, who had shared interviews and put themselves forward to help others.

As Julia Samuel says in her book *Grief Works*:

> Death is the last great taboo, and its consequence, grief, is profoundly misunderstood.
>
> An examined death is as important as an examined life. It shows us through vivid case studies that when we face our fears: the death of someone we love, our own death or being with bereaved friends, we are, paradoxically, better able to cope with them.
>
> When we feel bad, often our first instinct is to isolate ourselves and focus on what's upsetting us. Sometimes we really do need some downtime, but many times the best way to get out of the blues quickly is to turn our attention to other people. In being of service to others, paradoxically, we often find answers to our own questions and solutions to our own problems. We also end up feeling more connected to the people around us, as well as empowered by the experience of helping someone.

When Polly and I were funding our movie *Let Me Go*, we wanted to better understand generational trauma, the theme of Helga Schneider's story, and what happens when questions are left unanswered and grief is carried forward from generation to generation. Josh Cohen, psychoanalyst, author and professor at Goldsmiths, spoke with us and described it eloquently: 'Intergenerational trauma is the transmission of traumatic experiences down the generations. What distinguishes it as a clinical phenomenon is that it is rooted in silence, in unspeakability. The original trauma, more often than not, is an experience which cannot be represented to the person who suffers from it. So this silence, this lack of thinking, imagining and understanding, lodges in the mind of the victim and becomes part of their psychological makeup. Part of their way of relating, so the people who come into close contact with them, whether that's family members, friends, partners, will often feel they are running up against a barrier where whole regions of life can't be talked about. When this person goes on to have children, this is very much a shaping force.'

I have always felt that I was born into grief and have carried my mother's grief for her seven miscarried babies and two stillborn children (Edward and Mary) all my life. It has been voiced that I live the lives of my siblings, channelling their energy. It has had various consequences – one is that I have, way before Harry was born, always been fascinated by death and never scared of it, as a topic or inevitable outcome of our lives. The second is one that a dear childhood friend, Hattie Longfield, who was one of four children, expressed once: 'The reason you have such a capacity to love is because you were so wanted by your parents; they loved you unconditionally and you now pass that on.' It was such a lovely thing to say, particularly to a single child, and it made me think about my parents and their losses, and how my daughter Emilie was also born into loss, and our wish that Cam would not be left as the single child of bereaved parents.

I was pregnant with Emilie when my mother was diagnosed with cancer, and we were already decimated by Harry's diagnosis. Cam also only had six weeks of life before the bad news about Harry was given. Emilie and Cam have both experienced huge loss during their lives and carry the weight, but also, like me, the survivor's energy – the appreciation of life, health, friends and time. The importance of love, and love representing how much we grieve. In some ways life is enhanced in that way, but we feel things deeply which can be hard for people to understand. We have all found our own grief tribe – Cam and Emilie are often drawn to those who have lost, and I have been like that during my life too. Two of my best male friends, Jon Magnusson and Zander Mackintosh (godfathers to Harry and Cam respectively), experienced their own brothers' deaths, and while I wish that had not happened to either of them, what a gift for Cam and Emilie, for all of us, to have people closely in our lives who understand.

Learning from each other

'We cannot know your grief, but we can
walk beside you at every stage.'
Jacinda Ardern, Prime Minister of New Zealand

Rather than feeling wary of those going through bereavement, trauma and major life changes, I always feel it is the greatest privilege to be able to walk in their midst. You will never find more courage or awareness of the very essence of life than right there, in the community of the grieving. I always feel innately grateful when someone shares their sadness with me; I feel lucky to have a reminder of how precious life is.

I was lucky in some ways that my grief tribe started with the friendships I made at Helen House: the parents we met when staying there as a family, the people I met in attending their grief courses, but also by working there for twelve years, all the parents I came to know during that stage. If you are not in that position and the person you are grieving for died suddenly, you may not have immediately obvious resources at your disposal. In that instance I really recommend that, when you feel up to it (whether that is after weeks, months or years, there is no timeline), you look at joining a bereavement group. Nowadays there are death cafés and organisations like Cruse, The Good Grief Trust and many others, including those connected to certain illnesses, who will signpost you to find regular groups. It may not be a club you ever wanted to be in, but I can't underestimate the power of being able to listen to the stories of others in a community, even if you don't want to share your story. And friendships may be made there. Also bereavement retreats, days or weekends organised by different groups and charities can be hugely beneficial, as can yoga or meditation retreats – you will usually find others who are in a similar boat. Volunteering for a charity or organisation connected with your loss might help you to grow your grief community.

We can learn from each other and expand our knowledge – if we look at it like that, it takes away the fear and enables barriers to be broken down. We can feel less alone.

I'm always saddened in my talks and one-to-one grief guidance sessions when people say 'no one asked me how I was feeling', and others around them say 'I didn't know what to say'. It is led by a fear of saying the wrong thing; people tell me they are afraid that they 'might upset' the person. That person is already thinking of their loved one or situation every day, so you won't be 'upsetting' them, but helping them to release their grief and sadness by sharing it. Silence is truly deadly and this self-serving excuse that is fear just has to stop.

What is the worst that can happen when you reach out to someone in grief? Yes, they may rebuff you, but we have to get over that. So many times I have experienced bereaved friends and those I work with not wanting to or being able to share their grief at first, but by regularly letting them know you are there for them, eventually most people come to a stage where they do want to open up. I'm not talking about sharing everything, but at the very least having a coffee together occasionally, or an outing, shared experience, even a text! Absolutely anything will do, but please just keep on checking in with your friends, colleagues or family who are going through tough times. And remember, they are not 'better' yet; if you have truly loved, grief lasts a lifetime and needs acknowledging.

When grief equals love

More than two decades on from Harry's death, after much listening to the stories of others, talking and reading, my greatest realisation has been that the amount of pain we experience often represents the amount we loved the person who has died (or the passion for work or a relationship lost).

This realisation has helped me to find a balance between living with the trauma of my son dying alongside my love for life and wanting to live it well.

I don't want to be sad – I never did, and that is the dilemma for people living with grief. We want to grieve our loss and then live our lives, but the great shock is always that the loss doesn't change. So finding that balance of the two can take a lot of work and investigation.

If we are able to face the pain, thinking of it as love, somehow the two can meet and live alongside each other. They don't negate each other, but there is a match made somewhere along the line.

In my case the pain represents my love for my son, and it feels right that it should be experienced fully, but these days there is parity with my joy for living, breathing, loving and creating.

Mummy

To Mummy I hope
you Love this Love
from.

Harry.

Acknowledgements

The numerous friends who supported us through Harry's life and beyond, you know who you are – particularly Ben, Polly, Jon, Cath, Johnnie, Libby, Ann, Francie, Jayne, Martin, Elaine, Carol and Rosemary.

Sister Frances for sowing the initial seed of an idea many years ago that I should publish my grief journals one day.

Tom Hill and Johnnie Stebbings for their coaching at two very different stages of my life, but both leading to the work I do now.

Hugo Pickering, Erika Farwell, Cath Stebbings, Kate Gompertz, Jez Stone and Gaye Pool for their feedback before I submitted for publishing.

Everyone who was interviewed for this book – thank you for trusting me with your very personal stories.

For Dale and Hattie, beloved friends who were also far too young to die.

To all of you who have pledged and preordered this book – each purchase gave me courage!

To everyone at Unbound for your editing, publishing and design skills: thank you for making this such a life-enhancing process.

Hugo, for sharing our incredible family and a very happy life together for twenty-six years, alongside the immense grief challenges we faced.

Jez for our re-meeting after thirty years and sharing life together now. I am so grateful for this part of the journey.

To Cam and Emilie – for enabling me to get up every day after Harry died and giving me hope. I love you unconditionally, and I constantly learn so much from each of you. I am so proud of you both.

To my parents and Harry – you may no longer be here on earth, but you are with me every day.

'The Heavy Stone', quoted on page 151, is from the book *The Long Way Down, Poems of Grief and Hope* by Averil Stedeford, published by and available from Aspect Design. With thanks to Averil's daughter, Elizabeth Rolph.

The quotation on page 218 from 'Ta Moko' by Whirimako Black from *1 Giant Leap* by Jamie Catto and Duncan Bridgeman is reproduced with the permission of Jamie Catto.

The quotation on page 271 from *Grief Works: Stories of life, death and surviving* by Julia Samuel is published with the permission of Penguin Random House UK.

A Note on the Author

Lizzie Pickering is a speaker, a grief investigator, and a film and podcast producer. Following the death of her eldest son, Harry, in November 2000, she has used her personal and professional experience of navigating grief to offer guidance to companies and private individuals through presentations, podcasts and one-to-one sessions, helping people to adapt following major life changes.

In 2017 Lizzie produced the feature film *Let Me Go* with director Polly Steele, based on Helga Schneider's memoir of the same name. *When Grief Equals Love* is her first book.

www.lizziepickering.com

Unbound is the world's first crowdfunding publisher, established in 2011.

We believe that wonderful things can happen when you clear a path for people who share a passion. That's why we've built a platform that brings together readers and authors to crowdfund books they believe in – and give fresh ideas that don't fit the traditional mould the chance they deserve.

This book is in your hands because readers made it possible. Everyone who pledged their support is listed below. Join them by visiting unbound.com and supporting a book today.

Louise Browning

Claire Brydon

Guy & Ali Buckley-Sharp

Vicky Buckley-Sharp

Helen Bull

Emily Calladine

Eleanor Campbell

Alex Carter

Hester Carter

Maaike Carter

Jane Chapman

Glen Clancy

Holly Clark

Emily Clarkson

Francie Clarkson

Chris Coady

Katie Colcutt

David Cole

Hannah and David Cole

Kim Coles

Karen Colognese

Liz Cornish

David & Kass Court

Alison Cousins

Elizabeth Jane Coward

Lucy Crapper

Clare Cridland-Rutter

Marcus Cross

Violet Crudge

Lisa Cunningham

Ruth & Richard Cunningham

Kate Day

Laura de Bono

Angela de Ste Croix

Jayne Dear

Olivia Dickson

Marina Djurisic

Tania Dorrien Smith

Becky Dove

Lynda Dray

Lamorna Dudding

Erin Duffy

Timothy Dunn

Caroline Durance

Kathryn Edwards

Alex Egan

Isabella Egan

Rosie Egan

Alex Elmer Menage

Derek English

Catherine Evans

Joy Evison

Katharine Falcon

Sophie Fanshawe

Ina Focken

Kelly Foreshew

Rachel Foster

Joanna Frank

Dibby French-Constant

Lisa Fuller

Geraldine Gallacher

Daniel Gerring

Julie Giles

Catherine Gilpin

Tanya Gilson

Lydia Gockel

Emma Goldschmidt

Kate Gompertz

Renee Goossens

Jessica Govett

Pete Griffith

Tania Grose-Hodge

Katy Guest
Richard Gunton
Phil Gurin
Sara Hadley
Silva Hamze
Janet Hardie
Jane Harris and Jimmy
   Edmonds
Annie Harrison
Jane Hassell
Felicity Hayes
Ruth Hazeldine
Carey Heath
Tamsin Heatley
Georgina Hetherington
Francine Heywood
Ellen Hickie
Carmen Hillier
Francesca Hobart
Jamie Hodder-Williams
Fiona Hodgson
Cecilia Hojgaard-Olsen
Fran Hollywood
Rachel Hopkins
Kettivy Hor
Ed Horton
Jeremy Houghton
Jessica Houghton
Jo Howard
Sheila Hoy
Claire Hughes
Ellie Hughes
Richard Hughes
Peel Hunt
Caroline Hurst
Rick & Clare Jackman

Samantha Jackman
Neale Jackson
Jaffe and Neale Bookshop
Emma James
Joanne James
Jacquie Jenner
Ca Jm
Sally Johnson
Talitha Johnson-Lehman
Sharon Jones
Leslie Jowett Astor
Russell Kane
Carol Keith
Lucy Keith
Lucy Kelleher
Mim Kendrick
Dan Kieran
Amanda King
Liz Kingsbury
Rosemary Klee
Sarah Knowles
Sandra Kuchen
Simon Lacey
Emily Lang
Marjorie Lang
Susie Lawson
David Lightfoot
Cordelia Linacre
Hannah Lindsey
Sarah Lloyd
Richard Loftus
Zoe Lucock
Kate & Charlie Luxton
Kay Lyon
Trish MacIntyre
Kate Mackinnon

Alexander Mackintosh

Robert Mackintosh

Jon Magnusson

Rebecca Magnusson

Carri Mallard

Gill Mann

Elliott Mannis

Miranda Marks

Gill Marriott

Adam Mason

Helen Matthews

Stephen Matthews

Jonathan and Hannah Mayo

Lauren McAllister

Lucy McAndrew

Alice McColl

Lawrence McCrossan

Lucinda McFarlane

Marie McGinley

Sally McNair

Ainsley McNiff

Kim Meadowcroft

Emily Medley

Nicola Ménage

Charlie Milner

Claire Milner

Sophie Minter

Rachel Mitchell

John Mitchinson

Dee Montague

Zarrin Morgan

Philippa Morrison

Rupert Murdoch

Marie Murray

David Myerson

Tara Nash

Carlo Navato

Martin Neild

Hannah Nelson

Jessica Newell

Chris Newsom

Linda Nikolaou

Moi Nixon

Camilla Notman

Kerry Noyes-Lewis

Juliet O'Neill

Tara OBrien

Charlotte Orchard

Angela Osborne

Louise Padmore

Olivia Page

Kate Parker

Laura Parker

Nick Parker

Briony Partridge

David Pastor

Alex Pearson

Rebecca Perkins

Martin Perry

Nick Pettman

Sean Phelan

Esme Podmore

Justin Pollard

Laura Pollard

Catherine Pollitt

Gaye Poole

Fiona Porter

Rupert Potter

Tom Power

Molly Presly

Libby and Malcolm Price

Adrian Quest

Addie Quinnear
Nirvana Nadira Ramlakhan
Ros Randay
Susie Randle
Andrea Ratcliffe
Sam Ratcliffe
Holly Rebecca
Maria Rees
Min Reid-Richards
Jack Remmington
Georgia Reynolds
Danny Riding
Martin Ritchie
Katie Robins
Gill Robinson
Sancia Robinson
Christine Michéle Lucienne
    Roddier
Ellen Rodger
Tania Rotherwick
Kate Rudge
Adrienne Rutter
Kirsten Samuel
Jess Sanderson
Sham Sandhu
Sarah & Douglas
Charles & Katie Sargeant
Lyni Sargent
Grace Savage
Trish Schillaci
Jennifer Scotney
Mike Sell
Wendy Shaw
James Shingles
Jonny Shingles
Gill Siebert

Matt Siebert
Grace Simpson
Julia Simpson-Orlebar
Ann Sinfield
Tommy Skelton
Deirdre and Brian Skilton
Flora Smith
Linda Speddy
Sue Stapely
Cath Stebbings
Claudia Stebbings
Polly Steele
Juliet Stevenson
Jane Steward
Kieran Stiles
Francine Stock
Jez Stone
Nina Stone
Olive & Michael Stone
Damien Stork
Hannah Strickland
Diane Sutherland
Alice Sykes
Richard George Tailoring
Joelle Tamraz
Neil Taylor
Sarah Thiele
Sarah Thorn
Barbara Till
Naomi Tootill-Evans
Daniel Truell
George Truell
Katie Turfkruyer
Sophia Ufton
Judy Underhill
Kristina Ussi

Verena V.

Shirin Vahdat-Khah

Rose van Cutsem

Germaine VanGeyzel

Mark Vent

Edwina Vernon

Family Vernon—Purves

Liz Vinson

Saira Vögeli

Robin Walden

Susie Walker

Coby Walter

James Warburton

Tabitha Warley

Mark Watkin Jones

Meredith Watkins

Eileen Watt

Ernie Watts

Georgina Way

Tessa Webber Goldin

John Welch

Amadea West

Jervis Whiteley

Lucinda Whiteley

Sheila Astrup Whiteley

Domonique & Paul Wightman

Celene Wilkinson

Ali Wills

Yasmin Wills

Kay Winters

Michael Wood

Jade Lianna Woods

Annie Wray

Valerie Wright Goulet

Craig Yeaman

Joanna Yellowlees-Bound

Remembering

Gabriel Aitonje
Philip Alexander
Alice
Robert Allen
Ivor Arkinstall
Carol Atkinson
Stephen Bailey
Graham John Baines
Sheila Ballantyne
Victoria Florence Betts
Big Jr Richards
Alison Madeleine Bishop
Faith & Gustav Born
Tomo Brody
Sheila Campbell McNiff
Bill Cashmore
Rosemary Clinton
Oscar Cole
Dario Colognese
Dexter Constantine-
   Tatchell
Chloe Courtauld
Pippa Cowdrey
Margaret Dartnell
Jen De Costa
Derek and Sheila
Sylvia Dews
John Dudding
James Durrans
Sue Durrans
Elizabeth / Mum
Taffy Evans
For Tim Sinfield & Ella
   Greaney. Xx

For Tomo, forever loved and
   missed so much
Naomi Rebekah Franklin
Anne Gerring
Astrid Carmen Yvonne
   Geyzel
Misha Hannah Griffith
Natalie India Griffith
David Hall
Mike Hancock
Harry
Maxine Hayes
Tony Horton
Carol Ann Hughes
William Ingram
Cameron Jackson
Andy Johnson
Becky Johnson
Pooch Johnston
Pat and Peter Jones
Josh
Sally Kane
Marina Keeble
Aliba Keith
Mairead Kennedy
Geves Lafosse
Dale Langley Magnusson
Katherine Lennard
David Lightfoot
Lily
Lina
George Linacre
Cameron and Jackson
   Lister

Gillie Lund - Much loved
   Mother and Grandmother
Vanessa Lundahl
Angela Joy Mannis
Lyndell Mansfield
Stephen Matthews
Jasmine Milton
Mary Morley
Victor Morley
Giles Oldershaw
Elizabeth Mary Orchard,
   "Lizzie"
Harry Ottaway
Bill Perry, my dad
Jake Pirie
Andrew Quinnear
Harry Ramlakhan
Chris Rees
Peter Reid
Peter Stuart Reid
Lenny Anton Roddier
Roger
Rose
Pryana Shah
David Simpson
Tim Sinfield
Roger Skelton, with love
   as ever
Emily Smith
Joanna Smith
Sue Stapely remembering little
   ISABELLA
Maureen Stephenson
Jane Steward
JeanAnne Stock
Christopher Taylor

Freddie Taylor
Jack Taylor
Jordie Taylor
To All the Children I met
   through Helen House
Daniel Truell
George Truell
Eileen Ufton (My Mom)
Roger Underhill
Jim and Margaret Vinson
Mick Walter
Nicola Walter
Matthew Watkin Jones
Pauline Watkins
Tracy Watkins
Betty Whiteley & Dalal
   Wagokh
Rebecca Wilkinson
Jinks Wills
Julie Wills
Janet Winters
Henry Wiseman
Rita Wiseman
Patricia Withers
Maxine Vanessa Woods
Grant Yeaman